LUCKY AND GOOD

Risk, Decisions & Bets for Investors, Traders & Entrepreneurs

BY
JOHN SHERRIFF

Lucky And Good

♦♦♦
♦♦♦

TABLE OF CONTENTS

FOREWORD ix

PREFACE xiii

ESSENTIAL TERMS xvii

INTRODUCTION xxiii

CHAPTER ONE: DON'T BE A CHUMP 1

   THE CHAMP PROFITS WHERE THE CHUMP LOSES 1
      THINK RATIONALLY 4
      ...BUT RATIONAL THINKING IS NOT ENOUGH 4
      ESCAPE FROM CHUMPDOM 6

   INVESTOR, TRADER, ENTREPENEUR, OR PROFESSIONAL GAMBLER? 11
      LARD OR SHORTENING? 16
      TRADER VERSUS INVESTOR 16
      PROFESSIONAL GAMBLERS 18

   BUSINESS VERSUS GAMBLING 19

   FREE MARKETS 22

   LAW OF SUPPLY AND DEMAND 24

   COOPETITION 26

   FOUR STAGES OF BUSINESS 28

CHAPTER TWO: FIND IT 31

   NOTHING IS RISK FREE 32

   START WITH THE BIG PICTURE AND MACRO TRENDS ___ 35
      RECOGNIZE LONG-TERM TRENDS 37

LOOK FOR INFLECTION POINTS — 38
RECOGNIZE INFLECTION POINTS — 46
THERE'S ALWAYS A BEAR MARKET SOMEWHERE — 49
CONFIRMATION BIAS — 51
HOW DOES A TRADER GO SHORT? — 52
HOW DO THE OAKLAND A'S GO SHORT? — 55
HOW CAN AN ENTREPRENEUR GO SHORT? — 56
MULTIPLE DIMENSIONS = DEGREES OF FREEDOM — 60
RADIATION THERAPY — 61
NAVIGATION — 62
TRADING ON MULTIPLE DIMENSIONS — 64
ADDING DIMENSIONS AS AN ENTREPENEUR — 65
GAS BANK — 66
FIND THE RIGHT VALUE PROPOSITION — 68
AN EMPTY PICKLE JAR — 69
THINK IN OPPOSITES — 70
FLIES AT YOUR VACATION CABIN — 73
TAHOE, POLITICS AND DEBATES — 73
ENERGY PARKS — 74
COMMODITIZATION — 75
COMBINE AN INFORMATION ADVANTAGE WITH VOLATILITY — 80
WHAT IS AN INFORMATION ADVANTAGE? — 81
PARKING LOTS, CROPS AND CRAP — 82
AN INFORMATION ADVANTAGE WITH NO VOLATILITY IS USELESS — 83

CHAPTER THREE: DECIDE — 87
WELCOME FORKS IN THE ROAD — 88

FIGHT FOR FAST FEEDBACK 90

PLAY THE ODDS 95
FRAMING THE PROBLEM 98
SELLING COMPUTERS 99
STEALING BASES 100
PUTTING FOR DOUGH 100

THE NUMBERS MAY BE HAZARDOUS TO YOUR HEALTH 105
SMALL SAMPLES 105
SIGNIFICANCE OR COINCIDENCE? 106

CORRELATION IS NOT CAUSATION 110
CORRELATION 112
CAUSATION 113
BIG DATA 116
RELATIONSHIPS ARE NOT STATIC 118

SOME THINGS ARE LESS PREDICTABLE THAN OTHERS_120
TRADING WEATHER 121
MODELING HUMAN BEHAVIOR 124
COMPOUND FORECASTS 125
I COULD'VE GONE BAD (BEING AN ENRON EXECUTIVE
    DOESN'T QUALIFY) 129

BEWARE OF IDIOTIC LEVERAGE 131
THE MANIA OF LEVERAGE 135

THINK ON THE MARGIN 137

KNOW THE LONG AND SHORT OF IT 143
THE INDUSTRIAL VALVE BUSINESS 143
WALNUTS, LABOR COSTS, AND CEMENT 146

DO NOT IGNORE PRIDE OF OWNERSHIP 147

      90% OF THE VALUE OF GOLD IS THE "PRIDE-OF-OWNERSHIP"
          PREMIUM 149
      GARBAGE OR WINE BUSINESS? 150

DON'T JUMP THE GUN 152

FIGHT FRICTION COSTS 155
      LIQUIDITY VERSUS "LIQUIDITY" 156
      PLAYING A LESS THAN ZERO-SUM GAME 161
      I COULD'VE BEEN A HEDGE FUND MANAGER 166

DECIDE TO DECIDE 170
      GOLD VERSUS SILVER 170

CHAPTER FOUR: GO FOR IT 173

STRIKE WHILE THE IRON IS HOT 173
      THEN AND NOW 175
      SAN JUAN OPTIONALITY 176
      DIAMONDS AND THE GRIDIRON 178
      WEST COAST OFFENSE 179

DON'T PICK UP DIMES IN FRONT OF STEAMROLLERS 181

DON'T RUN OUT OF CASH 184
      CREDIT AND THE ENTREPENEUR 186
      THE COUNTERINTUITIVE CREDIT GAME 189
      BIG COMPANY CASH FLOW 192

AVOID GAMBLER'S RUIN 193
      KELLY CRITERION 195
      ALL-IN 199
      AND THE SURVEY SAYS… 199
      THE ENVELOPE PLEASE… 200

FIND FREE OPTIONS 202
      RECOGNIZE FREE OPTIONS 205

PUT YOUR SOCKS ON RIGHT	**208**
NATURAL GAS STORAGE	212
INTERNET HOTEL RESERVATIONS	215
THINK & ACT WITH THE BIG PICTURE AND LONG RUN IN MIND	**216**
BET YOUR BROTHER	217
BLACKJACK INSURANCE	217
CHAPTER FIVE: FIX IT	**221**
LIFE HAPPENS	**222**
GET LUCKY	**228**
VINEGAR IS SO SWEET	232
BE OPTIMALLY PERSISTENT	**233**
CHAPTER SIX: REAL-WORLD APPLICATIONS	**239**
APPLICATION ONE: LITIGATION FUNDING BUSINESS	**240**
HOW DO I FIND THE CASES?	242
WHICH CASES DO I FUND?	242
WHAT CAN GO WRONG? PLENTY!	244
WHICH PRINCIPLES APPLY	247
APPLICATION TWO: ENRON ONLINE	**249**
WHICH PRINCIPLES APPLY	251
APPLICATION THREE: SUTTON BRIDGE POWER PLANT	**255**
WHICH PRINCIPLES APPLY	258
APPLICATION FOUR: ENRON DIRECT	**261**
WHICH PRINCIPLES APPLY	263
APPLICATION FIVE: GOVERNMENT PENSION RETURNS	**264**
WHICH PRINCIPLES APPLY	270
APPLICATION SIX: ENRON CREDIT	**272**

CREDIT DEFAULT SWAP MARKET	273
OUR VALUE PROPOSITION	274
WHICH PRINCIPLES APPLY	278

APPLICATION SEVEN: COVERING YOUR LEGAL BASES — 280
    ADVICE FOR CIVILIANS IN THE LITIGATION WORLD — 280
    WHICH PRINCIPLES APPLY — 286

APPLICATION EIGHT: UNLOCKING THE FUTURE — 289
    WHAT IS THE OPPORTUNITY? — 290
    WHICH PRINCIPLES APPLY — 292

CONCLUSION IN A NUTSHELL — 295

EXHIBIT A: More (but not all) of the Current Macro Trends — 303

EXHIBIT B: Inflection Points — 307

EXHIBIT C: Calculations for the Short Putt — 311

EXHIBIT D: More Examples of the Long and Short of It — 313

EXHIBIT E: Sherriff's Core Business Principles — 317

ACKNOWLEDGMENTS — 319

ABOUT THE AUTHOR — 323

COPYRIGHT NOTICE — 325

FOREWORD

By Robb Sexton

I am the inventor of several technologies and products. The harsh truth for most inventors and entrepreneurs is that starting a business frequently requires an enormous amount of capital. Thus, investors become a part of your life. Sometimes, as in the case of the Flat Wire technology that I invented, investors own more of your creation than you do.

When we needed to raise capital, we had to decide whether to raise new, highly dilutive capital, or find a partner with complementary assets. We chose to license the global patents to the largest wiring company in North America. That company promised us, contractually, that they would give it their "best efforts" to commercialize and sell our technology.

The essence of our License Agreement was a commitment by this giant to use its extensive resources to globally maximize revenues for our Intellectual Property ("IP"—in our case, patents). We would receive a percentage of the gross margin of all sales as a royalty.

Flat Wire technology clearly had, and still has, the potential to change the game. It was a blue ocean, disruptive technology…but it did require an initial investment of many tens, if not hundreds, of millions of dollars to establish the market globally.

But our Licensee never lived up to its promises. It became clear that, if my company was ever going to receive a return on invest from our IP, we were going to have to fight it out in court. This is expensive, and takes years—believe me! We had the time, but not the money, to make it to the legal finish line.

Fortunately, I found a superb attorney who was willing to take the case on contingency, provided we paid for the expenses as we went along. But those expenses were substantial, and we didn't have the resources to pay for all the expert witnesses, depositions, and computer support required to review and manage millions of pages of discovery.

Prior to this, I had neither heard nor considered commercial litigation funding. But luckily, I found it. And it allowed my small company to run with the big dogs.

Certainly, the burgeoning litigation funding industry is creating nightmares for big business defendants caught red-handed with their hands in our collective cookie jars. Their normal tactics are delay, delay, and delay, in an effort that frequently works to outlast the little guy.

John Sherriff, along with other litigation funders, may now be the most important, field-leveling innovation ever created for small companies (and individuals) forced to fight big, well-capitalized companies in court. Is it expensive? Yes—but less so, in relative terms, and less costly, than venture capital.

So, John's very calculated decision to provide my company with litigation funding resulted in my meeting this man whom I have come to respect on so many different levels. His titles now have blurred into a wonderful hybrid: financier, partner, co-inventor, teacher, pupil, confidant, and most important, (and hardest to achieve,) my close friend.

You'll find no euphemistic or wishful thinking in this book. For investors and entrepreneurs who want to assess a bet, and then make the most of it once they "go for it," John tells it like it is.

As a serial inventor with hundreds of global patents and more than six companies, I have been guided by many of the forces and tenets that John conveys.

John, for all of his professional success and broad educational background, doesn't fall into the trap of thinking that he has acquired some privilege to judge others. Nor does he deny having earned the occasional "Chump" tag himself. I respect that aspect of John as much as anything else.

So, my biased, but honest, suggestion is that you take the time to not only read this book, but also to use it as a form of financial, investment, entrepreneurial, even a Business 101 mirror.

I also suggest that you don't take this book as just another quick business read. When I am thirsty, I love to guzzle ice cold water.

Foreword

When I want to reflect on the day, on my life, my joy or sorrows, success or failures, I enjoy slowly sipping a Dewar's and soda, tall, with a twist. The drink of choice is completely up to you. But, the preferred way to enjoy and learn from this book is slowly.

I promise that you will be entertained; you're also going to learn something.

Lucky And Good

♦♦♦
♦♦♦

PREFACE

> "It is what you learn after you know it all that counts."
> —Earl Weaver, 13-year manager of
> the Baltimore Orioles

On a Friday evening in the early summer of 2000, my wife Lorraine and I arrived for a three-day weekend at our hotel on the beautiful island of Capri, in the Gulf of Naples. As gorgeous as the location was, and at the risk of a possible divorce, I had almost cancelled the trip. It had been my worst trading week ever. My UK trading desk had lost over $100 million that week. I had only recently been named CEO of Enron Europe, and at this rate, it was going to be a very short gig.

I checked my voice mail, and found a message from Enron President (and soon to be CEO) Jeff Skilling, asking that I call him. Obviously he wanted to talk, but I was not looking forward to this conversation.

When Jeff came on the line, I said, "I guess you want to hear about our losses on the UK power book."

And he said, "No that's not why I called; but let me have it."

So I explained our positions, and how they had moved against us that week. He reassured me that he trusted my leadership and that direction that our business was headed. He also had good news: The board of directors had granted me, along with several others, options on our high-flying stock. Although I never made a dime off of those options (I did on some earlier ones), his vote of confidence improved the flavor of the wine and the pasta's aroma that weekend.

By the way, those UK trading positions, managed extraordinarily well by my colleague Richard Lewis, were enormously profitable over the years—even including that rough week. The positions were large, though, so when the market occasionally moved against us, it always hurt.

Lucky And Good

Later that fall, I had another, more personal, defeat that was much smaller—yet this latter story has been retold more times than my $100 million loss. It involved a single hand of poker played in the lobby of the Hill Country Hyatt, outside of San Antonio, Texas (remember the Alamo), where Enron was holding its annual and, ultimately, last management conference.

While playing Pot Limit High-Low Omaha, I had a very good high hand and a reasonably good low hand. As the evening progressed, the stakes had steadily grown. Then, it happened: I lost both ways to a player who turned over the "nuts," or a straight-flush wheel (Ace-2-3-4-5 of the same suit). In this one hand, I lost over $11,000—a tale which would go public in 2003, when it was described in the book *Enron: The Smartest Guys in the Room*. Since then, I have played plenty of poker but never again won or lost nearly as much on a single hand.

Over the course of my life, I have made hundreds of thousands of wagers—from five-cent poker bets to commodity plays that could make or lose hundreds of millions. Whatever the stakes, *they all involved risk.*

Taking risks, assessing the odds, making decisions, and placing bets as they relate to business, are the themes of this book.

As CEO of Enron Europe, and before that, as President and Chief Operating Officer, I ran one of the largest commodity trading organizations in the world. During my tenure at Enron, I did everything from making trades myself to managing large trading organizations. Over the years, my groups operated in: Western US natural gas; UK natural gas and electricity; European continental natural gas and electricity; Australian electricity; Japanese electricity (*you didn't realize that Australia and Japan were part of Europe?*); and Enron's worldwide oil, metals, and credit-trading businesses.

Since Enron, I have started several of my own businesses, which gave me the chance to apply the trading mentality to other areas of business. I'm convinced that what I have learned about risk and business "bets" can help other entrepreneurs, traders, and investors.

My target audience is primarily businesspeople looking for a unique opportunity, who must then decide whether or not to chance it. My goal is to provide you with insights gleaned from years of risk

taking, decision making, and placing bets—-and from coming out (mostly) on top.
 Enjoy!

Lucky And Good

♦♦♦
♦♦♦

ESSENTIAL TERMS

"Speak English!' said the Eaglet. "I don't know the meaning of half those long words, and I don't believe you do either!"
—Lewis Carol, *Alice in Wonderland*

In order to gain the most insight from this book, you need to know the terms of the game. Glossaries usually aren't found immediately after the Preface—but this time is different, and hence has another name. In the age of ebooks, it is simply more difficult to reference material located in the back of the book. I hope this helps you to better follow the action.

Bad Beat: A poker term for stealing defeat from the jaws of victory. Once ahead in a hand, another player's (improbably great) cards allow him to come from behind and beat you. It is a *bad beat* for you, and a brilliant play for him.

Bankruptcy Swap: A financial derivative (see definition below); one counterpart pays another counterpart a fee, or premium, to secure protection against a third company's bankruptcy. The "swap" price is based on the perceived probability that a company will declare bankruptcy during an agreed period of time.

Bid: The price at which a buyer is willing to buy an asset or financial instrument.

Bid-Offer Spread: The difference between the best posted sales price "offer" and the best posted buy price "bid." The narrower this spread, the more liquid the market.

Black Swan: A term coined by Nassim Nicholas Taleb; a totally unexpected event that creates major consequences. *Black swans* can be positive or negative, but are more often discussed when they are calamitous. These can include wars, natural disasters, epidemics, and government collapses.

Blackjack: A casino game, also known as Twenty-One. One of the most widely-played casino games in the world. The object is to

Lucky And Good

reach the highest total count in your hand without exceeding 21. If the player or dealer is dealt an Ace (which counts as either one or 11) and a ten (10, Jack, Queen, or King), this two card hand constitutes a *Blackjack*—the best possible hand.

Blackjack Insurance: When the dealer's "up card" is an Ace, the player may make a second bet of up to half his current bet that the dealer's down-facing card has a value of ten (10, Jack, Queen, or King). If the dealer ends up with a blackjack, the insurance bet wins, with a two for one payoff.

Bubble: A severe "inflection point" (see definition below) that develops when a price climbs absurdly higher until the trend can no longer be sustained and collapses.

Champ: One who is "good enough" to make money at the game.

Chump: One who is *not* "good enough" to make money at the game without an unusual streak of luck.

Critical Junctures: Historical, political and systematic inflection points that dramatically change the status quo. These include wars, epidemics, natural disasters, advancements in technology, and wholesale shifts in economic systems.

Derivative: A financial instrument utilized by two counterparts who bet on the value or change in value of another asset, index, or real-world variable. For example, one counterpart might bet that the 30-year Treasury yield will be greater than 4.25% on August 1, 2014, and her counterpart takes the opposite wager that the yield will be lower than 4.25%. A bet placed on the over-under points of the next 49ers game is a form of *derivative,* although few describe it as such.

Enron Online (EOL): Enron's online commodity trading system, launched November 29, 1999.

Entrepreneur: A business person who either creates a new business from scratch or runs a small business.

ETF (exchange-traded-fund): A publicly-traded investment. An *ETF* can hold a variety of assets from stocks, bonds, to commodities, and can be used to bet that an asset price will either increase or decrease in value. An *ETF* is similar to a mutual fund but, unlike a mutual fund, can be shorted and bought or sold during the trading day at the intra-day price (see definition of "short" below).

Exit Strategy: An investor's plans to convert an investment, trade, or business into cash.

Expected Value: In probability theory, the estimated weighted average of the potential results of a random variable.

Friction Costs: The costs associated with getting into and out of a transaction or investment. These include "transaction costs" (defined below), which are a subset of friction costs, plus bid-offer spreads and miscellaneous costs associated with buying and selling an asset or placing a bet. For example, the cost to drive to Las Vegas to place a bet on the 49ers is a friction cost but not a transaction cost.

Hedge fund: A private, actively-managed fund that invests or trades on behalf of that fund's investors.

Inflection Point: A dramatic reversal or change in the direction of a curve or trend.

Intellectual Property (IP): A technology, product, service, territory or market-based advantage such as a patent, trademark, copyright, know-how or trade secret, that gives an individual or company an exclusive competitive advantage.

Investor: One who buys and owns an asset, such as publicly-traded stocks, bonds, real estate, or privately-owned companies.

Independent Power Producer (IPP): A power plant developed and owned by a third party rather than by a traditional utility. These first gained prominence in the US in the early 1980s.

Less than Zero-Sum Games: Games, bets and businesses whose participants lose more money than others earn (in total), usually due to "friction costs".

Lions in the Grass: A term coined by John Mauldin; a subset of the "black swan." A major change or rare event anticipated by a few keen observers, and from which they profit.

Liquidity: This term has two related meanings. First, having enough cash, or access to cash, to pay the bills. Second, the state of having small friction costs for buying or selling an asset, or for a trader to enter into and then reverse a position. The more liquid the market, the narrower the "bid-offer spread," and the lower the costs to transact. Liquid markets cost less to make a trade in, and less to subsequently undo that same position.

Lizard Brain: Thinking that relies on that part of the brain that senses danger, where instincts and gut feelings—primal thoughts—guide decisions rather that "Rational Thinking". Also, used as a noun to describe a person who uses this style of thinking to make decisions.

Long: The term used for owning an asset and benefiting when a price increases. If I am "long" gold and the price increases, I make money. If I am "long" gold and the price declines, I lose money. This is the opposite of being "short" (defined below).

Margin: The collateral required by the market, necessary to assure participants that a trader/investor can make good on any potential losses.

Market Maker: One who provides market liquidity by both buying and selling an asset or financial instrument, generally profiting from the difference between the buy "bid" price and the sales "offer" price or the "bid-offer spread."

Offer: The price at which an asset or financial instrument is offered for sale in the marketplace.

Option: The right, but *not the obligation*, to buy or sell an asset or financial instrument at a pre-determined price during an agreed period of time.

Other People's Money (OPM): Portfolio and hedge fund managers invest and manage "other people's money"—not their own. Portfolio managers' compensation may not be perfectly aligned with that of their investors, creating a potential conflict of interest.

Poker: A family of card games that involve betting; the highest-ranked hand shown at the end collects the pot. Today, the most popular form of poker is Texas Hold'em.

Professional Gamblers: Gamblers skilled enough in certain games to earn a living playing those games. These days, they are usually poker players, but may also "work" in sports betting, horse betting and blackjack.

Rational Thinker: One who makes decisions based on the greatest likelihood of getting what she wants in the long run. The opposite of a "Lizard Brain."

Short: A bet that profits when an asset or factor drops in price, and loses when that asset or element increases in price. It is also used as a verb (i.e. to short the market). If I am short oil, I make money when the price declines; if the price of oil increases, I lose money. It is the opposite of being "long" (defined above).

Sunk Costs: Those costs that have already been spent. On a go-forward basis, they should be irrelevant.

Essential Terms

Texas Hold'em: The most popular variation of poker. Each player is dealt two "down" cards which distinguish his hand from the other players. Eventually there are five shared, or common, cards in the middle. The winning hand combines the player's two down cards with the five common cards in order to create the highest-ranking poker hand.

Time to Sell: Related to liquidity, it represents the time required to sell an asset. Liquid assets take less time to sell than less-liquid assets.

Tipping Point: An inflection point where one small element leads to wholesale change—the proverbial straw that breaks the camel's back.

Tolling Agreement: An agreement between the provider of a finished product (such as electricity or cheese) which allows the owner of raw materials to exchange the raw materials (e.g. natural gas or milk) for a finished product.

Trade Credit: Credit granted from a seller to a buyer, in lieu of demanding an up-front payment.

Trader: One who buys and sells financial instruments, such as stocks, bonds, commodities, and derivatives. Unlike an investor, a *trader* is willing to bet that a price will decline (in other words go "short").

Transaction Cost: Out-of-pocket expenses and fees paid to brokers, attorneys, and markets involved in completing a transaction. *Transaction costs* are a subset of "friction costs" (see definition above). Lower *transaction costs* lead to lower friction costs, which leads to greater liquidity in a market.

Transparency: The clarity apparent in the current price of an asset or derivative. One can usually see the price of a liquid large cap stock traded on the New York Stock exchange within a penny per share. If you know that a stock just sold for $21.12, you wouldn't try to buy the stock for $5 or $35.

Value Proposition: A unique combination of benefits, features, costs, and value offered by a business that distinguishes its products, services, and offerings from those of its competitors.

Vig ("Vigorish"): The amount of money retained by sports books in Las Vegas and similar venues; it's the gross profits before deducting operating expenses from the bets placed. If the casino accepts two offsetting $110 bets and ultimately pays the winner $210, it keeps the remaining $10—the vig.

Volatility: The measure of how much a price or variable has or will change over time.

Zero-sum Games: A game or market where the winners' profits equal the losers' losses. This is a market with no "friction costs" (defined above). For example, if I make a $5 bet with my brother that the total points in the first half of the 49ers game will be 27 points or less, one of us will make $5, the other will lose $5.

♦♦♦
♦♦♦

INTRODUCTION

"I'd rather be lucky than good."
—Vernon "Lefty" Gomez

Lefty Gomez, the 1930s Yankees pitcher, had the benefit of playing with both Babe Ruth and Joe DiMaggio (in different years). In reality, he was not only lucky—playing on teams good enough to win five World Series—but, as a seven-time All-Star, he was also very good. He was a Champ.

My ambition is a twist on Lefty's theme: be lucky *and* good in the risks you take, and the decisions and bets you make.

This book might have been titled, simply, "Be Good"; after all, my name is Johnny! We might have sidestepped entirely the "luck"

Lucky And Good

dimension because, the better you are, the luckier you tend to get. But that title is so dull that you never would have gotten this far.

Being lucky means being able to benefit from life's unpredictability. Some of this, you can influence; much of it, you cannot. If you are good, you are better able to position yourself for life's random walk, often getting luckier in the process.

Recognizing the difference between "being good" versus "just plain luck" can literally make or break your venture—but not everyone notices this critical distinction. Early success, for example, can blur the lines. Consequently, you may develop bad habits and a weak foundation on which to place your next wager. (My first hire as a manager was a home run; then I got cocky, and my second pick was a fiasco.) A new poker player or trader who makes all the wrong moves, but wins anyway, might never recover from his good luck in order to become a Champ.

On a short survey at SurveyMonkey.com, I found that, by more than a three to one margin (with a small sample size of 50), people would rather be good than lucky. I would rather be good as well, but I don't want to ignore luck either. Luck is one of those factors that I can neither guarantee nor significantly influence, but I'll take it, and hopefully not waste it when it comes my way. We'll spend some time on the "lucky" part, but more on the "good."

My advice is primarily set in the context of finding or creating opportunities, then assessing them, making decisions, and taking those actions that will make you a Champ in business, rather than a Chump.

You will notice that I use the terms "good enough" and "Champ" interchangeably. Likewise I use "Chump" as shorthand for "not good enough." By "good enough" I mean, capable of making money at your game. *Good* is relative, depending on what the game is and who else is playing. Many business writers discuss the importance of being the "best." *Best* is a subset of *good enough*.

However, if you can't reach the minimal threshold of *good enough*, then you're rarely going to get the chance to compete long enough to reach the ultimate goal of becoming the "best" before you run out of money, lose your job, or your spot in the batting order.

Introduction

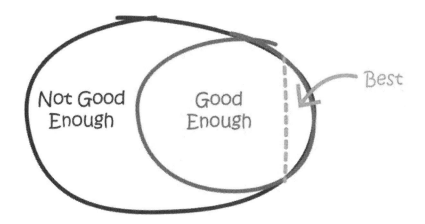

In poker, with all the players sitting at the same table, it can take hundreds, if not thousands, of hands before it becomes obvious who's the Champ and who's the Chump. And in the meantime, some of the Chumps may have improved their play. In a complex, international trading or investing market, it is even harder to figure out how the players stack up.

The most important thing to focus on is how well *you* are playing the game. About 400 years ago, Shakespeare wrote: "To thine own self be true." But without abundant objectivity and thousands of outcomes, you won't have enough data to know, precisely. Even with glaring evidence, the average Chump will ignore the results.

You can only take charge by constantly improving your game, your skills, and knowledge, to create an advantage.

*****

In case you haven't guessed by now, I have a passion for business, playing poker, and talking baseball.

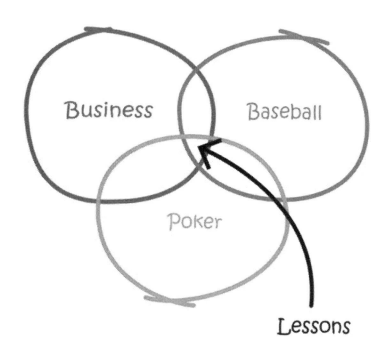

The business world is where I have had success: it's the purpose of this book. I'll employ many examples from sports and gambling in order to make you better at the "sport" (as Mark Cuban calls it) of business.

This book hopes to borrow from the best of baseball decisions, the world of poker, and my own business experience. I use these examples to illustrate how traders, investors, and entrepreneurs take risks, make decisions, place bets—and how you can use these principles to your advantage.

Now, let's deal the cards.

Introduction

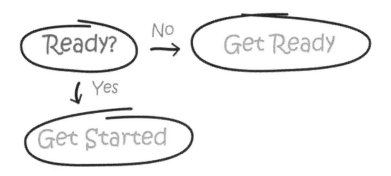

Lucky And Good

♦♦♦
♦♦♦

CHAPTER ONE: DON'T BE A CHUMP

"May the odds be ever in your favor."
—*The Hunger Games*

In his book *The Signal and the Noise,* Nate Silver tells the story of his being an internet poker player. In some of that market's busiest years, Silver was good enough to make a nice living at the game. But when Congress attempted to shut down the internet poker industry, many of the poorer players abandoned online play. Suddenly Silver found himself as the Fish (the poker expression for a Chump,) and started to lose to better players who he now faced more regularly, instead of the many Chumps who had formerly frequented his games. Silver was smart enough to switch to another market—election forecasting—where he reemerged as a Champ.

In this chapter, we will discuss the leading cast of characters that you may encounter in business. The principal characters are *Champs* and *Chumps*. What differentiates the two is the ways in which they make decisions based on their respective competitive advantages. All other classifications are supporting actors, and intended to clarify this primary distinction.

THE CHAMP PROFITS WHERE THE CHUMP LOSES

"Know your enemy and know yourself and you can fight a hundred battles without disaster."
—Sun Tzu

Lorraine was sure that the garage door was open. I was adamant that it wasn't. I had closed the garage door five minutes before. She had just returned from the garage after having opened it. I bet her $10 that the garage door was closed, and she quickly accepted. She had better information and was the Champ—I was the Chump.

Being a Champ requires satisfying two conditions:

- ❖ First, it means consistently thinking and acting rationally. Set aside any tendency to follow your Lizard Brain (see below).
- ❖ The second condition requires finding a market in which you can build a competitive advantage.

If you can pass these two tests, you can reach the threshold of "good enough" to beat the game. Satisfying only one of the criteria is a sure way to lose. Meeting neither test means it's time to start attending the weekly Chumps Anonymous meetings.

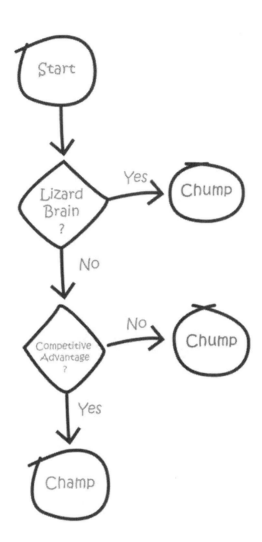

THINK RATIONALLY

Lizard Brain, n: that part of the brain that senses danger, where instincts and gut feelings originate; primal thoughts; subconscious or involuntary processes.—*Urban Dictionary*

If you can't get past your Lizard Brain and think rationally when making decisions, you are destined for perpetual Chumpdom.

Acting on instinct is a reptilian habit that has been engrained in our DNA for hundreds of millions of years. While this thinking might be ideal in fight or flight situations, it will not serve you well in business when making more complicated choices. The Lizard Brain is sometimes motivated by "that's the way we've always done it," or "I hate to lose"—or by a knee-jerk reaction that fails to question assumptions, goals, and metrics.

The Rational Thinker, on the other hand (or hemisphere), makes moves based on the greatest likelihood of getting what he wants in the long run. **Contrary to popular opinion, the best traders and professional gamblers not only care about, they <u>rely on</u>, the "long run."**

My advice flies in the face of the ways that many people actually handle risk, manage the downside, and place their bets (otherwise this book would not be needed). When you see the Lizard Brain symbol as you read on, pause and consider your current biases—**put your intuition on hold and *think*.**

... BUT RATIONAL THINKING IS NOT ENOUGH

You might be poised and ready to think about every bet rationally by putting your Lizard Brain aside. But even with the right thinking style, if you don't have a competitive advantage in the market in which you are betting, you fail the second test. A competitive advantage comes via a deep understanding and anticipation of your market—its trends, inflection points, players, rules, laws, regulations, barriers, constraints, and all the other factors that cause daily fluctuations and major shifts.

I have an attorney friend, whose advice about the prospects for lawsuit investments I really value. He is logical, pragmatic, and can articulate what can go wrong, and what the odds are. (He scored in the 99% percentile on his LSATs.) He is a Champ. And yet he likes to actively trade individual stocks where he exhibits an unwillingness to take his losses, and in which he has absolutely no competitive advantage. In this latter market, he is a not a Champ. (Notice my diplomacy here, probably the last time you will ever see it.)

Only a Chump makes a serious bet without an information advantage. Developing one is hard, analytical work, and may be nearly impossible in the biggest, most liquid world markets. Seek that advantage according to your strengths. **You will do far better as a Champ in the Southeastern concrete market or the California almond market than playing the Chump in the S&P 500 futures market.** Remember that, even though Michael Jordan was a Champ (undoubtedly the greatest) in the basketball market, he was "not good enough" to play professional baseball.

*****

When you sit down at a poker game with strangers, you have no idea if you are the Champ or the Chump. Over many hands you should gradually figure it out. If you can't figure it out after thousands of hands, guess what category you're in?

James Altucher tells this story about raising money for his hedge fund. A neighbor introduced James to her boss, a gentleman who managed a portfolio much larger than Altucher's. James thought this would be a great chance not only to secure a sizable chunk of capital, but also to earn the endorsement of this investing Champ.

When Altucher met this titan, they had a great chat, and Altucher thought they were really connecting. The Champ told James that if he ever needed a job, he would be glad to hire him, but finally explained that he couldn't put any money into Altucher's hedge fund. The man expressed his concern about not having control; the last thing the Champ needed was bad publicity and an unfavorable front page story in the *Wall Street Journal*. Altucher was obviously disappointed.

It wasn't until December 2008, that Altucher discovered, along with the rest of the world, that his neighbor's boss, Bernie Madoff, really was a Chump *and* a Crook—<u>not</u> a Champ. Financial analyst Harry Markopolos had suspected Madoff in 1999, and informed the SEC (US Securities and Exchange Commission)—but the government Chumps ignored Markopolos. It took almost a decade before the SEC and the general public figured out this fraud.

It usually takes time to separate the Champs from the Chumps.

ESCAPE FROM CHUMPDOM

Know what to avoid, or you may find yourself at the bottom of the food chain (the *dinner*, rather than the *diner*). The classic Chump is:

- overmatched,
- gullible,
- the prey,
- confused,
- below par,
- the green weeny,
- the dumb money,
- a pushover,
- the fish,
- lightweight,
- out-gunned,
- sucker in the game, and, as John Mauldin labels it,
- "a bug in search of a windshield."

The bug might find a nice warm windshield on a Mercedes parked in the shade, but will become very unlucky, if it lands on any old car (it doesn't matter the brand) traveling at 70 mph on the freeway—splat!

The Chump doesn't understand the contest well enough to compete, yet he doesn't recognize or accept this deficiency. In the technology world, for instance, the Chump might be smart, but too late to the party. (Think Microsoft's entry into the smartphone or tablet markets.) We have *all* been Chumps (hopefully past tense), probably more often than we'd like to admit.

As a Chump, you might have plenty of information, might have done lots of thinking about the opportunity, and given it the "old college try," but what matters is how skilled and knowledgeable you are *relative to your competition.*

Let's consider some typical Chumps.

- ❖ Amateurs with no relevant experience or education who put their life's savings into new restaurants. They do this despite the fact that more than half (reportedly anywhere from 60-90%, depending on the study) of new non-franchise restaurants fail within three years.

- ❖ Procter & Gamble, usually masterful when bringing new products to market, failed, in 1983, to successfully launch their Citrus Hill orange juice brand. They picked the wrong market, at the wrong time, to challenge already-successful Minute Maid and Tropicana. P&G was a distant third until they eventually pulled the plug on the OJ business.

- ❖ The vast majority of those who enlist in multi-level marketing programs.

- ❖ Most mutual fund managers of active funds: Over a 20-year period, about 80% of actively-managed mutual funds underperform their benchmarks, i.e., the overall equity market. **This is a case of Chumps managing money for other Chumps.** (At best it is a matter of upper-quartile Chumps investing for lower-quartile Chumps.)

- ❖ Anyone who buys a heavily-advertised training program that promises to teach others how to trade the stock market using technical trading "secrets". If you want to see real magic, enjoy a good Penn & Teller show in Las Vegas.

❖ Most of those who invested in a major US airline before about 2009, other than those who favored Southwest Airlines. Recent airline consolidations may reverse this trend.

❖ People who put their entire life's savings into Ponzi schemes orchestrated by Bernie Madoff and Allen Stanford. Learn from these victims, and ignore the concept of economic diversity at your peril. Investing some money with these crooks did not make them Chumps—going "all-in" did.

❖ Someone who has accumulated huge college student debt, while earning a degree ignored by the market, so is now working for minimum wage. Minimum-wage work does not identify a Chump, but having planned—or not planned—in a way that offers no better choices after such a huge investment, *does*.

❖ Most authors who actually expect to make any money directly off their books. Kudos to Agatha Christie, Danielle Steel, Mark Twain, J.K. Rowling, and J.R.R. Tolkien, who shattered this trend.

Fortunately, you are not predestined to remain a Chump. You have the ability to improve your play or simply switch to an easier game (like Nate Silver did).

Don't Be A Chump

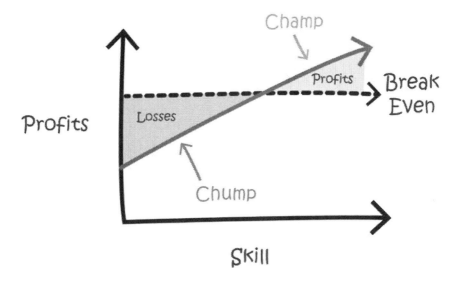

If you are the tenth-best poker player in the world, but happen to be sitting at a game with the nine better players, you are the Fish. But, the next night, if you enter a small local game, you may emerge as the Champ again (although you probably played for hundreds of thousands of dollars in the first game and quarters in the second).

Sure, you would love to play big stakes with the Fish, but it rarely works out that way. You might even be willing to play small stakes with the best players in the world, if you had a chance to learn from them for a minimal tuition fee. However, absent a strong friendship, the best are not going to be sharing their real insights.

Find your relative strengths (hopefully you have some) and play to them.

You might be a Champ in the market for 57 Chevys or South Miami real estate, but a Chump in the market for Honus Wagner baseball trading cards or independent film investments.

Wholesale US natural gas deregulation changed the markets dramatically during the early to mid-1990s. A newcomer with the right thinking style (non-Lizard), discipline, and access to market information could become a Champ in just a few years. If you are the

Lucky And Good

Chump in the market, you should root for dramatic change so that you can learn and adjust faster than the reigning Champs.

How does luck play a role? Any successful trader or poker player knows that there is randomness to almost any business or game (although, admittedly, a few games such as chess and duplicate bridge are nearly devoid of luck). Both the Champ and the Chump have streaks of luck, good and bad. But the Champ is better at identifying and separating outcomes based on skill rather than luck.

Joe Peta's entertaining book, *Trading Bases: A Story About Wall Street, Gambling, and Baseball*, discusses how he found opportunity in betting on baseball teams that had recently experienced bad luck. These teams should have won or lost more than they actually had, based on the runs they scored versus the runs they allowed. As a result, the odds tended to make them better trades because the betting public was generally ignoring the "luck dimension."

The best I can promise my readers with regards to luck is that, in the long run, you are likely to end up about average. That's where being "good enough" is so essential. The primary drivers for a Champ involve ***playing the game well to stay at the top***, and b***eing prepared to overcome bad luck at some point***. You control how well you play the game and how adept you are in handling the hot and cold streaks that are beyond your influence.

I recommend that you intentionally work at identifying and adjusting to the dynamics of luck and skill (the main focus of this book). As a blackjack player, if I am playing at an honest game in which I'm allowed to count cards and use a system (tested via tens of millions of computer-simulated hands), the casino doesn't ask me to leave, and if I play without mistakes, I can beat the game in the long run. But I might lose for several days in a row before I bounce back into the win column. As a trader in a unique smaller market (say, the market for trading California CO_2 emissions) where I might have a competitive information advantage, I am still not going to beat the market every day.

If I stay disciplined, maintain my competitive edge, get fast feedback, position myself to make many uncorrelated but favorable and reasonably sized bets, and keep my friction costs down—then I should win in the long run. Doing the opposite essentially guarantees losing in the long run.

Virtually every business outcome is the result of some combination of luck and skill. If you have been a Champ, but unlucky, you should stick with it. But if you have been a lucky Chump, you need to upgrade your game, switch to a game in which you can be the Champ (as Nate Silver did), or quit while you are ahead (an expression I typically hate). When a Chump gets unlucky, his life in the market is usually short-lived.

This book discusses how players make serious bets (those designed for profit rather than entertainment) based on where they think markets are headed. Finding the smart bet and avoiding the dumb one is within your power. And when you blow it (which you will), then learn, adjust, and move on. That allows you to consistently return to the pinball machine—with the chance to play again.

INVESTOR, TRADER, ENTREPENEUR, OR PROFESSIONAL GAMBLER?

People make different decisions, depending on their tolerance for risk, the perceived chance of loss, analytical skills, and time frame.

For example, in my lawsuit business, I buy a portion of a lawsuit's potential proceeds; this is an investment, not a trade. The secondary market (where I might unload my position) is weak and small; usually the only way out of the investment before the lawsuit either pays off or fails is to sell to another investor at a major discount (big friction costs) to the current value (which I have, so far, managed to avoid). Eventually, I will either get paid or lose my investment.

When Warren Buffett buys a company, his intent is to buy and hold forever. In my lawsuit business, a long-term investment might be three or four years, but I prefer cases that I believe will be resolved in 15 months or less. Investors who buy and hold forever care little about eventually selling the investment. **But plans and markets change, so, all things being equal, it's always better to have options for unwinding an investment—rather than not having this choice.**

Irrespective of your own mindset, you need to pay attention to the other approaches. There are two other key reasons for you to do so. You might be transacting business with one of the "others" or, one or more of "them" may be able to dramatically influence your market. **If am convinced as a trader that current housing prices are above fair value, I might be theoretically right; but if the investment community is massively bullish, I can still go broke betting against them.** If, as a trader, I am selling a power plant or gold mine, the ultimate buyer is likely to come from the universe of investors. As a natural gas trader if I am convinced that winter prices are too low and start buying, I can get burned if the producers decide they like the price and start selling.

Let's review the varying frameworks and mental operating systems for entrepreneurs, traders and investors. You can borrow concepts from each group that work in your business and, at the same time, seek out partners who possess valuable qualities you may lack.

An **entrepreneur** creates a new business from scratch, or runs a small business—think Mark Zuckerberg as he launched Facebook in 2004, or your friend who runs the corner deli. Most small businesses are relatively conventional (buying a franchise, starting a web development service, opening a dog kennel). To succeed, the safer bets (in this instance I mean a startup with a greater chance of being in business a few years later) rely on hard work, selling skills, good customer service, enough capital, execution of the fundamentals, integrity, and frequently copying what is already working.

Entrepreneur's Risk Scale

Some entrepreneurial endeavors entail more risk than others. Riskier bets require execution of the fundamentals just as much as the more conservative ones. But the riskier gamble on a unique and un-proven value proposition hopes to create a long-term competitive advantage, and a chance for an eventual home run.

A "value proposition" is a statement that defines the unique combination of features and services being offered. A "unique" value proposition is one that offers greater upside, but also more risk of failure.

One who has never worked in either the coffee- or food-delivery business is a long-shot to create a new business that promises to deliver 300 kinds of coffee to the customer's doorstep within fifteen minutes of ordering. And yet, almost all radical change comes from industry outsiders. Great examples of this include Amazon (originally a unique approach to the book business, but now so much more) and Apple, in both the music and cell phone businesses.

Long shots can offer tremendous value based on the upside, but the calculations and risk/reward profile are quite different from the safer plays.

Successful entrepreneurs combine realism and optimism. Too much of the former, and they never take a chance. Too much optimism and they only pursue long shots.

Entrepreneurs have both advantages and disadvantages compared to established businesses. On the positive side, they get to start from scratch, and look at things from a fresh perspective. Entrepreneurs don't have to do things the way they have always been done. And yet most entrepreneurs will fail because:

- Starting a new business is hard work.
- They must learn as they go.
- It's tough to raise enough money to get started so you have less cash to survive your screw-ups.
- It's more expensive and takes longer to bring your new product or service to market than you had expected.
- It's hard to convince most customers to try something new.
- Inertia favors incumbents.
- Making that first sale is very difficult.
- It is hard to get fast feedback.
- Constant adjustments are required—even quick responses and changes may not be enough as new business frequently works from a too-small sample size of experiences.
- Life happens!

Nassim Nicholas Taleb reminds entrepreneurs: "Most of you will fail, disrespected, impoverished, but we are grateful for the risks you are taking and the sacrifices you are making for the sake of the economic growth of the planet and pulling others out of poverty."

Thank goodness that, despite all these challenges, a few of you crazy entrepreneurs will still take the plunge.

*****

An **investor** normally buys and owns assets, such as publicly traded stocks, bonds, real estate, or privately owned companies. The

Don't Be A Chump

objective is to make an ongoing income, and eventually to profit from the asset's appreciation. Think Warren Buffett. When he buys a business, he searches for one that is well established, with a deep competitive moat; one that even a poor or mediocre manager can't ruin; one that will not face substantial changes to its business model during the coming decades. Warren Buffett prefers to avoid unproven value propositions.

In general, an investor usually goes "long" (expecting the price to go up) and rarely goes "short" (expecting the price to drop). Anyone who owns an IRA, savings account, or home is an investor. You are going long—wagering that your home will be worth more over time. You obviously don't want this investment to decline in value.

*****

A **trader** is someone who takes "positions" on things like stocks, bonds, currencies, or commodities (sometimes even baseball players), in which she bets that a dimension (frequently but not always a price) will increase or decline. Wall Street traders probably come to mind, but all over the world people trade in commodity markets, equities, debt, and the front offices of a few Major League baseball teams. Most traders are honest. But lately, the profession has gotten bad press every time a Wall Street hedge fund trader has been handcuffed and hauled off to court, accused of insider trading.

Believe it or not, one terrific illustration of a model trader is Billy Beane, General Manager of the Oakland A's. He is always slicing and dicing his team's makeup, pondering how every player's various dimensions might help his team win more games. Beane says: "Know what every player in baseball is worth to you. You can put a dollar figure on it."

Contrast his approach with Warren Buffet's intent to buy a company or stock, and hold it forever. Buffet owns part of the Omaha Storm Chasers, the Triple-A minor league baseball team in Omaha. Does Buffet espouse the same approach to player loyalty that he does to the companies that he owns? Does his team ever trade or sell a player? Probably. Is his team still playing any player that was on the team 20 years ago? I think not. In this rare instance, even Buffet is a trader.

Here's another difference. When you invest in your home, you always want the value to go up. Your position as an investor is "long." But a trader may be willing to bet that the value of the housing market or of an ounce of gold will go up *or* down—and if the trader is right, she will profit. Betting that something will drop in price is called going "short."

I acknowledge that the Urban Dictionary's definition is the view of many: *"Trader (tra'deer also pronounced treydor) is a form of profession on a distant planet far far away in a not very close future, that are [sic] eating children and are considered evil down to the bone."* And unfortunately "trader" sounds an awful lot like "traitor"—someone disloyal to his country.

LARD OR SHORTENING?

In his book *Lead With a Story*, Paul Smith recounts a market research story that has become folklore at Procter & Gamble.

It was 1985, and "Jim" was conducting an interview, trying to understand why a customer was using lard in her cooking, rather than P&G's shortening brand. The customer told him: "I know shortening is a lot healthier than lard. But it's better for my kids to buy lard."

Jim was puzzled. Shortening is healthier, so how can it be better for her kids to buy lard? The woman continued: "If I buy shortening, I can't afford to buy milk. Lard and milk is healthier than shortening and water. So I buy lard...and milk."

This mother thinks like a trader—comparing relative worth and different combinations, using a limited budget to create the most value for her kids. She knows the benefits and the price of milk, shortening and lard; if milk or shortening get cheaper or lard became more expensive, she would quickly change her recipes.

TRADER VERSUS INVESTOR

If I were required to identify the major attribute separating traders from investors it would be this: a willingness and requirement to change one's mind sooner, rather than later. (Some refuse to change their minds at all.)

A trader has the *benefit* of having made more mistakes than non-traders (is this a desperate attempt to turn lemons into lemonade?) He doesn't like being wrong, but he has plenty of history to remind him of the possibility.

A trader develops a hypothesis about how the market is going to move and how the odds favor a certain position. However, from that point on, having been wrong so many times, the trader continues to collect data which sometimes supports the original hypothesis but frequently contradicts it. Within minutes of placing a trade, the trader might be singing Toby Keith's song: "I wish I didn't know now what I didn't know then."

Relatively quickly (sometimes minutes, occasionally, months) the trader unwinds the trade. **Every so often, the data forces the trader to change her thinking so dramatically that she will close one position while simultaneously taking one exactly opposite from the original.** Such a reversal is virtually unheard of in the investing world.

Traders find themselves wrong more often than non-traders; therefore they also are more practiced in reversing course. The seasoned trader is like a Major League batter who takes a 95-mile-an-hour fastball on the elbow, and still crowds the plate on his next at bat. **The trader does not gauge success based on the frequency of being "right" versus "wrong," but rather, the amount of money made or lost cumulatively over a lifetime of bets.**

Investors are more bothered by the possibility of being wrong (losing), and when found to be wrong, struggle more to reverse course. The greatest US investor in recent history, Warren Buffet, rarely sells a major investment. Investors try to be extra careful about the decisions they make and the bets that they place because they don't plan on looking back and analyzing how well their bet is panning out for a very long time (in trader time).

PROFESSIONAL GAMBLERS

The **professional gambler** is a sub-species of the trader.

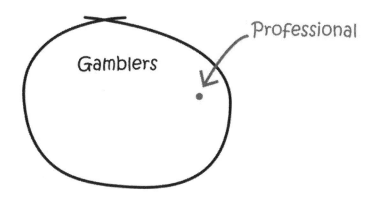

His "market" is usually the poker game, but can also include the blackjack table, sports betting, or horse race betting.

The term "professional gambler" brings up the stereotype of a riverboat gambler from Mark Twain's era—one that cheated to win. But today, there are at least four areas (sports betting, horse betting, blackjack, and poker) where honorable and smart gamblers play the odds and the psychology of the game well enough to make an excellent living. However, unlike professional gamblers, when traders, investors and speculators bet on price movements they generally add transparency and liquidity to a real-world market. By assisting the broad market to see the perceived changes in supply and demand, they help farmers decide which crops to plant, and oil companies decide if drilling for a new oil well is money well spent.

Entrepreneur, investor, trader, professional gambler: regardless of your attitude towards them, they all take risks with their money, and combine their time, insight and research to try to make a profit. This is all a very bottom-up process that usually creates value and efficiency. Alternatively, top-down, government-led pricing effectively guarantee the wrong price.

BUSINESS VERSUS GAMBLING

"The gambling known as business looks with austere disfavor upon the business known as gambling."
—Ambrose Bierce

You may be surprised by my unapologetic use of the terms "bet" and "gamble" in the context of commerce. But the odds in a given situation are just as important in oil trading as they are in poker.

The media portrays any trade, investment, risk, chance, or decision that goes wrong as a "bet" or "gamble." But that characterization can throw a subtle and negative bias on how entrepreneurs and investors make decisions. Conversely, the press portrays those risks that succeed as "strategic masterpieces," "strokes of genius," and "brilliant moves"—almost always in hindsight. The only difference is whether these bets won or lost—not if they were, in fact, smart. The media is generally incapable of recognizing that a losing bet may have been the best decision at the time.

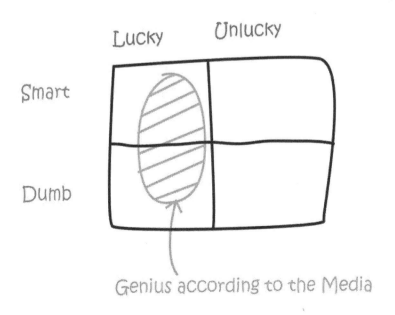

Lucky And Good

In business (and life in general), you need to appreciate that **sometimes smart bets lose, and occasionally dumb bets win**. As Michael Lewis said about the game of baseball in M*oneyball*, "There are lucky doubles and unlucky outs." If you can't come to grips with this truth, you might avoid decisions—and that in itself is a bad decision. To the media, though, gambling is dumb and investing is brilliant. Still, many of the processes for making smart decisions, managing capital, and cutting your losses are the same whether you are in business or are a professional gambler. Knowing full well that some will be uncomfortable, I intentionally commingle the use of "bet," "position," and "trade." I would love to find the sure thing for making a profit, but I have been totally defeated in that search. **My experience is that the only sure thing is the sure loss** (more about this later).

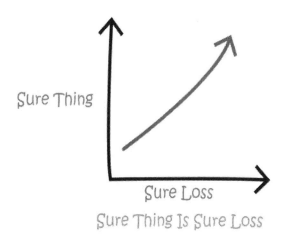

I know that if I roll the dice, I have exactly a one in thirty six chance of getting two ones (snake eyes). I also know that I have a two in thirty six chance of getting a one combined with a two (cross eyes). In business, one never knows the exact odds.

We can talk about decision making and placing bets, and put aside for now that in most business decisions, we don't know the exact probability. If we change the successful recipe of our soda drink (think New Coke), will the results be embraced by our customers? If we bet $800 million developing the Chevy Volt, will it be profitable? That is not to say that we won't make these estimates, just that they will be "best guesses," with varying levels of confidence, rather than exact odds.

Vanity Fair editor Graydon Carter overlooked the obvious similarities between these terms when he wrote, "Financial institutions like to call what they do trading. Let's be honest. It's not trading; it's betting." **But trading and gambling are not mutually exclusive, Graydon.**

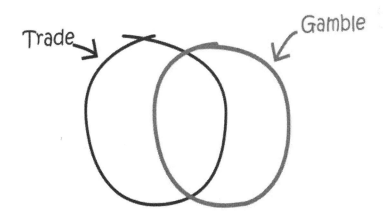

I am still waiting for a clear distinction between these terms. **Dictionary.com defines a gamble as "to stake or risk money, or anything of value, on the outcome of something involving chance."** Is there any question that chance is an element of trading, investing, or starting a new business? If you think not, then you need to find a less mentally-demanding line of work.

From a business perspective, I ask you why trades, investments, and enterprises involving risk (all of them) are considered wicked? There is no place to put your money that is risk-free, and if you want to park it under your mattress, you are destined to see your wealth gradually (and sometimes quickly) erode. Most states that run lotteries and horse racing spend taxpayer dollars to brag about the benefits of playing their games. Obviously, betting is not so evil when state-sponsored gambling boosts government tax receipts.

In general parlance, *gamble* more often refers to a game of chance where the player has a probabilistic disadvantage (i.e., slot machines, keno, craps, roulette, and lotteries); it is less often associated with professionals who have sufficient skill to regularly make money at games of chance (sports betting, horse betting, blackjack, and poker).

Although the odds are easily calculated for many gambles, I never know the exact probability of whether another player is bluffing. If I roll two dice, I know that I'm a 5-to-1 underdog to roll a 7. If I'm playing Texas Hold 'em poker, and there is only one card remaining (called the "river card") that will allow me to win the pot, it's obvious that my odds are 1 out of the 44 remaining cards (assuming I have only seen one other player's cards). But when my buddy Luther makes an all-in bet against me at the poker table, my assessment of it being a bluff is not so precise. Similarly, as an entrepreneur, I never know with confidence if a customer will prefer a certain feature by a 2-to-1 margin, or a supplier will reduce my price by 5% or 10% if I promise to double my volume. And I rarely know when a new competitor is about to appear on the scene.

As Nassim Nicholas Taleb reminds us: "In real life you do not know the odds, you need to discover them, and the sources of uncertainty are not defined." He goes on to illustrate how folks consistently overestimate their ability to handicap real-world outcomes. But not knowing the exact odds is no excuse to ignore them (Play the Odds).

FREE MARKETS

If you don't find yourself operating in free markets, you will find this book of little value. In that case, your money is probably better spent bribing (excuse me—donating to, or lobbying) politicians and regulators; or better yet, moving to a part of the world or a part of the market where free-market skills *are* rewarded. Maybe it's time to abandon the California cheese market, where wholesale prices are set by the government, and enter the California wine market, where prices are determined by market forces.

As an avid believer in free markets, I won't get into debating their role, other than to remind my readers that, in free markets:

1) Prices are set by participants using their own money.
2) Prices are set voluntarily between two parties without government interference.
3) Prices change continuously.
4) Prices change based on real-world fluctuations in many factors (some of which are not obvious).
5) Market-based prices offer more information value to the rest of the world than those prices set by governments. Transparent prices are valuable to almost everyone except those sellers who are trying to secretly charge some customers more than others for the same product or service.
6) If the market gets the price wrong, it adjusts at the speed of light when compared to a correction by a government bureaucrat or committee that has set a price too high or too low.
7) The relative value of different "things" is constantly changing and a free market recognizes, adjusts and communicates those ever changing relationships.

8) Prices benefit from the "wisdom of crowds."
9) Prices are self-correcting.
10) Traders and speculators play key roles in providing liquidity and transparency, thus benefitting all consumers. (These terms are reviewed later in the Fight Friction Costs section.)
11) Price fluctuations are messy.

LAW OF SUPPLY AND DEMAND

> "If desire for goods increases while its availability decreases, its price rises. On the other hand, if availability of the good increases and the desire for it decreases, the price comes down."
> —Ibn Taymiyyah,
> 13th/14th-century Mamluk scholar

Whatever your level of business acumen, this concept is so crucial that I want to review the nuts and bolts. It's a fact: usually-smart people often forget Economics 101, along with this essential law of supply and demand.

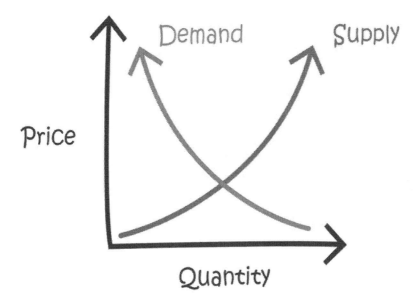

This drawing, the classic depiction of the law of supply and demand, has been used for decades to simply illustrate that, all things being equal:

1) When prices increase, more supply will be produced
2) When prices drop, less supply will be produced
3) When prices increase, demand for those products or services will drop, and
4) When prices decrease, demand for those things will increase.

This is fundamental to trading, investing, and any business. The difference between how Champs and Chumps regard this law is this: **an astute player never assumes, and normally roots against the possibility that the world's supply/demand balances will remain static**. It is always a horse race between Supply and Demand. Figuring out how the race will unfold is Job One for a trader, investor, or entrepreneur. **You win when you correctly figure out how the** supply/demand balance will change—before it is obvious to others and where you have enough confidence to place a big bet.

The most important lesson comes down to simply being on the right side of scarcity—using the law of supply and demand to your advantage, rather than your detriment. If you are selling, you want plenty of buyers and a scarcity of sellers. If you are buying, you want lots of sellers and few buyers. Inventors bringing a new idea to market will want to create a unique product or service with little possibility of substitution today and tomorrow.

A common misconception is that, just because something *should* get more plentiful or less expensive, it will. For decades the common logic of the solar photovoltaic industry has been that solar just has to get much cheaper because it is so important to our planet's future. While prices have dropped, that business is still unable to produce low-cost, reliable electricity for the average user, rate-payer, or taxpayer. Desired outcomes are irrelevant to determining whether it will, in fact, happen.

COOPETITION

In the mid-2000s, NASCAR driver Darrell Waltrip started using *coopetition* to describe how race drivers will sometimes cooperate by allowing one another to draft off of their cars. For example, when driving at 200 mph, one driver cooperates by allowing a second driver to snuggle right behind the lead driver's bumper, thereby increasing their speed and reducing wind resistance, fuel usage, and the frequency of pit stops for both cars. Despite this short-term cooperation, each driver's overriding goal is always to win the race.

This book is primarily about business competition, not cooperation—**but I don't for a minute want to downplay the importance of cooperation.** The hybrid term "coopetition" was first used about a hundred years ago and describes the phenomenon that, in nature and business, sometimes we cooperate and sometimes, we compete—with and against the same players.

Occasionally, Microsoft and Apple Inc. cooperate (for example, making Microsoft Word available on Apple computers). Yet most of the time, these two behemoths are fighting every inch of the way for technological market share.

Major League Baseball team owners come together to establish rules, select a commissioner, negotiate television deals, and decide when to add another franchise, all as a way of building the love of the game, and increasing the value of their individual businesses. Then they turn around and try to beat the other teams on the diamond.

Oakland Athletics general manager Billy Beane constantly tries to improve his team by trading one or more of his current players for those on other teams in a way that will improve his relative competitiveness. He can only sell a proposed trade to the other team if the other GM believes that the trade will result in more wins for his team. Let's say I have two outstanding first basemen and a poor second baseman. You have two outstanding second basemen and a poor first baseman. Do you think we might find a win-win deal?

If I am Billy Beane, I would rather improve the New York Mets in the NL East than one in the AL West, such as the Seattle Mariners. Why? Because the A's will not play the Mets at all during the 2013 regular season, while they will meet the Mariners at least 16 times. The important issue is not how good the A's are in absolute terms, but rather how good the team is relative to its daily competition that will determine if it wins 70 games or 100 games during the season.

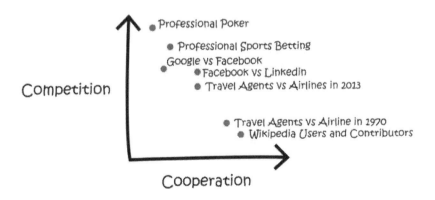

The balance between cooperation and competition varies. In poker, it is nearly 100% competition. In the natural gas trading market, there is more cooperation. And finally, development and continual upgrade of the Linux operating system and the Wikipedia encyclopedia are almost all about cooperation, with little competition.

The balance of cooperation versus competition changes over time, as well. In his book *On Innovation*, Terry Jones, who started working in the travel industry in 1970, describes how the airlines depended on and cooperated with travel agents. When Jones founded Travelocity as a subsidiary of American Airlines in 1978, that relationship started to morph, because the airlines began to view travel agents more as an expense and as competitors rather than partners. Jones says:

> **As online travel agencies continued to evolve, they captured $50 billion of the air travel business. In addition, airlines then got into the act and started recruiting travelers to come directly to their websites to book flights with their preferred carrier. Next, the airlines cut travel agent ticket commissions to zero (that's right, zero), dooming most leisure agents. In ten short years, more than eighteen thousand travel agents were out of business.**

Cooperation is not just sitting around the camp fire singing *Kumbayah*—it is central to most business success. But beyond acknowledging its importance, this brief discussion ends my coverage of the topic in this book. Let's get on with the principles that will help you *beat* the competition.

FOUR STAGES OF BUSINESS

In the next four chapters, we discuss the major stages of business and the principles that should be considered in each stage.

Find It—Find the right opportunity.

Decide—Objectively evaluate and tweak your idea or potential bet. It is essential to toss out the also-rans, and put your energy and money on the best prospect(s). Hedge fund manager and writer James Altucher says: "Write down your ideas but assume they suck." I have not consistently found such humility, but do realize that honesty, critical thinking, and objectivity are crucial at this stage of the game.

Go For It—You have "noodled" on your concept, researched it carefully, and given yourself the green light. Now you must implement it at full force. For an entrepreneur or small business, this is the hardest part. For a trader, this is sometimes as easy as a few keyboard strokes and mouse clicks.

Fix It—If you could simply sit back and receive your royalty or dividend checks from this point forward, it would be great, albeit boring (okay, not that boring)—but life is rarely that easy. Once you've executed your trade, investment, or new business, you are hardly ever at the finish line. As an entrepreneur, what do you need to change? As a trader or investor, what do you do with your position now that you have it? If things have gone well, how can you improve or double up? How do you build on your momentum? If you are stuck in the mud, how do you extract yourself? Your concept may have been a flat-out loser. So, when do you cut your losses and run?

Find It and *Decide* address the formulation of a business strategy that might succeed. *Go For It* and *Fix It* apply to the execution of that strategy. A great plan without first-rate execution doesn't hack it, and the opposite is true.

♦♦♦
♦♦♦

Lucky And Good

♦♦♦
♦♦♦

CHAPTER TWO: FIND IT

> "What makes a system successful is its ability to recognize losers and kill them quickly. Or, rather, what makes a system successful is its ability to generate lots of losers and then to recognize them as such and kill them off."
> —James Surowiecki,
> *The Wisdom of Crowds*

First things first! All business begins with finding an opportunity. This is the sexy part of commerce that I, along with many others, love to write about.

Some folks see opportunity at every turn, while others are engrossed with their one-and-only idea. The latter practice is perilous, because it is hard to be objective if you are working on your first, best, and *only* idea.

I love the *Shark Tank* television show, but when one participant pitched the idea of the Wake'N Bacon alarm clock, I figured this had to be one of his too-few ideas. The inventor loved the notion of waking up to the smell of bacon (he is obviously not married to a vegetarian like I am), so he invented a device that would start cooking bacon in your bedroom at the desired wake-up time. You awaken to that great smell of bacon, rather than an annoying alarm. Very unique, but not a venture into which I am going to put any money. I have had ideas just as silly (details to follow), so please don't come down too hard on the Wake'N Bacon.

Another inventor tried to get funding for a Bluetooth that would be surgically implanted in your neck. You would charge it at night by putting a needle in your neck, but every time you wanted a new phone, you'd need more surgery. (And you thought those two-year contracts with Verizon and AT&T were painful!) At the time the show aired, the guy was waiting for results from clinical trials and Food and Drug Administration approval. I won't be investing in this one, either (even if he gets the FDA nod).

I love wild and crazy ideas, though, because some of them just might trigger a ginormous opportunity for me. So, even though you might be laughing about the Wake'N Bacon alarm clock and surgically implanted Bluetooth, laugh in the spirit of "the possible" rather than in sarcasm and ridicule.

By 1997, Bruce Springsteen had over 350 recorded but unpublished songs. The Boss always had so many ideas that he had to work at focusing on a small subset of them whenever he released a new album. This principle might be thought of as *Find Them*, rather than *Find It*. You need to find enough of "them" in order to get the right "it."

NOTHING IS RISK FREE

"Playing it safe is probably the most unsafe thing in the world."
—Robert Collier

On March 16, 2013, the citizens of Cyprus gained a firsthand understanding of this principle, when the government announced a 6.75-9.9% tax on all bank deposits.

The government eventually backed down, and decided to confiscate money only from those accounts over 100,000 euros; but it imposed capital constraints limiting the amount that Cypriots could withdraw from their accounts (no matter the balance) each day, and the amount that citizens could send or take out of the country. Kostas Nikolaou, a 60-year-old pensioner, asked: "How can they tell you that you can't access your own money in the bank? It's our money, we are entitled to it."

The term "risk-free" is a myth, an illusion. The same goes for "safe." Nothing on earth is risk-free or safe—especially in business.

Find It

So, deal with it, handle it, and learn to profit from it, or go hide in the corner.

If you put money under the mattress and the house burns down, you lose. Even if you put your cash in a federally-insured bank account, you face the likelihood of losing value over time, because inflation usually exceeds after-tax interest returns. If you had put your money in a US checking account with zero interest and no services charges from 1957 until 2010, over those 53 years you would have lost 87% of your buying power—but it would have been considered "safe."

Okay, then, what about gold? How could that be a risky investment? If you buy gold, you have significant transaction costs to buy and sell, and the price can drop. (See a more detailed discussion about gold in Chapter Three.)

Buying wholesale and selling retail might seem like a good way to make money. If you buy ten widgets from party A for $100 and simultaneously sell the ten widgets to company B for $110, it sounds like you have locked in a profit. But what if company B declares bankruptcy before you get paid?

How about hedging? "When you reduce a hedge or hedge a hedge, isn't that gambling?" quipped Senator Bob Menendez on June

13, 2012, when trying to be clever during the Congressional hearings on JPMorgan's London trading losses.

My point is this: All business involves "gambling" or risk taking. Unfortunately, there are no perfect hedges in any arena. The only perfect hedge is to undo the original transaction with the same counterpart with whom you did the original deal. I might add that you also need to get a written waiver from him stating that he promises not to sue you.

A bank that lends a home-buyer $150,000 has no perfect hedge for that transaction, including convincing the new homeowner to pay back the loan. If the bank sells the loan to another bank or Fannie Mae, it still ends up with some legal liability. Witness all the fallout in 2012 by different state attorneys general, and the federal actions against the banking and mortgage-servicing industries. At issue were foreclosures using deceptive, incomplete, inaccurate, and sometimes fraudulent records costing these companies billions. I repeat: **There are no perfect hedges, and few mediocre ones, either**.

*****

"He has decided to play it *safe*," declared the announcer in the first game of the 2012 American League Championship Series, opining about Yankees' manager Joe Girardi's decision not to send Ichiro Suzuki on an attempted steal of second base. There were two outs, and Raul Ibanez was at the plate in the bottom of the 11th inning. **Attempting to steal a base may be a good bet or a bad bet (from a probability perspective)—but *safe* is the wrong word, and the wrong way to think about it.** There is one choice that has the highest likelihood of creating a win for the Yankees, and that is the right decision—the smart decision.

When decision makers have *safe* on their minds, they tend to ignore the odds. Interestingly, *S*abermetrics (the specialized analysis of baseball through detailed statistical analysis) strategies consider attempting to steal bases a poor bet, most of the time. So, I am not saying that it would have been smart to have Suzuki steal—simply that a manager can't afford to think in terms of *safe,* because there is no such thing. By the way, the Yankees lost that game to the Tigers in the next inning, so Girardi must not have played it *that* safe.

One characteristic common to both traders and entrepreneurs is a greater willingness to take on more risk than the Average Joe. And "risk" has many psychological connotations. In the context of business, we will spend much of this book discussing taking risk, managing risk, thinking about risk, avoiding risk, accepting risk, prospering from risk, and the psychology of risk. **Getting comfortable with taking intelligent risk puts you ahead of the game.**

START WITH THE BIG PICTURE AND MACRO TRENDS

"Do what you can, with what you have, where you are."

—Theodore Roosevelt

This principle demands that you start by studying the forest as a whole, rather than the individual trees, providing context for any business opportunity that you consider. Understand the major trends happening today—the demographic, economic, political, technological, lifestyle, and social trends. In some cases, the trader's cliché "the trend is your friend" can guide your decisions for decades.

The US has had long periods in which it was hard to lose by investing in real estate or the stock market. It was a bad idea to invest in a new typewriter- or electronic calculator-technology in the early 1980s. Investing in the personal computer business starting about 2000, or in an American coal-fired power plant from about 2008 were also losers. You would have been bucking major trends.

I recently overheard this statement: "I like the pharmas (pharmaceutical companies) because we have an overvalued market." Another blurb: "I think this market is ready for a correction, so here are three stocks to own." Wait a second—what are these "authorities" talking about?

Lucky And Good

 If you are bearish on the overall market, then tell me about the best stocks to short, not the stocks that will lose the least as the overall market drops. (See There's Always a Bear Market Somewhere discussion later.)

An investor who consistently put money into a variety of stocks in the US stock market from about 1983 through December 1999, would have done quite well (even with a few bad days along the way, like October 19, 1987 and October 13,1989). This secular (a fancy way to say "long-term") bull market in US equities was a winner for small investors, big investors, pension funds, and government tax receipts. The whole notion of "buy and hold" gained great popularity during this period.

Likewise, if you had bought most US real estate from about 1982 to 2000 and sold it by early 2005, you could scarcely have missed a profit. This was an age when you would have been challenged to find anyone, from your parents to your taxi driver, who would suggest that you could lose money by buying a home. It was very tough to bet against these secular trends and make money.

In contrast, a bearish macro trend was pointed out by Warren Buffett as he discussed the long-term trend of the airline industry: "The net wealth creation in airlines since Orville Wright has been next to zero." With a few exceptions (think Southwest Airlines) and a few brief stretches, investing in this industry has been a loser. Sure, "a rising tide lifts all boats," but an airplane doesn't float very well. With the continuing industry consolidation including the probable merger of US Airways and American Airlines (the merger has been opposed by the US Department of Justice, but I still bet it will happen), the United States will have an oligopoly in which the largest four airlines account for over 90% of the domestic market. So, this century-old macro trend may be coming to an end.

Before investing, trading, or starting a business, consider whether you are betting *with* a major tailwind or *against* a headwind. It's far easier to prosper while narrowing down your search for opportunities that benefit from the long-term trend than it is to find a short-term counter-trend opportunity. Now, if you think that a secular trend has reversed or is about to reverse, that's a different story, and the subject of my principle (Look for Inflection Points). But if the trend has not yet reversed, be very careful about jumping the gun (Don't Jump the Gun).

RECOGNIZE LONG-TERM TRENDS

How do Champs spot the long-term trajectory? How do they know when a trend is about to end? Do trends ever reverse once they pick up steam? Trends are easier to identify after they have been going for a few years, and when they will turn may not be predictable.

Here are just two of the many long-term trends we have seen over the last several decades:

- Since 1947, US birth rates have been dropping, and they have decreased in the rest of the developed world for the past few decades (no end in sight on this one).
- People in the developed world continue to live substantially longer lives. Today the average life expectancy for someone born in the developed world is between 77 and 83 years. When Social Security was established in 1935 and the retirement age set at 65, the average life expectancy for all Americans was about 62 years. (Obamacare might single-handedly reverse this trend, at least in the US.)

Exhibit A displays a longer (but far from complete) list of long-term trends. Some of these trends are decades long, and there is no reason that they should reverse anytime soon (i.e. the consistent increase in computing power per dollar spent). Other trends are sure to end at some point (such as declines in interest rates). **Rarely if ever do these long-term trends occur in a straight line. If they did, then it would be easy to figure out when they were finished.** Which other recent macro trends are driving the business world, and which will influence your next business bet?

*****

It's hard to profit by fighting a macro trend. So, if you're operating within a long-term trend of declining interest rates or increasing home prices that you expect to continue, *don't* fight it. Instead, look for the means to place a bet in sync with this trend. If you're bearish about the long-term real estate market, don't waste your time trying to find a great deal on a house to flip. Rather, seek out smaller niches that are aligned with your favorite macro trend.

Knowledge, or a well-founded hunch that a trend is shifting, creates a potential for success. That's why understanding the big picture and the current climate for your business opportunity is critical. Doing the groundwork may not be the most exciting part of your job, but without it, you might be forced to react to the market rather than to profitably anticipate its twists and turns.

LOOK FOR INFLECTION POINTS

> "This is not the dot.com situation ... you are not going to see the collapse that you see when people talk about a bubble. And so those of us on our committee, in particular, will continue to push for home ownership."
> —Congressman Barney Frank, June 27, 2005

In his book *Lead with a Story*, Paul Smith relates a story about the diaper business. In the summer of 2000, he was charged with developing a five-year strategy recommendation for Procter & Gamble's disposable diaper business.

Smith began by reviewing nearly 40 years of P&G's disposable diaper history. (The disposable diaper was first patented in 1948.) From the beginning (1961), P&G had enjoyed a near-perfect correlation between volume of sales and profits—the more they sold, the more they made. Between 1983 and 2000, that correlation ceased to exist. Smith's question: "What could have happened in 1983 to forever change the nature of this higher-sale/higher-profits industry?"

Since this date is soon after my three sons' graduation from diapers, I can relate to 1983's changing market.

My oldest son, Brian, was born in 1976, and his mother and I were on a tight budget. So we alternated between using cloth and disposable diapers. Disposables were obviously much more convenient, but more expensive. By the time my youngest son Mike was born in 1980, we had a little more money, so we always used disposable diapers. We weren't alone. By 1983, the date that Smith points to as the year the relationship between sales and profits disappeared, disposable diapers finally reached a virtual 100% market share (cloth diapers were history). There were no more profits (total industry wide) to be had by convincing parents to switch from cloth to disposable. In the diaper business, this was a major inflection point, creating a need for a different strategy.

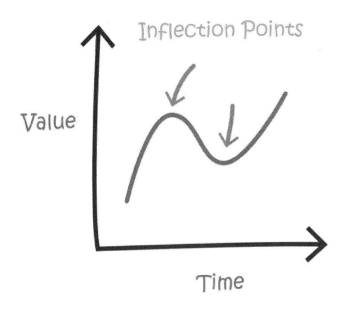

An **inflection point,** or turning point, is a dramatic reversal or change in the direction of a curve or trend. An inflection point can be

Lucky And Good

precipitated by something out of the blue, or it may arise by consensus when the market collectively discovers that a price is set either too high or too low.

Inflection points are often caused by arbitrary government action. For example, in 2013, California instituted a new Cap and Trade system for trading carbon dioxide which offers emissions flexibility through purchased offsets, like planting trees in urban areas. But the offset mechanism is limited to 8% of a plant's emissions. The regulations also set an arbitrary minimum value on each allowance (the right to emit CO_2) at $10/ton in the state-managed auctions.

Another synthetic inflection point (and horrible description) is "an acceptable level of risk." What in the heck is this? It means that a company or government states that it is A-OK to have 1.5 deaths per 100 million automobile miles driven (which is about where we are today). In the 1920s, the ratio was well over 10-times that high. Accepting this artificial boundary can distort our thinking—and suppress the speed at which we lower the death rate by yet another 90%.

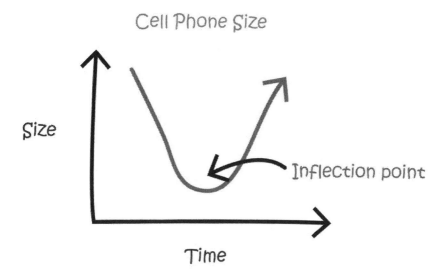

We see inflection points in the world of product development all the time. For example, the size of cellular phones hit a dramatic inflection point. For the first two decades in cell phone history, they consistently got smaller. The big, bulky units the size of a small loaf of bread were scaled down over the years into sleek pieces that easily fit in the palm of your hand. But then something changed. Cell phones began to be used for accessing e-mail and the internet, and new models continually evolved to support more complex applications. As that shift happened, the market started to demand a bigger screen.

Deer populations are an example of inflection points in nature. An optimum density of deer, considered by environmentalists to be 15 to 20 deer per square mile, contributes to ecological balance. But now that the number of natural predators such as wolves and mountain lions has decreased, and the popularity of hunting has dropped, deer populations in some parts of the US have exploded out of control. Some areas now must support hundreds of deer per square mile, which wreaks havoc on the vegetation, not to mention creating health problems. Once a distribution of animals reaches this biological inflection point, it can be difficult to check the population before it causes an ecological blight. Sorry, Bambi!

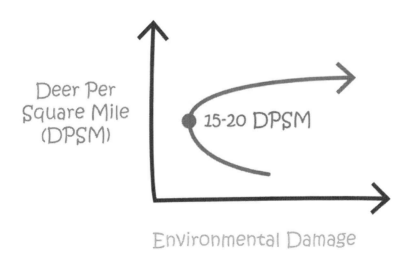

How about the collateral damage? In the US, deaths from accidents involving deer exceed the human death toll caused by sharks, rattlesnakes, bears, and alligators combined. Automobile accidents involving deer result in about 150 deaths and $1.1 billion in property damage annually in the US, not to mention plenty of aircraft accidents on runways when deer wander across.

A **bubble** is a severe inflection point that develops when a price climbs absurdly higher until the trend can no longer be sustained. This phenomenon may not be recognized until the bubble suddenly bursts. Many times, a bubble reflects a new and exciting technology that is sure to change the world, such as tulip breeding, railroads, or the internet. Even though the new technology is changing the world, the law of supply and demand eventually kicks in, and the bubble turns to trouble.

A **tipping point** is when one small element leads to wholesale change—like a single snowflake that is just enough to cause an avalanche. Malcolm Gladwell's book *The Tipping Point: How Little Things Can Make a Big Difference* defines it as "the moment of critical mass, the threshold, the boiling point."

On June 28, 1914, Archduke Franz Ferdinand, heir to the throne of the Austro-Hungarian Empire, was assassinated by a Yugoslav nationalist; this became the tipping point that led to World War I. Will the September 22, 2013 German federal election be the tipping point that leads to massive changes in the euro market? If not, what will be the tipping point that marks that point in time where the euro begins to unravel?

A social-network tipping point occurred in April 2008 when the number of users on Facebook surpassed those on MySpace. (A year earlier, MySpace had about two and half times as many users as Facebook.) Most people didn't need or want both systems, and the main criterion for their choice was based on which website they were most likely to find their friends. The continued prospects for MySpace are not promising: as of February 2013, it only ranked 220th for total web traffic.

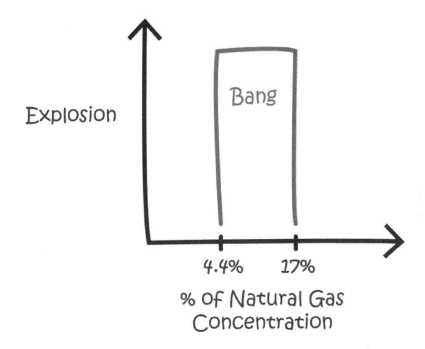

In the natural gas industry, one tipping point that is always a safety concern relates to gas leaks. A natural gas leak requires two elements to create an explosion: the right concentration of natural gas in the air, combined with a spark. When the gas initially leaks and the concentration is less than about 4.4%, there is not enough fuel in the air to burn. But as it continues to leak and the concentration level grows toward 17%, the danger is real. At these concentration levels, sometimes even the spark from a doorbell can set off an explosion. And then, just as quickly, once the concentration level exceeds about 17%, there is too much fuel to ignite. Two separate and quite sudden inflection points exist along this curve.

Critical junctures are political and systematic inflection points in history that dramatically change the status quo. These include wars, revolutions, epidemics, natural disasters, advancements in technology, and wholesale shifts in economic and political systems. Critical junctures frequently coincide with inflection points in determining various market prices. Critical junctures can be either positive or negative events, depending on how they affect your life and your business.

For Major League baseball players and owners, the end of the reserve clause was a critical juncture. In 1975, Andy Messersmith and Dave McNulty won an arbitration decision against Major League Baseball. The arbitrator ruled that, after a contract expired between the player and the team, the team only had an exclusive right to the player for one more season. After that, if the team and the player had not signed a new contract, the player was a free agent. A new era was born—a clear inflection point in the power of players to negotiate a higher wage. As a result, the average salary of Major League players grew from $44,676 in 1975 to $3.3 million in 2012 (an increase slightly above the rate of inflation), and the average player was quickly lifted from Chump to Champ (even if he was playing for the Cleveland Indians).

*****

Bubbles are the most dramatic inflection points because, with the exception of those few traders who are short, most of the economy's participants end up losing. In addition, Big Government tends to step in with a prescription that is worse than the ailment. Bubbles eventually burst as prices simply exceed the fundamentals by some massive degree. The most profound impacts of bubbles and crashes on the markets during the last century include:

The 1929 US stock market crash. The Dow peaked at 381.7 on September 3, 1929. On October 28, 1929 (Black Monday), the market dropped 13%. The next day, the Dow lost another 12%. This led to the Great Depression. By July 8, 1932, the Dow closed at 41.22, the lowest level since the 19th century. So, if you had an average stock portfolio during that period, you lost about 89% of your value (peak to trough).

The depression began in the US after the stock market crash, and then spread to the rest of the world. International trade dropped by about 50%, partly because of an increase in import restrictions and tariffs like the Smoot-Hawley Tariff bill, which passed on June 17, 1930. Although the legislation was meant to protect American jobs, the overall effect, exacerbated by the retaliatory responses of other countries, was to deepen the depression worldwide. Construction was nearly halted in many countries, and some agricultural crop prices dropped by as much as 60%.

The 1989 Japanese stock market and real estate crash. The Nikkei 225 (the stock market index for the Tokyo Stock Exchange) peaked on November 29, 1989, at almost 39,000. As of late-August 2013, that same index is 13,636. In 1989, real estate prices in Tokyo's Ginza District peaked at prices of about $20,000 per square foot. By 2004, prime "A" commercial space had slumped to less than 1% of the peak, and home prices had dropped to less than 10% of their peak prices.

The 2000 dot-com bubble. This grew on investor enthusiasm for the new world of the Internet during the late 1990s. NASDAQ (the stock market index that focuses more on technology companies) peaked (intraday) at 5,132.52 on March 10, 2000. At the height of the bubble, it was possible for a dot-com company to have an initial public offering (IPO) with few sales and no profit—only a "revolutionary business model" as an incentive to buy shares.

In a typical example, Boo.com spent $188 million in just six months trying to create a global online fashion store before going bankrupt. Of course, there were far more IPOs than profitable business models. The collapse stretched into 2002 when the NASDAQ dropped close to 1,000.

The 2005 US real estate bubble. This bubble accelerated in early 1997, and during the next eight years, average American home prices increased by over 125%. As the bubble gained steam, mortgage companies relaxed their lending standards, and unqualified home buyers could borrow 100% of the price of their homes. These "subprime" buyers kept all the upside price appreciation with no downside. This was a terrific free option for the buyer (Look for Free Options), but a horrible deal for lenders and taxpayers.

In mid-2005, national home prices peaked at about 190 on the S&P/Case-Shiller National Home Price Index. By early 2011, this same index had dropped about 35%. Seems mild compared to what happened in Tokyo or the dot-com bubble, doesn't it? This would not have made the top 100 list, except for the relative size of the real estate market—and how highly the US financial sector and the federal government were betting on US real estate, not to mention the tremendous amount of leverage used in buying that real estate.

The 2008 US banking crisis. The US housing bubble led to this fiasco, which contributed to a worldwide global financial crisis, still underway in parts of Europe. I call this calamity "Idiocy Cubed." The stupidity and, in some cases, dishonesty of borrowers, the mortgage industry, and the government converged and reinforced one another.

Bubbles create tremendous opportunities, but it's hard to schedule one, and especially tough to predict their peak. They happen when millions of people collectively go a bit nuts. The first recorded bubble was Holland's tulip mania, which peaked in 1637. At the top of the bubble, a single tulip traded for 10 times the annual earnings of an average tradesman. "Mania" is just as good a word as "bubble," and clearly depicts the mass frenzy in the market. After the fact, the insanity is obvious, but during the escalation, a broadly-shared delusion perpetuates the trend.

In a bubble, the thinking is that there is bound to be someone else who will pay even more for your house, your dot-com stock, or your tulip bulbs, with little regard to the underlying economics of the ridiculous price. This reliance on the "greater fool theory", however, is of no use once the bubble pops.

RECOGNIZE INFLECTION POINTS

OK: I have convinced you to be alert for inflection points. But how do you know when you have identified the real thing?

Let's start by reviewing a few historical cases.

Inflection points can be characterized by the reversal of a price, but may also be fundamental shifts seen at critical junctures. Cultural and technological change or exogenous events (like the 2011 Japanese earthquake and tsunami, or the 2010 BP oil spill) are examples.

Historically a few significant **non-price inflection points** have been:

- ❖ The giant asteroid that hit the earth about 65 million years ago and wiped out dinosaurs, thereby helping mammals (and eventually humans) to flourish.
- ❖ Gutenberg's invention of the printing press in 1440.

- ❖ The Renaissance from roughly the 14th to the 17th centuries, beginning in Italy and disseminating through Europe, as the invention of movable type spread new ideas faster than ever before.
- ❖ The Industrial Revolution, which began between 1750 and 1770 in England with the development of the steam engine.

*****

Price inflections are almost always a sign of a price going too high or too low, relative to fair value. Theoretically, a price could fall suddenly to its fair value and then stop, but I can't recall that ever happening. In signal processing, control theory, electronics, and mathematics, "overshoot" is when a signal or function exceeds its target. The market's target is fair value, but it tends to overshoot it in both directions. As prices get too high or low relative to the fundamentals and intrinsic value, they overshoot—eventually creating new inflection points and opportunities.

*****

As I write this, a few inflection points may be developing that will affect investments. I offer these prospects in the spirit of John Mauldin's "lions in the grass" or financial analyst Gary Shilling's "great calls," in the hope that my readers will evaluate the situation and make the right bets. I apologize that they are generally so negative. These potential impacts on the **global market** might send out big ripples:

- ❖ Cyprus, Greece, Spain, Italy, Ireland, Slovenia and/or Portugal might exit the Eurozone.
- ❖ The proliferation of weapons of mass destruction puts these tools in the hands of madmen and failed governments like North Korea.

In an uncertain **domestic market**, these potential inflection points could also have far-reaching consequences:

❖ Several US states (Illinois and California, in particular) may lose their ability to borrow because of their huge debts, unfunded pension liabilities, and massive deficit spending, all combined with some terrible management. California's Governor Jerry Brown declared early in 2013, "The deficit is gone. For the next four years we are talking about a balanced budget. We are talking about living within our means." It would be great if that were the case, but I will bet against the governor.

One of California's hidden liabilities (among many) is the amount owed to their employees for accumulated vacation time. As of early 2013, the average state worker had saved up 53 days of vacation, and the total liability, should this ever have to be cashed out, was about $3.9 billion. In the midst of this climate came a recent increase in the maximum state income tax to 13.3% for the wealthiest residents. Do you think a few of these folks might leave the Golden State?

A recently retired friend told me, "it was always our plan for my wife and me to move to Thousand Oaks, CA after retirement. Once we did the math and considered the unknowns, we opted to stay in Texas." So, not only is California losing entrepreneurs, retirees, and taxpayers, they are not getting many to replace those who are heading for the exits.

❖ Many public pensions, from Social Security to the California Public Employees' Retirement System (CalPERS), are grossly underfunded and may soon reach crisis levels. As local governments delay the pain, we will ultimately see failures like the city of Detroit, which declared bankruptcy in July 2013, setting the record (at the time) for the largest city bankruptcy in American history. I will go on the hook and predict that they will not hold this record for long. I discuss this "opportunity" further in Chapter Six, Real-World Application 5: Government Pension Returns.

Exhibit B has a more complete list of potential upcoming inflection points.

THERE'S ALWAYS A BEAR MARKET SOMEWHERE

"Selling short, in the minds of most investors, is unpatriotic to motherhood and apple pie."
—Dr. Gary Shilling

Most people can only think in terms of "going long" or buying "stuff." In order to qualify as a trader and differentiate yourself from a "long only" investor, you must be able to make short bets. **The capacity to go short also helps you keep an open mind.** In fact, if I were to interview you for a senior trading position, I would ask about the most profitable short positions you had ever taken. A stumble on this question would disqualify you.

The concept of shorting stocks may have been first devised by Dutch merchant Isaac Le Maire, in 1609. Once the largest shareholder in and governor of the VOC (also known as the Dutch East India Company), he had been forced out of the company and began to short its shares. Soon, however, the States-General of the Netherlands imposed restrictions prohibiting short selling. This became the first (in a long line) of intermittent government interference against short selling.

The concept of making business decisions based on a premise that certain prices would drop goes back thousands of years. When investing in a journey, spice traders were shorting both the cost of spices at their point of origin, and their cost of transporting those spices back to their ultimate markets. Farmers throughout the ages have shorted the cost of seed and gone long the finished produce.

In 1949, Alfred Winslow Jones established the first unregulated fund that went both long some stocks and shorted others—the first "hedge fund." The term is now used for a fund that makes any combination of market bets, long or short.

Lucky And Good

    Famous short seller Jim Chanos, (well-known for shorting Enron), notes that both sides of trading (going long and going short) require the same kind of analytical skills and discipline. The short seller, however, must resist the "giant positive reinforcement machine"—especially in popular investments like stocks and housing. The pundits are rooting so unabashedly for rising stock-and housing-markets that the average investor must wade through a sea of propaganda to determine which position to take. The financial media, the analysts, and Wall Street clearly have a bias for going long, and a bias against going short.

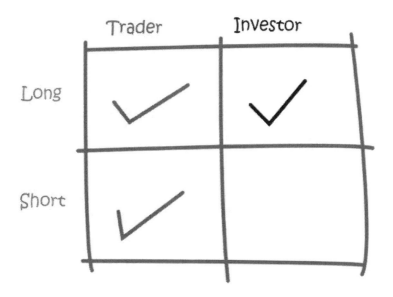

    Equity markets apply higher friction costs for those going short than for those going long. This is primarily because the short seller is fighting against long-term inflation (an influence that favors the longs), and must also pay the dividends for the stock that she is borrowing. So, you have to be right more often in shorting stocks in order to make the same returns that you would have gotten by owning them. This may be why, on average, only about 2% of the US stocks in play have been shorted. Most other markets (interest rates, currencies, commodities) don't give this same edge to the longs.

To benefit from thinking like a trader—and add to your roster of potential business opportunities—consider adding short positions to your repertoire. If you plan to short equities, though, you had better turn off the financial television coverage. The media is so gung-ho about rooting for higher prices that it will be tough to stick to your guns while hearing their never-ending "go-long" message.

CONFIRMATION BIAS

"The moment a person forms a theory, his imagination sees in every object only the traits which favor that theory."
—Thomas Jefferson

Psychologists study a phenomenon known as "confirmation bias," a term first coined by English psychologist Peter Wason. "Confirmation bias" is our natural tendency to collect data and more easily remember information that *confirms* our current beliefs, and dismiss that which *contradicts* our beliefs.

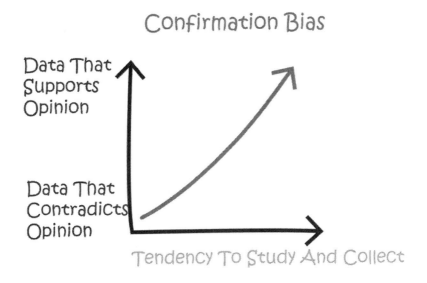

In another variation of confirmation bias, we collect data that supports what we *want* to happen. This was probably a factor in the 2012 presidential election: conservative pundits predicted a large Romney victory; liberal commentators predicted an Obama triumph. Liberal pundits were not more objective than their conservative brethren; in both of the prior Bush wins, commentators also forecasted a win for their candidate.

An unwillingness to go short puts you at greater risk of being wrong when you're long. Why? Because you were never neutral when you analyzed the market, and even your go-long bets are the result of an intrinsic bias of which you're unaware. I listen far more closely to a "buy" recommendation from a short seller than a perma-bull.

The good news? Traders have a remedy for confirmation bias: seriously considering the short position, and reflecting more completely on both the pros and cons of the long position; it's the capitalist's remedy for confirmation bias.

When the shorts bet that a stock price will drop or that government debt will lose value (think: Greece, Detroit, Stockton, Illinois), the general media often respond by depicting the shorts as the devil incarnate. But prices can go up *or* down, and the traders who are willing to short a stock or a market price help reduce the chance that we will have a market bubble with devastating consequences.

HOW DOES A TRADER GO SHORT?
(Traders may want to skip this section.)

Well, it depends. Typically, in order to short a stock, a broker helps a trader "borrow" shares from an investor, then sell those shares to a second investor who wants to buy them. At some point in the future, when the trader needs to "cover" his short (cancel out the position), he will buy the same number of shares on the open market, *hopefully at a lower price than he sold them for*, and return them to the investor who lent him the shares. (A share is a share. They're fungible like dollar bills; you don't have to pay a loan back with the same bills you borrowed.)

Brokers and the investor lending the shares charge for their services, and transaction costs are usually higher than a traditional purchase or sale. In addition, if the investor lent shares that are due dividends during the trader's borrowing period, the trader has to compensate the lending investor for the dividends, as well. This explains why the total friction costs are higher on a short equity position than a long one.

When a trader wants to short a stock, he must put up margin—cash—to insure that the counterparts get paid if the short position goes wrong. For example, if the trader wants to short 10,000 shares of a stock priced at $20 per share, then he must put up 150% of the value of the shares for initial margin, so, in this case, $300,000. If the stock price subsequently goes up and the trader wants to keep his short position, then he must deposit additional funds into the brokerage margin account.

Theoretically, this kind of short position has the potential for "infinite losses." Imagine this scenario: you shorted Apple at $7 in early 2003, and didn't cover it until the price hit $705 almost a decade later. On a million shares! You might not be in business any longer, after having lost $698 million. (I know I wouldn't be.) That's not just a lost decade; it's a massive losing decade! However, those traders who started shorting Apple stock when it hit its recent peak of $705 have done very well, as the price recently saw a low of less than $400.

If you want to go short but simultaneously limit your potential losses, you can also buy a "put." A put gives you the *option* (which means there's no obligation) to sell the stock at a given price during a defined period of time. Buying an option has a known maximum loss, and a potentially, big gain.

For example, let's say that BP PLC (formerly named British Petroleum) is selling today at $34 per share. You might be able to buy a put by paying a premium of $1 per share to have the right (but not the obligation) to sell shares of BP for $30 for the next four months. If the BP share price drops to $29, you break even, because you paid a $1 premium, were able to buy the stock for $29, and then sell it to the other counterpart for $30. (This example ignores transaction costs, which are fairly small.) In this case, you can lose at most $1 per share.

If BP drops to $25, you earn: ($30-$25 = $5) - $1 (premium paid) = $4.

In equity markets, there is growth in the use of exchange-traded funds (ETFs) to short indexes and segments for equity and debt markets. For example, PSQ (an ETF managed by ProShares) shorts the NASDAQ 100, SH (also ProShares) shorts the S&P 500, and SDOW (Proshares) shorts the Dow Jones Industrial Average.

ETFs also can be used to short commodity markets like the DGZ, which shorts the price of gold. Other ETFs short long-term US Treasuries.

It's important to note that the trader has a limited loss when he buys a short ETF, because his losses are restricted to what he invests in the ETF. With no daily margin requirements or cash movements for the individual investor to manage, administration is also easier than in conventional short transactions. You pay for that convenience, of course: The annual fees are normally higher for a short equity ETF fund than a long one. For a typical long S&P 500 ETF, you pay about 0.1% per year, whereas for a short S&P 500 ETF, you pay around 0.9% per year (Fight Friction Costs).

For decades, (and in some cases, centuries), commodity traders have used futures markets to short commodities like oil, gasoline, natural gas, silver, and copper. In fact, the first modern organized futures exchange began in 1710 in Osaka, Japan, where they started trading rice. In 1848, the Chicago Board of Trade was opened in the US, and the first corn contracts started to trade in 1851.

When trading in today's futures markets, the trader must first post margin. The amount of margin required is typically set by the futures exchange (i.e. NYMEX or CME) based on the recent volatility in the price of the commodity. As volatility increases, the cost of margin increases; as volatility falls, the cost of margin usually drops (but is limited by a minimum amount).

Investors repeat the mantra, "There's always a bull market somewhere." I want my readers to consider the equal and opposite proposition: **"There's always a bear market somewhere."** A trader should start out neutral on a market, and be willing to go long or short, depending on what she's seeing.

HOW DO THE OAKLAND A'S GO SHORT?

In *Moneyball*, Michael Lewis does a wonderful job of describing how the Oakland Athletics added economic rationality to drafting and trading players. A baseball team wins by scoring more runs than its opponents. They are long runs scored and short the runs scored by their opponents. But there is a cost to hiring and keeping players who score runs, and who prevent the opposing team from scoring runs (based on defense and pitching).

Oakland's moderately-sized sports market limits the total payroll dollars that the A's can spend. The New York Yankees, for instance, usually spend at least three times as much on their payroll. Billy Beane, Oakland's general manager, looks for ways to produce more runs for his team, and to allow fewer runs for their opponents, *while simultaneously being limited by a small payroll.*

As I mentioned earlier, Beane places a dollar value on every player: Major/Minor-League pros, and potential amateur draftees from around the world. This value is based on their expected contributions to generating runs and preventing opponents from scoring runs. He compares his valuations to that of the general baseball market. Then, he tries to keep and trade for those players with the greatest economic value to his team for the lowest cost—while trading away players who are valued more highly in the general baseball market than with the A's.

Beane is long any player that he drafts, trades for, or is already an Oakland Athletic. If players in his organization are overvalued by others, Beane can get "flat" that player by selling or trading him. But how can he short a specific player? Well, nowadays, he can't, because of Major League Baseball's prohibition against gambling. But if the League threw out that 1921 rule (obviously he should not be able to bet against his own team or players), then Beane could find a number of bets from which his ball club could benefit financially, if a player on another team did poorly.

For example, he could take the under bet in Las Vegas on the number of home runs that Albert Pujols (now with the Los Angeles Angels) will hit in the 2013 season, or the number of wins that Matt Cain will secure for the San Francisco Giants during the month of

May. But this betting provision ain't gonna happen any time soon—actually, as Pete Rose will attest, probably never.

If you don't work for a Major League team, you could also short a player by purchasing fantasy sports insurance at the website fantasysportsinsurance.com, which promises to "lessen the disappointment and aggravation of losing your top fantasy player(s)". Unfortunately, this bet has an incredibly high friction cost, with an insurance premium of roughly 10% of the potential payoff.

HOW CAN AN ENTREPRENEUR GO SHORT?

An entrepreneur might apply this principle when he signs a contract to deliver a product that he does not have in inventory, knowing that he can have it produced and delivered. This is a form of going short by selling high and buying low, although, in this instance, the entrepreneur is probably not counting on the price of the desired good or service dropping. But he still faces the same risk/reward. Like any short seller, if the market moves against the entrepreneur, and his production supplier wants to raise the price before he has placed his order, then he will make less than expected or might even lose money. Likewise, if the price of production drops after the entrepreneur has made the sale promise, but before he has placed the order, he will make more than expected. High fives!

The traditional start-up model is to manufacture a thousand widgets and then try to sell them. This is going long. The smart trader/entrepreneur at least considers the option of making the sale *first*, and *then* producing or buying the products to meet the order. Later on, as the enterprise gets bigger, it will likely require a minimum inventory because many customers might need the product immediately. But that's a good problem for a later day.

There was a period in Dell Computer's early business life when they would take an order and get paid via credit card for that order before they manufactured and shipped the product. Michael Dell was selling high and buying low (a great way to build cash). It helped that his cost to manufacturer the PCs was—and continues to be—in a secular bear market, in which the cost of technology almost always drops. So, going short on component costs usually paid off (with a rare exception being the period after the 2011 Thailand floods). Early on, this macro trend benefited Dell, but more recently, PCs have gotten so cheap that margins have become razor-thin—creating a different obstacle to profitability.

*****

Most investors only think in a narrow fashion: *I will be long stocks or not; buy bonds or not; I will buy a home or not. If I don't buy stocks, bonds, or a home, my only alternative is to put my money in the bank.* Not enough business people consider the possibility of going short the equity market or any other market or dimension.

If your belief and value system extends only to "going long," and you can't find it in your gut to sometimes go short, you'll miss half of the world's opportunities. You can't short half of the world's assets (we discussed how Billy Beane can't short a specific baseball player), so there are fewer assets and factors that can be shorted. However there are so few traders and investors willing to go short, I would hypothesize that the number of moneymaking opportunities are about the same as for going long.

*****

I have already mentioned the book *Trading Bases: A Story About Wall Street, Gambling and Baseball (not necessarily in that order)* by Joe Peta. If you enjoy my book, his should be your next Amazon download. If you don't care for mine, don't despair, download and read *Trading Bases* for another swing at some of the same topics.

I had the chance to chat with Joe about a phenomenon that he discusses in his book—the bias of Wall Street equity traders to go long at the beginning of the year. He points out that, when you are managing other people's money (OPM), your interests are usually not perfectly aligned with your investors' (Buffet is an exception). If the risks and rewards were completely in sync, it wouldn't matter if it was January or December: a portfolio manager would always go short when he thought prices were headed lower, long when he thought prices are on the rise.

But most of the time, Wall Street as an institution (media, investment banks, hedge funds, politicians, regulators) is biased to root for and bet on rising prices. That's because "The Street" makes more money on average when prices head higher. The industry loves bull markets. Try listening to a few hours of CNBC or Fox Business, and count the number of bullish statements versus the number of bearish ones (month in/month out, year in/year out, bull market or bear market).

Peta explains why Wall Street equity traders need to win in both absolute and relative terms. In managing OPM, they compete against others to get and keep that money to manage. He also discusses how much harder it is to play well when you are trading from behind (where you have lost money or done poorly, compared to other money managers)—especially relative to your competing portfolio managers, thanks to the extra psychological baggage (loss of confidence, money worries, and pressure from the boss).

If a portfolio manager goes short at the beginning of the year and wins, then he is in the minority, and has won both in absolute and relative terms. If he goes long and wins, then he is up in absolute terms, and perhaps average in relative terms. Should he go long and lose, then he would be at least about even in relative terms. So, on the relativity scale (which Peta thinks carries more weight than the absolute scale), the average Wall Street portfolio manager is not really playing from behind at all. But the big no-no is to have gone short at the start of the year and lost, because then he is a loser in both absolute and relative terms. This is where his chances of being shown the door or losing investors become a factor.

Peta does not suggest that this is the rational way the market should operate, or that this phenomenon is necessarily in the investors' best interests; he simply states that it is the reality as he sees it.

This bias may provide some explanation for the "Sell in May and go away" bandwagon. If there is a collective bias to go long at the start of the year but not the end of the year, it would make sense that, on average, if you know nothing else, you would be hesitant to fight this macro trend.

Another interpretation of this Wall Street bias is that it hurts more to be a Chump among Champs than it feels good to be a Champ among Chumps. Similar to the logic that it hurts more to lose a bet than it feels good to win.

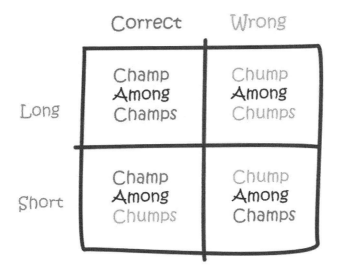

My advice relative to managing your own money is simple: Go long when you think prices are rising, and go short when you think they are falling. But if you are trading equities rather than commodities, you can't simply ignore these industry biases, or you may be broke by May.

MULTIPLE DIMENSIONS = DEGREES OF FREEDOM

> "I should have preferred to have taken players in exchange for Ruth, but no club could have given me the equivalent in men without wrecking itself, and so the deal had to be made on a cash basis."
>
> **—Red Sox owner Harry Frazee, justifying his cash-only sale of Babe Ruth to the New York Yankees in 1919**

Bobby came running in to the kitchen and proclaimed, "I've sold the dog!"

His mother said, "You did what?", and then, "How much did you sell him for?"

Bobby answered, "$10,000!"

So his mother asked, "Where's the money?"

Bobby responded: "Well, I didn't get cash—I got two $5,000 cats."

Maybe Harry Frazee might have learned something from young Bobby about exploring more dimensions than simply cash. Did he ever consider half cash and a few players or future players, or the right but not the obligation (an option) to acquire one of the Yankees in the future for a fixed price?

Before the sale of the Bambino, the Red Sox had been one of the most successful teams in the Majors, having won five World Series titles out of the first 16. After this deal, the fortunes of the Red Sox faded, and they failed to win another World Series until 2004.

Thinking in multiple dimensions (or degrees of freedom) can be as simple as opening your windows at night rather than turning on the air conditioning. Or planting a tree that will provide shade in the summer, but won't block the sun's warmth after its leaves have fallen in winter. How about adding wheels to your suitcase, or a Bluetooth sensor to your toothbrush?

The more dimensions that you explore, the greater the chance of finding one or more on which you have confidence in placing a bet. **Adding dimensions to your value proposition means that you do not have to accept all the constraining factors that your competitors do.**

The Greek fable of the Trojan horse was an early application of this principle. The Trojan War (which began in 1194 BC), saw the Greeks' attempt, for 10 years, to invade and take the city of Troy. Finally, they shifted dimensions, building a huge wooden horse and hiding a few soldiers inside. The Greeks then pretended to sail away, and the celebrating Trojans pulled the "horse" into their walled city. That night, the Greek soldiers left their hiding place, opened the gates of Troy, and let the rest of the Greek army in to destroy the city.

RADIATION THERAPY

Radiation therapy works to kill cancerous cells by shooting irradiated beams (usually x-rays and electron beams) at a tumor. To treat cancers deep within the body, the challenge is to apply the right amount of radiation to the tumor without killing all the healthy tissue around it.

Lucky And Good

Radiation Treatment

If you take a radiation gun, or medical linear accelerator, and simply use one beam at a fixed angle, then all the tissue along the path (good and bad) gets the same amount of radiation. But if you use multiple beams, or rotate a single beam from multiple angles while focusing on the tumor, the cancerous cells get many times the radiation of the surrounding healthy tissue.

In this case, shifting the path of the radiation beam from one dimension to three creates the possibility of doing the most good with the least harm.

NAVIGATION

Man has been sailing for at least 7,000 years, and may have been using dugout canoes for up to 45,000 years. But the skills of designing, building, and operating ships were of limited value without the critical science and art of navigation.

The progress of navigation relied on several broad innovations: global and celestial charts and maps, compasses, clocks, speed-tracking devices (think speedometer), dead reckoning, triangulation, radio and electronic signals, and today's global positioning system (GPS). It was a combination of these new dimensions that increased the functionality, accuracy, and flexibility of navigation.

An early fusion of these techniques was dead reckoning, which combined maps, compasses, time pieces, and speed-tracking devices. A sailor would begin with his "fix," or knowledge of his starting point, and then keep track of where he was headed by noting the direction, speed, and travel time in order to approximate where he was, later in the voyage. But the longer the trip (without confirmation of where he actually was), the more the cumulative errors added up, and the bigger the difference between the estimate and reality. These cumulative dead-reckoning errors are analogous to the cumulative errors of some complex computer simulations today. Computer models start at a given point in time and then simulate, day by day, or second by second, how some factor in the world is going to change. Small error builds upon small error to produce sometimes grossly inaccurate forecasts. For example, 30-day weather forecasts are grossly unreliable, even with today's supercomputing power.

The second major innovation in navigation was the concept of triangulation, based on Euclidian geometry. If I see two separate landmarks and draw a line on a map (at the precise angle) from where I am to those visible points, I know that my location is where the two lines intersect on the map. Triangulation methods required tools to measure angles (like the sextant), and the visibility of a landmark or identified star.

Finally, as triangulation on radio and electronic signals combined with greater timekeeping accuracy (culminating in the atomic clock), we evolved through a number of navigation techniques (Omega, VOR, LORAN), culminating in today's global positioning systems (GPS). Each of these electronic and radio systems relied on the basics of the past, including an accurate clock and multiple known points on which to triangulate. And, of course, GPS required a fast, compact and inexpensive computer to do the required calculations in real time.

All this, and it only took 45,000 years. By comparison, a little over a hundred years seems like such a short time since we started flying.

TRADING ON MULTIPLE DIMENSIONS

You can't schedule a great trading position, so a trader needs to consider several dimensions in order to find an opportunity on which she is willing to place a bet. What if you only went long NYMEX oil futures contracts for the prompt month (the earliest month being traded)? Or, what if you had no conviction that prices were going up or headed south for a sustained period? A narrow focus on only one or two dimensions might not reveal any opportunities for a very long time. And yet, trying to stay current on too many dimensions or too many markets may give you an information advantage on none of them (relegating you to Chump).

As a natural gas trader, I was always looking for another dimension to increase my chances of finding a potential winner. I could go long or short the overall natural gas market for the next month. But what other dimensions could I bet on, for the US natural gas market? Here are two: long or short volatility (by buying or selling options); long prices at the Henry Hub in Louisiana (the delivery point for New York Mercantile Exchange futures trades) versus short the California border (called a "basis trade").

You can be long prices in years one and two, and short prices in years five and six. I could be long prices for the first half of the month, and short prices for the second half of the month. I could be long natural gas prices and short oil prices. I could be long short-term volatility and short long-term volatility. There are no limits to the combinations.

In the oil market I can be short the NYMEX contract based on delivery in Cushing, Oklahoma, and long the ICE Futures in London (formerly the International Petroleum Exchange) contract, which is based on delivery in the North Sea. This type of trade tends to work when tensions escalate in the Middle East, and loses steam when things settle down (on a relative basis). This bet is less profitable when the Western Hemisphere's oil supply is growing faster than its demand.

A typical investor who is bullish on oil probably thinks only in terms of buying Shell Oil, Chevron, or, perhaps, going long on oil ETF. But not enough traders, investors, and businesspeople consider things like spread (or "pair") trades, in which you buy one and short the other, such as long Apple while short Microsoft, or long gold while short silver. Or in the oil realm, you might go long Chevron and short Shell. If I were bringing young traders into a trading desk, I would require each of them to give me a daily "pair" to see how they were thinking in an unbiased fashion, not to mention giving me a good idea or two.

Think back to the 2000 AOL acquisition by Time Warner. It was the ultimate spread trade between an email and dial-up internet service, and a conventional media company. Time Warner simply bet exactly the wrong way. AOL bet correctly by exchanging part of its position for a long traditional media position at the peak of the internet bubble. Because the value of their franchise was vastly overpriced, the AOL investors lost money as well, just not as much as they would have lost without the deal, and not nearly as much as original Time Warner shareholders lost.

Later on, when the combined company, AOL-Time Warner, spun off the AOL business, they were then going flat (neither long nor short) the AOL internet business.

ADDING DIMENSIONS AS AN ENTREPENEUR

Entrepreneurs need to find ways to expand the dimensions in which they choose to differentiate their product or service. This does not always involve offering more choices and options to customers. Conformists always want to add services (the customer is long services, and the company is short services) and options (making the customer long choice). But remember how successful Southwest Airlines was by *reducing* choices. They started by offering no assigned seating, and peanuts instead of meals. Their product was short choice and short extra services. Recently, Southwest has reversed that practice slightly with a major advertising campaign about how "bags fly free" on their airline. (They continued to provide free baggage when most other airlines started charging for it.) They have allowed their customers to go long baggage but continue to stay short meals—a great multidimensional trade.

Ray Kroc used the same strategy when he began what would become the McDonald's empire. He reduced customer choice by focusing only on the top proven menu items: burgers, fries, soda, and milk shakes. He went short variety and long consistency and low prices. Interestingly, as McDonald's has grown to the world's largest restaurant franchise, they have added numerous choices, while others (like In-N-Out Burger, a Western regional chain) stayed closer to McDonald's original formula.

GAS BANK

Enron's original success in the commodity business came as the US natural gas market began to deregulate in the 1980s, based on a concept called "Gas Bank." The Gas Bank was a four-legged stool, with Enron relying on these dimensions. The ability to:

1) receive, transport and deliver physical natural gas;
2) trade and provide risk management services to buyers and sellers of natural gas;
3) finance natural gas producers; and
4) provide both a competitive buy and sell price, as a market maker, for most natural gas trading points. (I have never seen much discussion of this point—I think it happened somewhere in Enron's basement gym, but it was before my time, and I don't know how it happened. It was really BIG, though.)

By 1990, as a result of several Federal Energy Regulatory Commission orders, more than 75% of the US market was conducted through the spot market, rather than through long-term contracts.

Investment banks, at the same time, were generally not trading, scheduling, or moving physical natural gas, so they could not compete on physical natural gas deals. Having schedulers and enough of a North American logistics network to buy and sell natural gas at virtually any point in the US and Canada was no small matter. It was not necessarily a 24-hour-per-day job, but it definitely required dedicated and knowledgeable staffing 365 days a year. And since the investment banks weren't moving physical natural gas, they were at a major disadvantage in providing risk-management services (via options and fixed price transactions) to the market.

These risk-management services allowed customers to lock in prices, and hedge against unfavorable price movements. They also partially protected small producers against the chance that prices would get so low that they couldn't meet their cash needs. Early critics suggested that no one would ever transact because, when prices were heading up, producers would wait, and when prices were dropping, buyers wouldn't commit to long-term contracts. Of course, this same faulty logic would mean that no stock, currency, bond, or piece of real estate would ever get sold.

One group of buyers desperately wanted and needed long-term contracts—the new independent power producers. They were building natural gas–fired power plants, and generally could only secure 15-year project financing if they lined up both a 15-year power sales agreement and a 15-year natural gas purchase agreement.

When Gas Bank first emerged, the investment banks were shying away from financing small natural gas producers, because prices were low and the small producers were struggling financially. Enron had a major advantage, based on its ability to physically take delivery from the producers and to guarantee a fixed price.

The company also shifted another dimension by structuring its producer finance transactions as purchases of natural gas in the ground—not as loans (similar to how I structure my lawsuit funding transactions today). This structure allowed the company to purchase natural gas from companies with terrible credit because Enron purchased the natural gas, rather than simply having it as collateral for a loan. Even if the producer went bankrupt, Enron owned the natural gas. And once it took the physical gas, Enron could get the full market price for it—whereas an investment bank, lacking the national trading and scheduling infrastructure, would typically lose value selling it.

The fourth element of Enron's model is that it acted as a market maker in most of the US markets. For the heavily-traded points in the country, Enron would provide a reasonably tight two-way market (a price at which you could sell and a price at which you could buy) on the same contract for natural gas. This meant that Enron trading desks would tend to get the first phone call and the last one—far more action than any other trader, marketer, or producer.

These four dimensions (physical delivery, risk management, finance, and market making) allowed Enron to catapult into a dominant market position. Working only one of these dimensions would have been far less profitable and garnered only a fraction of the market position. In a liquid, transparent market, it is virtually impossible to make money competing for a commodity business on a one-year contract based solely on price—unless you can profit from the subsequent price movement. By 1992, Enron was the:

- largest buyer and seller of natural gas in North America;
- manager of the largest portfolio of fixed-price natural gas derivatives in the world; and
- largest supplier of natural gas to the electricity industry in North America.

A few years later, based on extending this model to electricity, the company was the largest buyer and seller of electricity and natural gas in the world.

FIND THE RIGHT VALUE PROPOSITION

When deciding on the right combination of services (or lack of services) for the price charged, entrepreneurs need to be able to think in multiple dimensions. By adding up all of these choices into your business offering, you have defined your "value proposition." **Creating a winning value proposition lies at the heart of business strategy.** There are thousands of combinations and permutations for any potential value proposition, when you stop limiting yourself to the dimensions that the incumbents dominate. The value proposition defines what market you will "play" in and how you expect to win.

As I have mentioned, the best value proposition is one that you can shout out consistently and loudly to the entire world, including your suppliers and competitors. It is great if the proposition is not only a unique and ultimately winning combination, but also one that your competitors will either ignore or mock because they don't think it will amount to anything. That gives you the chance to execute on it without much competition.

Don't look for kudos for the brilliance of your unique value proposition, though, because wildly successful value propositions are rarely lauded by the industry when they are first unleashed. Short-term media acclaim feels better, but once they declare your genius, you will soon have hundreds of competitors.

AN EMPTY PICKLE JAR

This story has been told in variations over the years to make several points, but it reinforces the notion of multidimensional thinking:

A teacher stood before her class. When the class began, she wordlessly picked up a very large pickle jar and filled it with tennis balls. She then asked the students if the jar was full. They agreed that it was.

Next, she picked up a box of small marbles and poured them into the jar. She shook the jar lightly. The marbles rolled into the open spaces between the tennis balls. Again, she asked the students if the jar was full. They all nodded in agreement.

Then the teacher picked up a box of sand, and poured it into the jar. Of course, the sand filled in the gaps. She asked once more if the jar was full. The students responded with a unanimous "yes."

Finally, the teacher produced a couple liters of water from under the table and started to pour the liquid into the jar, which effectively seeped between the grains of sand. The students couldn't help but laugh.

Let me ask you this. Is the jar now full? If I promised you a million dollars, could you think of anything else to cram into the jar? What would it be, and how would you go about getting it in there? Every time the teacher asked if the jar was full, the students were challenged to change dimensions, but failed to do so.

It is the process of shifting dimensions that adds value to your product or service and positions you for greater market share and profitability.

THINK IN OPPOSITES

> "I will not make age an issue of this campaign. I am not going to exploit, for political purposes, my opponent's youth and inexperience."
>
> —Ronald Reagan, when asked during the 1984 presidential debates if, at age 73, he was too old to be president

It was February 5, 2012, and the New York Giants were trailing the New England Patriots in the Super Bowl 17-15. The Giants, led by Eli Manning at quarterback, were driving the ball towards the end zone in the late minutes of the game. They were eating up the clock, and positioning themselves for an almost certain game-clinching field goal just as time expired.

I have seen this situation hundreds of times before, and Patriot's coach Bill Belichick was the first and only one whom I have ever seen handle it differently. He thought in opposites, in order to give his team a chance to win.

He told his defense to let the Giants *score* on the next play—and the Giants did. When Giants running back Ahmad Bradshaw was about to cross the goal line, he had second thoughts about scoring so easily, but his momentum carried him in for the touchdown.

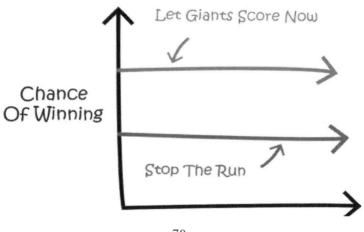

Belichick had unemotionally (setting aside his Lizard Brain) assessed the odds, and thought his team had perhaps a 1% chance of getting the ball back via a turnover, or of the Giants missing the field goal. But he realized that his team's chances were slightly improved (perhaps to 2-3%) if he got the ball back with some time on the clock, and if his (future Hall of Fame) quarterback Tom Brady could take the team down for a final game-winning score.

The Patriots didn't succeed on their final drive and, therefore, lost the game 21-17. But the Belichick decision was analytical, rational, and the right call—even though it didn't pay off.

Sometimes smart bets lose.

Belichick is often described as brilliant when his ideas work, and arrogant when he fails. This is one of the reputation risks that anyone takes when they make the unconventional move. Of course, the more Super Bowl titles he piles up as head coach (Belichick's teams have three, as of this writing), the more the detractors move on to criticizing new mavericks (like the 49ers' Jim Harbaugh).

*****

If your only tool is a hammer, every problem looks like a...? But guess what: when you think of the hammer as your one and only tool, you are probably thinking about using it to pound the nail. Right? Well, how about using the claw on the hammer to pull out a nail? This is the essence of thinking in opposites.

Considering opposites defies conventional thinking, and is an especially valuable skill for entrepreneurs. It combines the art of skepticism and the practice of doubt. Entrepreneurs and businesspeople should consider this principle whenever they try to solve a problem. **It means questioning assumptions, and accepted beliefs as you search for opportunities.** Bob Knight sums it up in the title of his latest book: *The Power of Negative Thinking.*

Here's yet another warning—it takes a strong ego to pull off this kind of thinking because, if your departure from the status quo stalls or fails, you will get a load of criticism from the Monday-morning

Lucky And Good

quarterbacks, and they might not even wait until Monday. Of course, when the gamble pays off, you are a genius.

Going into the final week of the 2012 NFL season, questions arose about San Francisco 49ers coach Jim Harbaugh changing starting quarterbacks. (He replaced Alex Smith, then leading the NFL quarterback ratings, with second-year QB Colin Kaepernick.) On *CBSSports.com's* weekly power rankings, the comment was, "There are now major issues about the quarterback change. Was it arrogance?" And just before the 49ers' first post-season game, a *San Francisco Chronicle* sportswriter wrote, "Right now, Harbaugh's hubris isn't sneaking up on anybody."

What in the heck does arrogance have to do with it? Harbaugh's decision may turn out badly, or might look brilliant in a few years, but it had nothing to do with hubris. It would be interesting to see what these same writers would have written about Bill Walsh, when he was defying conventional wisdom.

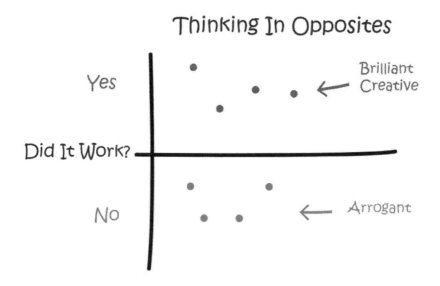

One more note. We won't have a final analysis of Harbaugh's decision for several years, when both Kaepernick and Smith have retired. Colin Kaepernick had a magnificent game against the Green Bay Packers a few days after the San Francisco Chronicle writer pointed out Harbaugh's "hubris". In his first playoff game against the Packers, he ran for 181 yards (an NFL record for quarterbacks in a single game), two rushing touchdowns, and threw for two more touchdowns as the Niners beat the Packers 45-31. He then led his team to a win over the Atlanta Falcons. And, even though the Niners lost a close Super Bowl, Kaepernick played well in that game too. The jury is still out ... and it should be.

FLIES AT YOUR VACATION CABIN

If you were trying to reduce the number of flies on the deck of your lake cabin, you would be better equipped to solve the problem if you first thought in reverse about how you might *increase* the fly population.

What are some ideas for growing the number of flies in your backyard?

1) Put out old scraps of food.
2) Create pools of standing water.
3) Get rid of birds, spiders, and bats, all of which eat flies.
4) Optimize the temperature to contribute to their reproduction.
5) Encourage flies to reproduce (e.g. date nights for flies, or tax subsidies for flies with big families).

It's the thinking in reverse that gives you additional insight into the original problem, and provides opportunities for ultimately reducing the number of flies.

TAHOE, POLITICS AND DEBATES

At Lake Tahoe, one of the most visible environmental challenges is preserving the clarity of the pristine lake. In 1968, one could see a white disk submerged to a depth of 100 feet. Today, the visibility is only about 70 feet. So, if you want to improve water clarity, how might you go about solving the problem? I would suggest starting with the inverse question: How can we reduce the clarity of the lake?

A great debater can argue either side of a case. The best attorney can effectively argue for either the plaintiff or the defendant. A real trader can go long or short. They can all zig *and* zag.

We all know that politicians can flip-flop, and they get criticized for doing so. But would you rather have a leader who cannot change his mind? Unless they already agree with us, we all want politicians with a capacity to change their positions when they gather more insight into an issue—assuming they legitimately do so, rather than wanting to simply increase their chances at reelection. The US would have lost far fewer lives in Vietnam if President Lyndon Johnson had reversed course earlier.

This dynamic applies to much more than the price of real estate, equities, currencies, and bonds. As an entrepreneur (or an "intrepreneur," the term used for entrepreneurs who work within large companies), you can test this thinking on the opportunities you see. There are times when you dislike an opportunity so much that you might seek success in an approach that is exactly the opposite of the idea being pitched. And the contrary idea might be the winner. **As Peter Thiel, co-founder of PayPal, said: "It is better to be right than to be contrarian. But being contrarian is very often a good heuristic for finding what is right."**

ENERGY PARKS

In the mid-1980s, I was working for Pacific Gas and Electric which, at the time, was the largest gas and electric utility in the United States. CEO Dick Clarke wanted to develop "energy parks" in our service area. The idea was to create a new industrial zone with a centralized steam distribution system used by the tenants of the energy park, and the park would use energy-efficient cogeneration technologies to produce electricity. I got the assignment. But, within a few weeks of taking on the task (a promising job for a young person, from a career perspective), I determined that the idea was not only a no-go, but was exactly the opposite of what we should do.

The problem was that, at the time, our marginal cost of generating electricity was about three cents per kilowatt hour (kwh). The all-in cost for electricity from a new energy park cogeneration plant (owned by PG&E or the customer) was actually higher—about four cents per kwh (Think on the Margin). Society would be worse off by one cent per kwh, and the penalty would be shared by anyone who made the investment, as well as our other customers, who would have to share some of the common costs among a smaller base. Remember that one cent might not seem like much, but when you're selling billions of them, they add up fast.

Coincidentally, I learned during my research that we were losing several large customers who were installing self-generation. So, after explaining the situation to my boss and to my boss' boss, we had a chance to tell it like it was to the CEO.

The rational business answer was that we should do exactly the opposite of building an energy park (although we were diplomatic enough to phrase it differently). Instead, we suggested that we negotiate special retention rates for those customers who were considering installing their own generation. Our rate to the largest customers was about 4.5 cents per kwh, while our marginal cost of generating the power was three cents per kwh. If large customers could make their own power for four cents per kwh, they would probably do it.

We got the OK from the CEO to start negotiating rates that were about the cost of customers generating their own power at four cents per kwh; that way, they could invest instead in another part of their business. It was a bit more complicated than that, because we had to negotiate a contract with the customers, and then, one by one, get them approved by the California Public Utility Commission. But it helped delay additional generation until it was needed, years later.

Some conspiracy theorists might argue that I was simply setting the stage for the energy crisis that started in 2000, but I will remind them that these agreements were never longer than five years and, at this stage of my career, I had never even heard of Enron. The whole idea was that, when things changed, these companies would build the power plants because the economics would then be "right."

COMMODITIZATION

In his book, *Behaving Badly: Ethical Lessons from Enron*, Dennis Collins describes Enron's value proposition as "find an untapped area of business, buy some assets, don't worry about initial costs, and get the revenue numbers up." During my eight years at Enron, I never once heard "untapped area of business" or "get your revenue numbers up." I *always* heard, "increase your profits." And Collins' interpretation was never what I thought, although it might accurately describe the implementation of Enron's 1999 investment in its water business, Azurix. I never had anything to do with that business, so please accept that this opinion is based on what I have read, rather than any special insight.

I don't know how other senior officers discussed it, but here was the way I always thought about and described our business model. One of the first questions I always asked myself when considering a new market was whether we could commoditize it—although we rarely used that exact language. Commodities are bought and sold on the basis of price alone. This is exactly the opposite of how most businesspeople think. They are always trying to make their product and service unique, hard to copy, not fungible, and hopefully more profitable than a mere commodity. Warren Buffett sums up the *conventional* wisdom by saying, as he has on numerous occasions, "We like companies which buy a commodity and sell a brand."

But at Enron, we usually took the opposite approach as we entered the natural gas, electricity, coal, shipping, pulp and paper, bankruptcy swap, or weather derivatives markets. **To commoditize a market we tried to accomplish four things:**

1) **Create and gain industry acceptance of standardized contracts.** This meant that, if we bought 10,000 MMBTUs of natural gas in the Permian Basin (Texas) and sold it the next day, we already had a standardized master contract in place, and did not have to haggle over terms and conditions, like when the seller got paid and the specifications for the natural gas. We always pushed for an industry-wide standardized contract so that everyone had to live up to the same terms and conditions. This made the asset fungible and the deals easier to transact.

    These standardized contracts were not biased to buyers or sellers. (We were both.) Prior to this method, utility buyers would try to use their monopoly power to slant contracts in their favor. And the big oil companies would do the same, to slant their contracts in favor of the seller. **But having different contract terms and conditions for those you are buying from and those you are selling to is a recipe for bigger friction costs and added risk.**

2) **Provide transparency and liquidity to the market.** We were the leaders in this effort to ensure that more participants knew the price of the commodity. Before we were online, you could call up one of our many trading desks and request a price. You might ask, "What's the October market for California border natural gas?" and our trader would tell you it was $3.00 by $3.02, which meant that we would buy from you at $3.00 and sell the same thing to you at $3.02 per MMBTU. With only a $.02 difference, you knew that you weren't getting hosed.

Prior to Enron providing this market-making function, you would need to shop around to see what various producers were selling at, and what buyers were willing to buy at. Of course, the difference between these two prices tended to be much wider than the tight two-way prices that we were showing once Enron jumped into the game. **Because we were the easiest, quickest source of information on current prices, however, we tended to get the first call and the last call before the counterpart transacted.**

3) **Make it easy for others to buy and sell.** That way, a transaction could be as easy as "I am buying 10,000 of September Permian for $4.23," and the response on the recorded line was "You're done." All in a few seconds, for a $1,269,000.00 transaction. We ultimately made the process even easier when we provided a mechanism to transact online with a single click of the mouse. Our thinking was that, in the process, we would create a dominant position with more liquidity for ourselves. **By** *giving* **liquidity we would** *receive* **even more liquidity, and have more counterparts to buy and sell with than our competitors did.**

We also planned to create information and trading advantages by knowing more about the markets and their directions than anyone else. We expected to make large directional bets when we thought a price was going up or down, or if two prices were going to converge or diverge (although we did not make this intent public). In some ways, our market maker role was a loss leader (depending on how one allocated the costs), to set us up (with liquidity and information) for the "swing-for-the-fences" positions that we believed in, based on extensive analysis and better information.

4) **Add other dimensions to large structured trades** (see the Sutton Bridge Real-World Application in Chapter Six). We also planned to offer financing services, giving us the capacity to do huge transactions for which we would have few competitors—a position with the potential for enormous profits.

A challenge with this value proposition (as I have defined it) was that not all of our employees understood it, and the public didn't grasp it at all. Even some senior managers didn't appreciate it.

As I mentioned before (Multiple Dimensions = Degrees of Freedom), the best value proposition is one that can be communicated to employees, suppliers, customers, and competitors across the board, and will not be weakened even though everyone knows about it.

A great value proposition hits the competition like a tsunami that travels below the sea at 500 mph, with a wave that is visible only a meter above the surface. As this enormous volume of water nears the shoreline, the ocean's depth shifts from thousands of feet up to sea level, transferring all of that energy into a powerful impact with land. It is a devastating "black swan"—as Nassim Nicholas Taleb calls an unanticipated risk—because you can't see it coming.

A value proposition that has the same kind of power can beat the entrenched players when they are unprepared for its impact.

Senior management frequently tried to position Enron externally as a "logistics" company. No one wanted to be labeled as "trading" to the investing public, because trading was deemed dangerous and speculative, and carried a share price with a lower multiple on earnings. A logistics company (think FedEx, when it was hot), on the other hand, would generally get valued at a higher multiple and share price for the same earnings. This sleight-of-hand meant that there was no uniform vision of Enron's value proposition. The company *was* a logistics company, but only secondarily. The real goal was to make money with the unique value proposition of commoditizing markets, and only part of that job involved being outstanding at logistics.

Enron's approach generally annoyed the established players, such as the German and US utilities and large natural gas producers—that is, until their traders wanted to know a current price. Then, they would put their irritation aside and check out the price to buy or sell for virtually anything they wanted to transact on via our trading desks, and eventually through our Enron Online system. We became an addiction to the rest of the market.

This method worked, and Enron became far and away the largest buyer and seller of natural gas, electricity, and commodities in the world. If we considered Enron North America and Enron Europe separately, Enron North America was clearly the largest buyer and seller of electricity in the world (by itself). And Enron Europe was number two (by itself), far outdistancing the bronze medalist.

*****

This principle, Think in Opposites, also applies to trends in the price of oil, public pension obligations, government spending, government debt, public education, auto mileage figures, and the value of a college education. It is closely related to the earlier principle: There's Always a Bear Market Somewhere.

I'm not the first person to encourage contrarian thinking. In one of my favorite *Seinfeld* episodes, George decides that every decision that he has ever made has been wrong. While meeting at Monk's café, Jerry advises him, "If every instinct you have is wrong, then the opposite would have to be right."

George is convinced, and decides to Think in Opposites rather than what naturally occurs to him. Later in the episode, when he meets a beautiful woman, he introduces himself: "My name is George. I'm unemployed and I live with my parents."

Remarkably, it works; she's impressed with his honesty, and agrees to date him.

Thinking in opposites is a creative way to solve problems. You should not act in opposites often, but the very process of considering such an extreme stretches the mind and expands the possibilities, making it easier to consider everything in between. Thinking in opposites may not be popular, and may get you labeled "arrogant," if you are wrong. But it is an essential thinking style if you care more about results than the accolades of the herd.

COMBINE AN INFORMATION ADVANTAGE WITH VOLATILITY

> "Most people won't put in the time
> to get a knowledge advantage."
> —Mark Cuban

Unless you're selling options, having an information advantage in a market that never moves doesn't do a darn thing for you. I buy for $2.00 and can sell for $2.00. The price is $2.00 today, $2.00 tomorrow and $2.00 the next day. It's impossible to make any money or to lose money (other than the friction costs discussed in Fight Friction Costs).

Likewise, *not* having an information advantage (aka Chump) in a volatile market is a recipe for not only losing money, but also going broke. Think of the poker adage: "When you sit down at the table, look around for the sucker. If you don't see one, then it's you." A ruthless take on competitive advantage.

WHAT IS AN INFORMATION ADVANTAGE?

It is the acquisition—and the *understanding*—of the right data at the right time. Even if you amass the information you need, it's not always easy to interpret what that data means.

You will almost always have a race of supply against demand. Figuring out who will win this race—and by how much is crucial. Having the data without fundamentally understanding the market is *not* an advantage.

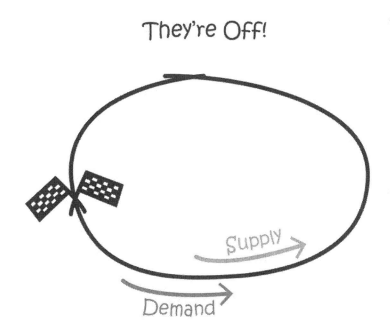

To provide real benefit, an information advantage needs to be substantial. It has to be enough to get you out of the "not good enough" territory. Knowing just a smidgen more than an average player is usually not enough to even cover the friction costs. I'm talking about knowing about supply/demand dynamics, market rules, and the changing choke points *in far more detail than everyone else* so that you can seriously cash in.

And here is the challenge: In most very big liquid markets, like the S&P 500 or the NYMEX oil futures market, it's tough to create and sustain a real competitive advantage, even for a huge player. Even if you're in the top quartile, you may still be a Chump because no market promises a minimum quota of Champs.

On the other hand, in smaller markets—like the Western US natural gas market, just evolving during the early to mid-1990s, and the UK electricity market, which changed rapidly in the late 1990s—it is easier to get the information edge. Those markets had plenty of electronic information available (usage, consumption, energy flows), and yet the big investment banks and hedge funds were not pursuing them. Those two markets also had periods of substantial volatility. This combination allowed some new players (including Enron) to make great profits.

Here is the twist: You will have less total information about the Western US natural gas market than about the US stock market. **But having a big information *advantage* in a smaller market is more valuable than gobs of information but no discernible advantage in a larger market. It is the "information advantage" you have relative to the rest of the market that matters.**

PARKING LOTS, CROPS AND CRAP

Gaining an information advantage can be expensive, even when vast amounts of accurate electronic information are available.

For example, there are companies that use satellite technology to track the number of cars in retail parking lots in the US. They use this info to estimate retail sales by region and retailer, and compare year-over-year sales (ahead of quarterly earnings announcements) simply based on the traffic. Imagine how this will change when the estimates become accurate enough to analyze how many are new Mercedes versus 10-year-old Chevys. And, as more auto companies build GPS tracking systems into their vehicles (for example, GM's OnStar system), companies like GM are selling some of the information (usually within privacy-policy boundaries) to data crunchers (Champs), who use it in clever ways to understand changing trends before the Chumps do.

One crop research company, Lanworth, analyzes commodity-crop production using infrared and microwave images, a relatively inexpensive process when done on a large scale. If you needed to predict the future price of corn or soybeans, and had big money riding on getting the call right, you would gladly pay for this kind of information. Imagine the costs involved if, instead, scouts had to drive around manually recording the height of corn fields across America.

In the late 1990s, we hired an aerial photographer to fly over all the big power plants in the United Kingdom. We were looking for just one thing: how many porta potties were at each site. Porta potties meant that the plant was coming down soon for maintenance, which would tighten supplies and push electricity prices up.

We also investigated—but never pulled off—using a remote electromagnetic detector that could be placed near large transmission lines which might, together with other monitors, give us instant feedback on changes in the supply/demand balance. We hoped to learn more about power plant availability which obviously would affect our market positions.

In the US, if a major new pipeline was going to change the supply/demand balance by bringing in more natural gas from Canada, we sometimes hired scouts to physically view the construction progress, and talk to the crews about how things were going. The owners of the new pipelines could not be counted on to be as forthcoming about the headway on their construction. To us, knowing when a new natural gas transmission line would start flowing was important because, when the new line went operational, it would immediately *increase* prices in the area near the pipeline injection point and *decrease* them at the pipeline delivery point. Gaining this intelligence was costly, so the stakes had to be big enough to justify the expense.

AN INFORMATION ADVANTAGE WITH NO VOLATILITY IS USELESS

Let me define the concept of volatility.

The words *danger, risk,* and *volatility* are frequently mixed up and conflated. Volatility in trading parlance is a measurement depicting how much a price or measurement has moved, is moving, or is expected to move, either up or down. Historic volatility is a measurement of how much a price has already moved during a specific time period. Traded volatility is the level that is priced into options as the aggregate market assessment of how much prices are likely to move in the future. Note that past performance (or volatility) certainly does not predict future performance (or volatility), **although many novices will mistakenly assume so.**

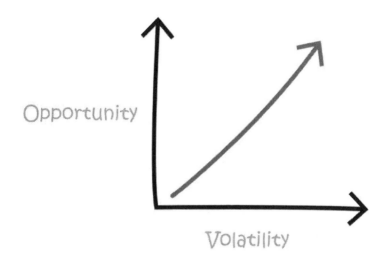

Volatile markets are perceived as riskier than less volatile markets. The traditional risk models that use "value at risk" measures specifically place a larger risk factor on higher volatility.

Prices can be volatile and trending up, or volatile and trending down. But politicians and the media tends to report only about volatility when it's moving prices in an unpopular direction—such as gasoline prices increasing or the stock or housing market dropping. Here is a typical quote reporting "unpopular volatility: "The central bank of Latin America's largest economy (Brazil) said late on Thursday that it would launch a currency intervention program worth about $60 billion to ensure liquidity and reduce volatility in the nation's foreign exchange market." But, alas, the central bank is not trying to reduce *all* volatility—just volatility that weakens the value of their currency. Interestingly, it was not long ago that they had announced their intention to weaken their currency to protect their manufacturing sector. They just can't make up their minds.

I believe that most investors, traders, and entrepreneurs go broke not because they analyze a market, bet on it, and then get it wrong, but because they simply ignore the possibility that the volatility or trend might suddenly *change*. The out-to-lunch crowd (perhaps with a martini or two) has experienced smooth sailing, and is oblivious to a threatening storm.

The danger is when you are going along assuming that volatility will stay low, or more frequently, not making any assumption at all, and suddenly, *Bang!*, the world changes. You are short oil, and the Strait of Hormuz gets shut down. Or you are long US equities, and a terrorist attack hits New York City.

Some of these bangs can be predicted and some cannot be anticipated at all. The weather forecast business is still not very good at forecasting when a tsunami might hit Japan; earthquake and volcano predicting businesses are still in their infancy.

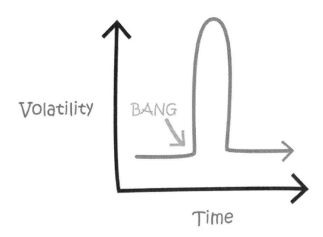

Lucky And Good

Interestingly, the Chicago Board Options Exchange trades an index called the "VIX," which is the implied (or traded) volatility of S&P 500 index futures. This gauge increases as options get more expensive, and drops when options get less costly. But the financial press likes to label this index the "fear index," implying that greater volatility is dangerous and less volatility is safe—a bad way of looking at the world. Here is where my advice differs from the conventional wisdom. **Coming from a trading background, volatility is my lifeblood.**

No volatility means no way to make money other than selling options and betting that volatility will remain low.

It is hard to orchestrate a volatile market. But you can anticipate one if you know when a dramatic change in the supply or demand is about to occur (via an information advantage). Information is one thing, but an information advantage is another. Simply collecting and reviewing all available data doesn't provide you a competitive advantage. You need to find a way to understand the relationships and data that others are missing.

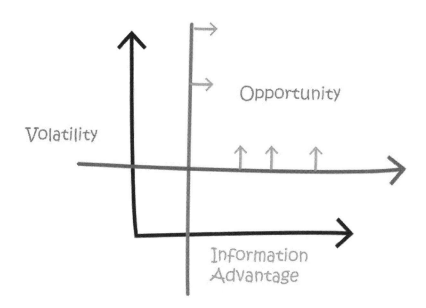

CHAPTER THREE: DECIDE

> "The sobering reality is that the grandest revelations often still need work."
>
> —Jonan Lehrer,
> *Imagine-How Creativity Works*

So you have finally found the next great idea. Should you pursue it?

Finding an opportunity only gets you to the one yard line...with 99 yards to go. Thinking about the opportunity, analyzing it, collecting the data, and getting feedback are the next steps in determining whether you go for it. The way in which you make decisions is make or break.

Considering an opportunity is the rational evaluation and improvement of that idea, trade, or investment. At this point, your adrenaline level needs to be lowered, your critical thinking ramped up.

Making informed and intelligent decisions is central to success for traders and investors; if they do nothing else well, they can prosper by being good at this stage of the game.

WELCOME FORKS IN THE ROAD

*"I took the one less traveled by,
and that has made all the difference."*
—Robert Frost

As an entrepreneur, you are *the* decision maker (head honcho). You get far more practice than your college roommates who are working for established companies. To begin with, you decide to open up shop. You create a value proposition and find customers willing to give your new business a chance. You either raise capital or, more likely, put most of your life savings at risk. And, once you receive feedback from prospective customers, you probably have to decide if and how you will adapt the business plan.

As an entrepreneur, what risks do you take? When do you bet on the favorite? When do you take the long shot for a chance at a much bigger payday? How are others likely to think about exactly the same problems? How do you present the possible outcomes to your customers, partners, and suppliers?

Every fork in the road is a chance for the Champ to gain ground on the Chump. Young traders and young entrepreneurs have plenty of opportunities because they arrive at many crossroads. What to do next? Where to turn now?

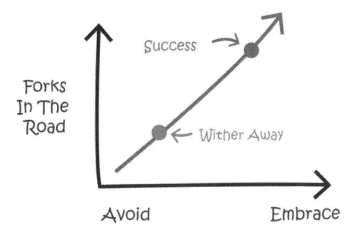

Interestingly, Warren Buffet tries to avoid buying businesses that are facing important turning points because he understands that every major decision can derail a company. His lower-risk approach has paid substantial dividends (in generating investment returns, but not on the innovation scale). He tries to buy businesses that have such a competitive advantage, you could have your lazy, good-for-nothing brother-in-law (to be clear: I don't have one of these) running the business and it would continue to flourish.

But what has worked so well for investor Buffet makes less sense if you are getting started as an entrepreneur. Champs prefer Yogi Berra's advice: "When you come to the fork in the road, take it." I suggest a more assertive mantra: **"Find a fork in the road and take it!"**

Traders and entrepreneurs actively seek out forks in the road because forks create opportunities. Without forks in the road, everyone is going in the same direction, so it is hard to tell the Champs from the Chumps. A fork in the road can be a price inflection point (gasoline prices double), a change in technology (tablet sales overtake personal computers), or new legislation. (Obamacare changes the entire nature of health care insurance in the US.)

If, like most of us, you are starting with little or no capital, forks in the road are your primary currency. Each decision gives the Champ a chance to distance himself from the Chump. But if you don't get to make any more decisions than Buffett's brother-in-law, then you are likely to end up where you started—unless you marry "well."

FIGHT FOR FAST FEEDBACK

"Solve it. Solve it quickly, solve it right or wrong. If you solve it wrong, it will come back and slap you in the face, and then you can solve it right. Lying dead in the water and doing nothing is a comfortable alternative because it is without risk, but it is an absolutely fatal way to manage a business."

—Thomas J. Watson (1874–1962), former president of IBM

Were it not for fast feedback, "Dilbert" creator Scott Adams would have quit producing his comic strip. He first syndicated his work in 1989, working double duty at Pac Bell while his readership grew. He attributes his success to the fact that he included an email address with his satirical work so he could get feedback from his readers. An inspirational letter from a fan persuaded him to keep trying when he nearly gave up drawing.

The faster you get feedback from potential customers and investors, the better. Lack of speed kills. It shouldn't take a month to learn that 50 other companies are already pursuing the same business concept as you are.

Decide

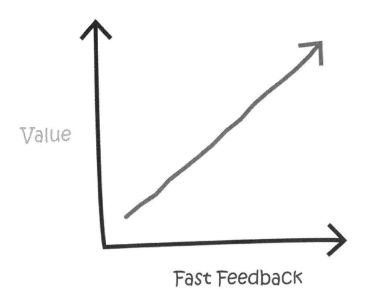

Fast Feedback

Fast feedback allows you to learn, adjust your strategy and tactics, and improve your business model. Imagine yourself competing in a 50-meter target pistol contest. You carefully made your first shot, but would be unable to see the results and adjust your shot for another 20 years (slow feedback). Only then could you find out how close your last shot was to the bull's eye. After 80 years, you might not have the strength to hold the pistol steady, but you would finally know the results from your first four shots.

Spanish clothing retailer Zara, founded in 1975, built its strategy around fast feedback and quicker response, rather than lower production costs associated with outsourcing to China or Vietnam. The company launches about 10,000 new designs each year, which can go from the back of an envelope to store shelves in just two weeks. Clerks and store managers worldwide tell Zara designers in real time which fashions are selling, what customers are complaining about, and what shoppers are asking for. These in-house designers then create new styles "on the fly," send them to Zara's flexible and highly automated factories, and have new products in the customers' hands faster than anyone else. The company doesn't have to order 20,000 new women's blouses three months in advance; it can try a new item in a few stores and then adjust, based on how that fashion sells. Today, Zara has more than 1,600 stores on every continent except Antarctica, with annual revenues over $9 billion. Zara's former chairman, and owner of nearly 60% of its shares, was named the third-richest man in the world on the Forbes March 2013 list, with an estimated net worth of $57 billion.

Innovations such as email, and shared cloud files via Google Drive and Dropbox.com, have made it so much easier to give and receive fast feedback. The Dropbox founders created a video mockup of their product, and shared it far and wide, asking for feedback on features and design before investing to develop it. New contractors in the construction business are wise to cut their teeth on small time-and-materials jobs before placing a big bet on a large fixed-price contact.

Need feedback? Easy-to-use free survey tools such as Surveymonkey.com allow you to create a simple survey and gather basic statistics in no time flat. After reading this book, I hope you won't bet the farm on a five-question survey of 50 of your closest friends. But it can be a great tool for getting a rough idea about what people are thinking—fast.

Geoffrey Moore is a high-tech consultant and venture partner in Silicon Valley, and author of several marketing books including *Crossing the Chasm*. He advises entrepreneurs developing a new product to try and sell it to another company before it's finished. This goes against the natural inclination of most inventors. While you might feel more confident presenting a finished product, you miss the opportunity to integrate the prospect's early feedback into your design. Incorporating this user feedback also vastly increases the chances of making a sale to that company when the new and improved product is ready for prime time.

*****

Most junior traders start in liquid, fast-moving markets in which they transact frequently and get swift feedback. Why would I want a young trader working for me making long-term bets or investments that might require years to evaluate? Years later, the young trader can hardly remember why he made the trade in the first place. Slow feedback dramatically reduces his chance to adjust and improve. There is a huge advantage in getting feedback through winning and losing, adjusting tactics and strategy, and getting better the next time. The trader who can only adjust once every few years learns at a much slower pace than one who can adjust and learn hourly.

Speed counts, and so does the quality of the feedback. Getting fast feedback goes beyond asking your mother how much she likes your idea.

Entrepreneurs first need feedback on a new business plan. Here is where a network of friends providing honest feedback and suggestions comes in handy. Too many idea generators think their concepts are so "rare and valuable" they can't risk telling anyone about them.

The truth is, there are many more ideas out there than entrepreneurs who can get them up and running. Most people don't have time to rip off your brilliant plan, and those who would do so are generally too lazy to bother. It's better to share your thoughts and get responses early on in the process than to work in a vacuum, with input from too few people. I am not advocating being a blabbermouth—I just favor getting fast feedback over keeping your proposition top secret.

Let's look at some examples of **fast and slow feedback:**

- ❖ After every telephone sales pitch, telemarketers get the sale or fail right away. Compare this to sales cycles that require years to close, like selling jumbo jets to airlines.

- ❖ An infomercial can provide feedback within minutes after being presented on television. If the infomercial generates sales, you quickly buy more air time. If the infomercial doesn't work, it's back to the drawing board--tonight.

- ❖ Those who invest in offshore oil platforms requiring five years to permit and three years to build. A solar farm that needs three years to permit and a year to construct, must consider long term variables. What will the price of oil be by the time your platform is up and pumping? Today, oil may sell for $100 per barrel, but in three years, it might be $40. Can you predict the price of electricity in four years, when your wind farm is finally producing power?

- ❖ A major automaker commits hundreds of millions of dollars to develop an electric car. The project is based upon predictions that, in 10 years, when the car goes to market, US gas prices will consistently be over $5 per gallon, but electricity prices will stay low. Fast-forward 10 years, and gas prices are hovering at only $2 a gallon, while electricity prices have tripled. Ouch!

- ❖ Compare a new design prototype being built in China that won't be ready for four months, versus one built in your own garage in a week or two. This example points out a negative trend for America, as we have outsourced so much manufacturing and prototyping capacity to China.

- ❖ A new smartphone application might be up and running in a few weeks. Then users can give you feedback.

- ❖ A high school graduate sets off for college intending to earn a PhD in history, and eventually to teach at the state U. Unless the student continues to research and check on job/pay prospects, she may later find herself, after ten years of toil, facing a very bleak job market. This is slow (and painful) feedback.

- ❖ In 1992, the Maastricht Treaty established the euro as the replacement currency for the participating countries, as of 1999. It worked flawlessly for the first eight years; then the engine sputtered. This was slow feedback. But once the process was in motion, there was no turning back. It may eventually collapse. (As I write this, I can't conceive of the euro surviving as is, although many would disagree.) The euro was the equivalent of the "all-in" poker bet, with a decade or two wait before knowing whether or not you won.

- ❖ An internet poker player can play hundreds of thousands of poker hands in a short time before ever sitting down at a live game. She is no longer relegated to being the Fish, as her predecessors were 30 years ago. This is fast feedback. Of course, this also means that the veteran's information advantage can erode much faster than in years past (Strike While the Iron is Hot).

I am not suggesting that you absolutely avoid long lead-time investments, just recognize the added risk.

*****

Collecting and adjusting to feedback takes humility and an ability to listen to and sift through others' advice. Asking for feedback early and often is a start. Even harder is asking follow-up questions and adjusting to what you are hearing—even when you don't like what you hear. Gauging the quality of the advice takes some finesse, as well.

Leveraging Time

Receiving and acting on fast feedback leverages the most important dimension of all—time!

PLAY THE ODDS

"The race is not always to the swift nor the battle to the strong, but that's the way to bet."
—Damon Runyon

It was Week 10 in the 2009 NFL season. The New England Patriots had a fourth-and-two on their own 28 yard line, with two minutes eight seconds left in the game and a six point lead. If the Pats punted the ball, the Indianapolis Colts (and future Hall of Fame Quarterback Peyton Manning) would get one more shot at scoring a

Lucky And Good

touchdown for the win. If the Pats made the first down, they could run down the clock and virtually guarantee a victory.

If you're the Patriots' head coach, do you go for it, or do you punt?

Pats Head Coach Bill Belichick (first introduced in Think in Opposites) went for it, came up short, and lost. Here's what the Monday morning quarterbacks had to say:

- ❖ "One of the most bizarre coaching decisions in the history of football..."
- ❖ "The NFL has outlawed gambling. Clearly, New England missed the memo."
- ❖ "The Patriots took one of the biggest, most mystifying gambles in memory Sunday night, and paid the price when it backfired."
- ❖ "Each and every week we see bad coaching decisions in the NFL, but never, and I mean never, have I seen one as dumb as the decision Patriots coach Bill Belichick made Sunday."
- ❖ "The worst coaching decision I've ever seen Bill Belichick make."

Brian Burke, who operates Advanced NFL Stats, a blog about NFL statistics and decisions, has a different analysis of Belichick's decision. Based on the odds of making a first down, and the chances of the Colts scoring if they got the ball, he estimates that the Pats had a 70% probability of winning the game if they punted, and a 79% chance if they went for it on fourth down.

Brian Burke, Bill Belichick, and I all advocate playing the odds. But don't expect kudos for making the smart but unconventional decision when it fails.

*****

If you are playing a game, you might know the odds. However, in business, you never know them exactly. But you can still take your best shot at evaluating your chances. You must use what you know to gauge the range of possible outcomes and the likelihood of any one of them coming to pass.

Let's review a concept called "expected value." In probability theory, the expected value—or mathematical expectation—of a random variable is the weighted average of all possible values that this random variable can achieve. This formula is not meant to predict an exact outcome (e.g. the number three will be rolled on the dice); it instead suggests an aggregate of many potential outcomes. You assign a probability to each prospect in order to estimate the average outcome. This is "probabilistic" evaluation.

For example, if I were going to receive $1 for every dot on a single dice I rolled, what would the expected value of the dice roll be?

It would be ($1 +$2 +$3 +$4 + $5 +$6)/6 = $21/6 = $3.50.

In other words, my expected value would be $3.50 for each and every roll. If I can roll the dice ten times a minute, I can expect to earn an average of $2,100 an hour (not bad work, if you can get it).

Alternatively, if I were going to receive $1 times the square of the number of dots that I rolled, what would the expected value of each roll be?

It would be ((1*$1) + (2*$2) + (3* $3) + (4*$4) + (5*$5) + (6*$6))/6= $91/6 = $15.17 per roll.

Now, if I can roll 10 times a minute, I can earn $9,102 per hour. You'll have to drag me away kicking and screaming—even if I have to pay for my own drinks.

This next simple drawing shows an example based on "investing" $10, with a 25% chance of losing the $10, a 20% chance of making $5, a 30% chance of making $10, and finally a 25% chance of making $20.

Lucky And Good

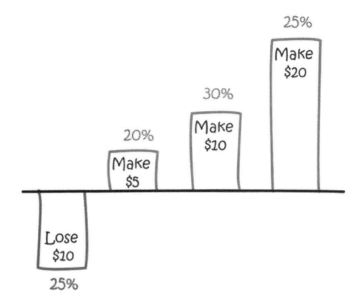

If this is how you assessed the odds, your "expected value" would be:

(25% * - $10) + (20% * $5) + (30% * $10) + (25% * $20) = $6.50

So, in this case, I am risking $10 for an average profit of $6.50. In real life you don't get many bets this easy. If you won't take this opportunity each and every time (except when you face the risk of ruin), you are wasting your time reading this book.

Taleb correctly points out that, in the real world, we don't know the exact odds, but by at least thinking through various possible outcomes and giving it our "best guess," we can get closer to the value of making one choice versus another, based on our own assumptions.

FRAMING THE PROBLEM

The way in which you look at a business opportunity can affect your outcome. As financier J.P. Morgan once said, "No problem can be solved until it is reduced to some simple form. The changing of a vague difficulty into a specific, concrete form is a very essential element in thinking."

Let's explore the framing of problems by considering two questions that come from the work of Daniel Kahneman:

Would you accept a gamble that offers a 10% chance to win $100 and a 90% chance to lose $10? (($100 * 10%) - ($10 * 90%) = $1)? $1 is the "expected value," and here it is positive.

On the other hand, would you pay a $9 fee to participate in a lottery that offers a 10% chance to win $100 and a 90% chance to win nothing? (($100 * 10%) - $9 = $1)? Again, $1 is the expected value.
These two examples, framed differently, describe nearly the same problem. Both have a positive expected value of $1 with a worst case possibility of losing either $9 or $10. But the first opportunity describes the chance as a "loss," and the second one calls it a "fee" or "expense." A bad outcome is much more acceptable to non-traders if it's framed as an ordinary expense, rather than as a loss. People hate to "lose."

 But you will be cumulatively "luckier" over a lifetime if you learn to suck it up and take either of these bets every time you get the chance. This is how some people have done it:

SELLING COMPUTERS

In the early 1980s, my brother Jim was a computer salesman for Hewlett Packard. He had a customer who wanted to buy a system based on a third-party software package that Jim and the customer thought would meet their needs. But the customer wouldn't buy the hardware without seeing the software demonstrated; the start-up software company would only fly out for a demo if Hewlett-Packard agreed to reimburse their $750 air fare should the sale fall through. HP wouldn't accept that potential liability.

Jim figured to make a $4,000 commission on the sale, and estimated that, if the software was demonstrated, he had about a 50% chance of closing the sale. So he called up the software vendor and said that he would personally pay the air fare if they didn't make the sale.

Jim's expected upside was 50% * $4,000 = ($2,000 pre-tax) with an expected downside of 50% * $750 = ($375), leaving him with a net expected value that was a positive $1,625 (pre-tax). So Jim did something that many would not: He took the chance, and it eventually had a happy ending when he closed the deal. Jim is a Champ. I doubt that, should Jim find himself in France and if President Francois Hollande (a real Chump) has his way by increasing the top marginal income tax rate to 75%, Jim would make the same gamble.

Doing the numbers and making the smart bet is always the way to go, whether the bet is $750 or $100 million. The more you practice thinking and acting this way on smaller bets, the better prepared you will be for making the bigger decisions.

STEALING BASES

What problem are we trying to solve when deciding whether we should attempt to steal a base? Stated this way, the answer is more clear.

In baseball, Sabermetrics suggests that an attempted stolen base usually results in fewer total runs scored for the offense, except when the base runner has a success rate greater than about 70%.

And yet, a baseball manager whose team is in a tied game in the bottom of the ninth inning must reframe the problem. In the first inning, the best strategy is one that will create the most runs (on average). In the bottom of the ninth inning with the score tied, the best strategy is one that has the highest probability of scoring one or more runs, not necessarily the strategy that will score the highest average number of runs.

PUTTING FOR DOUGH

When calculating the expected value, it is critical to focus on estimating the most important variable. Getting secondary variables right while missing the more significant ones can spell trouble.

In *Moneyball*, Michael Lewis describes how many old-school baseball scouts paid too much attention to foot speed along with other, sometimes irrelevant factors: did the prospect "look like a baseball player"; was he self-confident enough to have a good-looking girlfriend; how "smart" was the player? As if the textbook smarts of players like Babe Ruth, Joe DiMaggio, and Willie Mays had any connection with their contributions on the playing field.

Are you measuring the right variables in your business? Consider this theoretical (at least for me) example about focusing on what is important:

Imagine you are making a difficult, slightly downhill, eight-foot putt on the 72nd hole of the U.S. Open. The hole is a par five. If you sink it, you will have a birdie four and be crowned the new U.S. Open Champion. If you barely miss and tap it in for the par five, you will go into a sudden death playoff with Tiger Woods. Because you have played better than Woods this final day and he has struggled, you figure that your chance of beating Woods in sudden death is 70%. (You probably don't want to discuss this estimate at the post-tournament press conference, regardless of the final result.) The last thing you want is to leave your putt short. The expression "never up, never in" applies tenfold here.

Based on that strategy, you normally play the putt to go 30 inches past the hole (we'll call this the "30+ putt") if you miss. This approach has a smaller chance of falling short, but a bigger chance of ending up so far past the hole that you might miss the second putt (for par) and ultimately take three putts to score a bogey six. (Being "short" and "long" have entirely different meanings in this example than in the rest of this book.) Let's say that, with this approach, the probability of a birdie four is 80%; the probability of a par five is 10%; and the probability of a bogey six is 10%.

Alternatively, you are also considering striking the putt with enough speed so that, if you miss it, you expect to roll the ball 18 inches too far. (We'll call this the "18+ putt.") Let's say that this approach has a 60% probability of a birdie four; a 40% probability of a par five; and no chance of a bogey six. (Please bear with me on this assumption, even if you are as bad a putter as I am.)

If you are interested in the calculations, see Exhibit C at the book's end. Given these assumptions, the 18+ putt gives you an average score on the hole of 4.4 and an 88% chance of winning the championship. With the 30+ putt, the same math gives you a 4.3 average score but only an 87% chance of winning the championship. In most evaluations, a percent or two is all that separates the Champs from the Chumps. In Olympic track-and-field or swimming finals, how often have you seen a medalist beat out an also-ran by a hundredth of a second?

When you consider the odds in making a decision, start with what you are trying to optimize. **You cannot optimize more than one dimension** (despite what Congress thought when they gave the Federal Reserve the dual mandate of reducing unemployment and fighting inflation). (But no one ever claimed that Congress was very good at arithmetic or budgets.)

Your thinking should be different on the first hole of the first round of the tournament than on the 72nd green. The 30+ putt has an average score improvement on just this one hole of 0.1 strokes. That doesn't sound like much, but used consistently over 72 holes, it adds up to 7.2 strokes. On the first hole, you take the approach that gives you the lowest expected score. But on the 72nd hole, you want to play the hole in a way that gives you the highest chance to be the U.S. Open champion. Interestingly, in this example, each goal (playing for the lowest average score versus playing to win the championship) dictates a different putting style—and a different decision.

Players with the lowest average scores do better financially on the PGA tour than those with just slightly higher average scores (both high correlation and high cause and effect). At the end of the 2012 PGA season, Rory McElroy was ranked number one, with an average 18-hole score of 68.9. To see a full stroke difference between competitors, you'll find Steve Stricker at number 16, with an average score of 69.9. A one-stroke difference between two golfers over the span of a season had a huge impact on where they finished. You'd have to drop all the way down to number 76, Jonathan Byrd, to find an average score of 1.8 strokes per round *higher* than number-one McElroy. For the season, McElroy earned $8,047,952 and Byrd made $1,616,789, all based on 1.8 strokes per round better play.

When used on the last hole of the tournament, the 18+ putt gives you the best chance of winning the U.S. Open—but consistently choosing the 30+ putt gives you a 1.8-stroke better scoring average per round of golf. Again, you cannot optimize two dimensions at once. **You have to choose the stroke based on the circumstances.** These choices represent tiny scoring differences, but cumulative tactics add up—over the course of a single round of golf, over 72 holes for the U.S. Open Championship, an entire season, an entire career, or an entire business lifetime.

I am confident that most of us would want to go with the strategy we thought offered the highest probability of winning the U.S. Open—a rare opportunity involving prestige, endorsements, and automatic qualifying for other tournaments. I also want to acknowledge that, for this kind of decision, every putt involves a vast array of instinctive factors. Professional golfers are not pulling out their iPads and doing calculations; they intuitively consider how best to strike the ball, based on years of practice and hundreds of thousands of putts. The pro has to stay relaxed and focused, slow his breathing, listen to his caddy, but ignore the crowd and cameras—and then judge the speed of the green, the undulations and slopes, and the dangers of going too far.

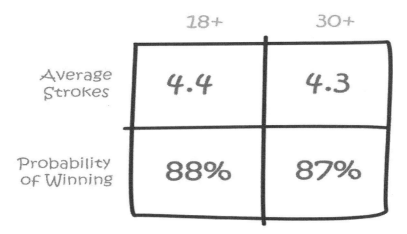

Here's another factor considered by the media and some decision makers that should never enter into the equation: The 30+ putt also has a 10% chance of resulting in a bogey, ensuring a tournament loss.

This outcome would be viewed as a "choke," a total embarrassment for the golfer. The aggressive nature of striking the ball harder means that the player might forever be seen on television replays crumbling on the final hole. Although this strategy shouldn't be selected anyway, it should be discarded based on the best chance to win the tournament, not the risk for public embarrassment.

This is analogous to many business decisions as viewed by the media. For example, as a mobile handset company, BlackBerry struggles to find a recipe for competing against the iPhone and Android phones. The company may find that they are down to one final big bet—the Z10 and Q10, introduced in early 2013. Their choices are no longer about not looking foolish or being average, but rather, Can they survive? Time will tell how their new device is accepted in the market. (Reports in early July 2013 indicated that these smartphones may have only sold about three million units during the first quarter of 2013.) If you are a shareholder, you wanted them to make the "hard" choices despite the reputation risk to management, but that happens less often than it should. This is where managing normal psychological factors can help you to act boldly and correctly, once you have properly framed the problem.

So, before you collect oodles of data and study the odds in boundless detail, make sure to carefully define the problem and identify the most important variables. Albert Einstein understood this when he said, "If I had an hour to save the world, I would spend 59 minutes defining the problem and one minute finding solutions."

♦♦♦
♦♦♦

Decide

THE NUMBERS MAY BE HAZARDOUS TO YOUR HEALTH

"The results of a new study are out this week saying that New Jersey is one of the most livable states in the country. The study has a margin of error of 100 percent."
—Conan O'Brien

How many television financial analysts have you heard say something along the lines of: "We are bearish because the last two times the VIX closed below 15%, the S&P 500 has suffered plunges of over 5% in the two months following that event." I don't know about you, but I am not going to go all-in based on a sample size of two.

 These observations may be pure coincidence. So, instead, focus on the logic of why this has happened, and why these circumstances are likely to result in the same pattern next time.

SMALL SAMPLES

Listening to a San Francisco Giants-Atlanta Braves baseball game, I heard National Baseball Hall of Fame announcer Jon Miller mention that red-hot Angel Pagan had been hitting .489 over the last seven games. His seasonal average was only .289. Seven games is also a small sample size (although I was already becoming a big Pagan fan).

Hasty generalization is the process of making a rushed conclusion without considering all the variables and the amount of data you possess. Absent the discipline of statistics, this may lead to jumping to broad conclusions regarding survey results from a small sample group that does not adequately represent an entire population.

Statistical significance is based on a mathematical assessment of whether observations reflect a pattern rather than just chance, the fundamental challenge being that any partial picture is subject to observational error. In testing, a result is deemed statistically significant if it's unlikely to have occurred by chance. In these instances, "significant" does not mean "important" or "meaningful," as it does in everyday speech; it means that the numbers represent a proven pattern in which you can be confident.

SIGNIFICANCE OR COINCIDENCE?

Hasty generalizations can lead folks to believe that a coincidence depicts some greater truth, pattern, or rule of thumb. However, sometimes the numbers cloud what is really going on—a mere quirk in the grand scheme of things.

"One Is the Loneliest Number" – Three Dog Night. On September 2, 2006, on the first pitch of his first Major League at bat as a Cleveland Indian, Kevin Kouzmanoff hit a grand slam. Kouzmanoff is one of only four players to hit one in his first Major League at bat. The fourth and final (so far) player to match this accomplishment (and only the second to do it on the first pitch) was Boston Red Sox rookie Daniel Nava, on June 12, 2010, at Fenway Park against the Philadelphia Phillies.

But that was as good as it got (it obviously couldn't get any better) for both of them. Kouzmanoff went on to play for the San Diego Padres, Oakland A's, Toronto Blue Jays, and Colorado Rockies through 2011, and have 2,748 at bats and get 84 more home runs. Not bad (from a guy that never made it to Majors in Little League), but not quite up to his debut. After his first trip to the plate, he had a career AB/RBI (at bats/runs batted in) ratio of .25, which is the lowest and best theoretical possibility—it means that he got four runs batted in for every at bat. By comparison, Babe Ruth had 2,217 RBIs in 8,399 at bats, so his ratio was (8,399/2,217) = 3.788. Kouzmanoff slipped a bit after his first at bat.

Nava has had three years in the Majors (2010, 2012, and 2013), and, as of late August in the 2013 season, a total 794 at bats. Since his first at bat, when he had a career 1.000 batting average, his career batting average (as of when this book was published) is a more ordinary .266.

"Two Is the Loneliest Number Since the Number One"– Three Dog Night. Johnny Vander Meer was a Major League pitcher for the Cincinnati Reds, Chicago Cubs, and Cleveland Indians. He was a promising young player early in his second season when, on June 11 and 15, 1938, while pitching for the Reds, he became the first and only Major League pitcher to throw two consecutive no-hitters. He was riding high, but things were never again quite as bright. Over his entire 13-year career, he went on to only a 119-121 record, although he did manage to get voted an All-Star four times, and was a World Series champion in 1940.

Switching to golf, the odds of the average amateur golfer having a hole-in-one ("ace") on any par three is roughly 12,500:1. Yet, when I was playing a few years ago, the course marshal came by to tell us that one of the other players on the course had just made his second hole-in-one in that round of golf! I still await my first.

Sometimes 16 Is a Small Sample. Since 1940, the winner of the last NFL home game before the presidential election has usually predicted which party would win the presidency. Whenever the Washington Redskins won their last home game, the incumbent party would win. It happened for 16 elections in a row, through the 2000 election. But if you started betting big on this phenomenon, beginning with the 2004 election, you would have lost two out of the next three times.

Sometimes 30 is a Small Sample. Phil Garner was 30 years old, and playing in his sixth Major League season. He had played in Little League, high school, college, and the Minors, but had never hit a grand slam in organized baseball. On September 14, 1978, while playing for the Pittsburg Pirates, he stepped up to the plate in the seventh inning with the bases loaded, and finally got his slam. When he arrived home, his wife was upset because she had missed the game. Garner told her not to worry: if she came to the game the next day, he would get another. And he did.

Sometimes 56 is a Small Sample. On May 15, 1941, New York Yankee Joe DiMaggio started one of the most celebrated streaks in any sport. "Joltin' Joe" hit safely in every one of his next 56 games. He hit well during this streak (.408), and yet the random nature of the record is truly phenomenal. In a 2009 article on *Science20.com*, Josh

Lucky And Good

Witten described his findings regarding DiMaggio's streak, based on millions of computer simulations. Two of his conclusions stand out:

1) Given DiMaggio's career statistics, the "Yankee Clipper" would, on average, have a streak of at least 56 games once every 1,100 careers. (If you could clone him and those around him, and play in the same stadiums with the same umpires, managers, teammates and opponents.)

2) Assuming the historical Major League batting average of .262 for all players who have played the game, the chance that someone would have this same streak (in the entire history of baseball) is roughly 5%. So it was extraordinarily lucky for DiMaggio to have done it—but not nearly so exceptional that *somebody* did.

Sometimes 63 Is a Small Sample. In the mid-1980s, my brother Jim had a system that seemed foolproof. His analysis indicated that the price of dividend-paying utility stocks consistently increased for the three-day period starting five days before the ex-dividend date. (That's the first date after the declaration of a dividend on which the buyer of a stock is not entitled to receive the next dividend payment. In this case, "ex" is similar to "ex-wife.")

Jim would buy the stock and sell it three days later. He used money from his home-equity line of credit, and was buying all the stocks with the maximum margin. After the system worked flawlessly for the first 63 times, he was ready to quit his day job, and add even more leverage to his "system." But then, one day, it didn't work, and he lost all of his gains on the next two trades. Later, my brother did some further analysis and found that, because the stocks had been steadily increasing during this period, had he simply bought the stocks and held them during those six months, he would have made a nice, but unimpressive, profit. Warren Buffet would have been proud of Jim's eventual conclusion.

Even a Million Is Sometimes a Small Sample. Another phenomenon is the way traders can gain confidence from computer runs involving millions of iterations that should be statistically significant. If I take a random set of variables (ones that follow a bell curve, which not all variables do), and run a statistical analysis on the results, I can find out how a given strategy would have done during

108

Decide

the last several years. It will show me how bad my bad days would have been, how good my best years would have been, and it will all be in black and white, impossible to dispute. This is great "hindsight trading."

If I could run tests on millions of different trading algorithms, I might find that one in a million combinations was consistently profitable during the last five years. But why was it profitable? And for the next five years, this lucky algorithm might be just as unlucky.

The past decade has seen an explosion of software trading systems (especially for equities) that allow you to back-test a trading algorithm with hundreds of variables. These might be relative strength indexes, moving averages, and stochastic oscillators, to name a few, each of which you get to iterate; for example, you can try factor X1 with levels of 1% to 99% in 0.1% increments. Then you can test the second factor, X2, in levels between 25 and 50 with increments of 0.1. So, when all is said and done, after a quick set-up and a few hours on the computer, anyone can test literally millions of different algorithms. If nothing looks good, you can test another million algorithms, and it will be hard to eventually not stumble across an *apparent* winner.

If I play the lottery with about one in 14 million odds against me, and I get to play it 14 million times, I have a reasonable shot at hitting the winning number.

So, the figures can help or hinder you. Just pursue them as far as you can reasonably go, and take the results with a grain of salt. Here are four fun examples from Correlated.org. They are not statistically valid, because the sample is the universe of people who voluntarily participated in their surveys—and the survey size is relatively small.

- ❖ 15% of people who dislike mayonnaise are good dancers, compared with 29% of people with any mayonnaise preference.
- ❖ 82% of people with tattoos prefer hot weather over cold, compared with 63% of people in general (based on a survey of 114 people with tattoos and 579 people with or without tattoos).
- ❖ In the general population, 70% prefer big dogs to small dogs. But, among those who would rather have a lock with

a key than a combination lock for their locker, 83% prefer big dogs (based on a survey of 149 people who prefer a lock with a key for their locker and 393 people total).
- ❖ 59% of all people surveyed don't wear pajamas to bed. But, among those who prefer Bill Clinton over Hillary Clinton, 79% don't wear pajamas to bed (based on the answers of 142 people who prefer Bill Clinton over Hillary Clinton and 390 people in general).

The moral of this story is: be skeptical about the numbers; be suspicious when the dataset is small; look beyond "averages," and seek out the logic and drivers behind the numbers. There are plenty of valid interconnections and relationships for you to find and understand.

CORRELATION IS NOT CAUSATION

"Repeat after me: correlation is not causation, correlation is not causation, correlation is not causation ..."

—Nathan Green

Okay—I repeated it, Nathan. Now, let's dig a little deeper.

A European reporter visiting the US about a hundred years ago missed this point when he wired his editor back home: "My God, you'll never believe the sort of money there is in running public libraries."

The reporter was in America doing a profile on steel magnate Andrew Carnegie, who is often regarded as the second-richest man in history (adjusted for inflation) after John D. Rockefeller. Carnegie had spent his last years as a philanthropist promoting and funding public libraries across the United States. The reporter got the cause and effect backwards, as many reporters do.

Decide

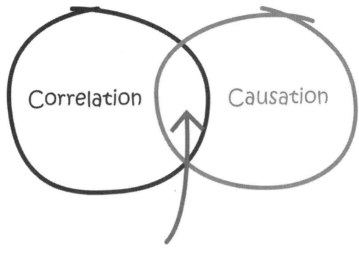

If you understand this principle, you're ahead of 90% of your competitors. Think about this, and how most stories are reported. Contrary to much of the news spin, you will realize that, while a correlation may exist between two separate events, there often is no cause/effect relationship.

 The average story never even suggests that two events might be correlated but that one does not cause the other. This common misperception weakens many people's general thinking, to their detriment. Here is a perfect example:

A caller named "Donna" phoned the Y94 Morning Playhouse radio program to air her frustrations about three separate deer-related car accidents in which she was recently involved. As she shared her tale of woe, she clearly demonstrated how easy it is to confuse correlation with cause and effect. Donna complained, "My frustration

Lucky And Good

is that Minnesota and North Dakota Departments of Transportation would allow these deer crossings in such high-traffic areas. I mean, I've even seen them on the interstate."

Here, she made a serious error.

"Why are we encouraging deer to cross at the interstate? I don't get it," Donna said to the astounded radio hosts.

CORRELATION

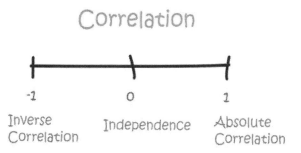

Let's define correlation. It's a statistical measure (with values between -1 and +1) that indicates to what extent two variables move in synchronization—or two events happen together.

A correlation of +1 indicates that the variables are absolutely correlated and move in total lockstep. A correlation of 0 shows that they are totally independent and are not correlated, and that there is no pattern in which they occur together. A correlation of -1 means they move undeniably in opposite directions (inverse correlation).

Two examples of **zero correlation** (independence) are:

- ❖ the relationship between annual rainfall in Mongolia and the chances that the next Super Bowl winner will be from the NFC (You will have to take this one on faith since I have no supporting data.);
- ❖ the relationship between IQ and the last four digits of your social security number. (I haven't bothered to prove this

one either; perhaps the last four digits of my social security number are not high enough.)

An example of **absolute correlation** is:

- ❖ the speed of a moving automobile and the amount of damage the auto will cause in a collision.

Three examples of **inverse correlation** are:

- ❖ low IQ and probability of being accepted to Harvard;
- ❖ being short and the chance of starting as a center in the NBA;
- ❖ being very tall and becoming an Olympic gymnast.

CAUSATION

The challenge in making decisions based on correlation is that an apparent correlation may not indicate a cause-and-effect relationship. You must distinguish between the symptom and the disease—what causes what, and whether one predicts the other.

The inverse correlation examples above reflect both negative correlation and a cause-and-effect relationship. Causation is when a second event (B) is the result or consequence of the first event (A). It's the relationship between a set of factors that cause or prevent another phenomenon or effect.

Frequently, however, A and B may be seen together because, perhaps, event C, which you may not even be aware of, caused both A and B to occur. But even though events A and B are correlated, it does not mean that A and B have any cause and effect on each other.

Let's say that Adam and Becky both commute in their own cars from the same part of Marin County, down Highway 101, across the Golden Gate Bridge, to the financial district in San Francisco. They usually leave at about the same time each morning, and arrive at work within minutes of each other. Their commute times are highly correlated. But one day, when a truck overturns on the Golden Gate Bridge (event C for "crash"), both Adam and Becky get to work two hours late. If you knew how long it took Adam to get to work on that given day, it would give you a strong clue about how long it took Becky. But there was no cause and effect relationship between Adam's commute time and Becky's. It was event C that caused *both* A and B.

Causality *may* mean that A causes B but B does not cause A. Think about the correlation between the size of a fire and the number of firemen fighting the fire. Increasing the number of firemen will not make the fire larger. But as the fire gets bigger, more firemen usually show up to battle it.

A recent study found that those who smiled sincerely most often lived the longest. I am not sure how they determined which smiles were sincere and which were not. But is it the smile that extends longevity? Or are there other factors, such as happiness and better health, that extend life spans, and also bring a smile?

The fallacy occurs when one sees two events occur together often without understanding the real-world dynamics that might make A cause B or B cause A. For example, having a fever and being ill are highly correlated (a classic symptom and disease). While being ill might cause the fever, the fever, did not cause the illness.

The Obama 2012 campaign kept harping on the notion that Bill Clinton raised taxes, and Bill Clinton's economy was strong. (Clinton did, however, benefit from low oil prices, no large wars, a boom in the housing industry, and the internet bubble.) Therefore, Obama asserts that raising taxes will improve the economy. Obama is guilty of mixing up cause and effect with correlation—and his mistaken conclusion is also based on a very small dataset. (If you are an Obama supporter, you probably didn't make it this far, anyway.)

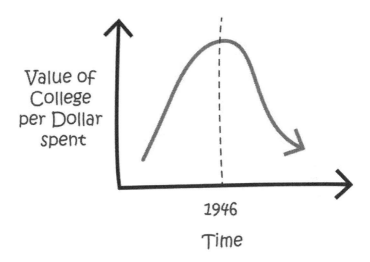

Another study, published in the August 2012 issue of *Health Affairs,* declared: "College graduates live a decade longer than high school dropouts." For men, the gap was 12.9 years, and for women it was 10.4 years. The average business reporter (sorry to be pickin' on you) might simply suggest that, to lengthen people's life spans, we insist that everyone stay in college until they graduate. That amateur logician misses fundamentals like:

- ❖ College graduates, on average, have higher IQs than high school dropouts.
- ❖ College graduates, on average, get more jobs that entitle them to better health care benefits than high school dropouts.
- ❖ The average college graduate has a job that involves less physical risk than jobs filled by high school dropouts.
- ❖ A smaller percentage of college graduates are smokers.

Similarly, it has been asserted that graduating from an Ivy League college and financial success are strongly correlated. But, is this cause and effect? In the November 12, 2007, *Forbes* told how Princeton researcher Stacey Dale had studied high school graduates accepted to Ivy League colleges. Dale found that those who instead chose to attend local state universities or colleges did just as well financially as those who attended the Ivy Leagues. So the cause-and-effect relationship *may* simply be that being smart enough to be accepted at an Ivy League college bodes well for future financial success (again, we are talking averages here). Perhaps the extra $200,000+ that the Ivy League colleges charge for an education is not such a great investment after all.

Here are some examples of plausible cause-and-effect relationships:

- ❖ Bill was late for school because his alarm clock didn't work.
- ❖ As a result of the Iran oil sanctions, Iran was prevented from exporting as much oil as usual, and the world supply of oil dropped.
- ❖ Because natural gas prices fell, coal prices had to drop: natural gas–fired power plants produced electricity so economically that it was displacing coal-fired electricity.

By not examining relationships carefully, people miss the boat. Do not assume too quickly that because A and B are correlated, one causes the other.

BIG DATA

Now that I have convinced you that correlation is not causation, let's take a U-turn, and consider some of the emerging benefits of studying correlation in massive datasets. In their recent book *Big Data: A Revolution That Will Transform How We Live, Work, and Think*, Viktor Mayer-Schonberger and Kenneth Cukier make some thought-provoking observations about how massive datasets are changing the way in which many business decisions are made. The book's central propositions are: 1) big datasets are allowing nonobvious but useful relationships to be discovered; and 2) correlation is beginning to get far more respect as a decision-making tool.

Big data holders vary, from Google (the biggest), Facebook, the IRS, and Twitter, to online travel companies, credit card companies, and the National Weather Service. When this data is conveniently recorded in an easily analyzed digital format, it is referred to as "datafied" by Mayer-Schonberger and Cukier. The difference between datafied and non-datafied electronic data lies in how the information can be tracked, computed, tabulated, summarized, and compared.

For example, an image of the Bill of Rights can be captured and saved in digital files. But unless it is processed in some way (for example, via optical character recognition), it is impractical to use computer algorithms to analyze the content. On the other hand, a Microsoft Word version allows a user to easily check spelling, count the number of words, and allows for more manipulation and processing—everything from language translation and synonym suggestion to "autocomplete" functions.

The big data Champs like Google (processing over 3 billion search queries per day at the end of 2012) and Facebook (handling 2.5 billion content-shared items per day as of mid-2012) have a huge advantage in searching their datasets for hidden relationships—after all, everything resides on their servers in a convenient form. Twitter, with over 340 million tweets a day as of this writing, has a formal program to sell some of its data. Twitter uses resellers like Datasift, Gnip, and Topsy to help them monetize the value of their content, and manage access to the datasets, without wreaking havoc on the security and response time of systems that house the data.

Outsiders sometimes employ web-scrapping systems (which use optical character recognition to convert the words and numbers in images to datafied words and numbers) to search through online data and find relationships, rather than buy it from the proprietor. Most data owners discourage this process, via legal routes and CAPTCHA systems ("Completely Automated Public Turing Test to Tell Computers and Humans Apart"—those annoying tests that make users decipher a hand-drawn word) to keep the internet bots out. The data kings don't want third parties getting a free ride or bogging down the system response time for their regular customers. And most of all, they don't want these alien forces to hack their security. Of course, there are privacy issues that the data kings have to respect as well.

What Mayer-Schonberger and Cukier explain very clearly is that, **when massive datasets are used, many things can be learned and sometimes predicted based only on seeing the correlation between two factors—not the cause and effect.** We see that, when condition A exists, B is likely to happen. Amazon learned that when many readers buy a book like *Big Data,* they will also buy a copy of *The Signal and the Noise* (fairly obvious). Because they can look at all the permutations and combinations, they also find cases where buyers of certain photography books also buy books about dog training (less intuitive) with just a gentle suggestion on their web site.

The correlations found within massive datasets can sometimes help one determine what is going to happen without knowing why.

Unfortunately, when big government advocates see correlation with no evidence of cause and effect, they mistakenly think they can accomplish something that they can't. They start planning to tweak (not tweet) the first variable (say, school breakfast programs for the poor) to increase the second factor (learning). For years, the "experts" thought that eating a good breakfast improved school children's ability to learn. As we later discovered, the more important correlation was really between a child not having breakfast and missing school altogether. As the Statistical Assessment Service at George Mason University revealed, a good breakfast improves education results only for a malnourished child. For a well fed (or overweight) child, there is no cause-and-effect relationship with more learning.

A study published in the December 2010 *Journal of Health and Social Behavior* showed that those who graduated with better grades from high school reported healthier lives. So, if we were simply to give every high school student all A's, could we eliminate Medicare? Since college graduates smoke less than non-graduates, the central planners use this as yet another reason to send everyone to college.

RELATIONSHIPS ARE NOT STATIC

Perhaps as important as the difference between causation and correlation is this: **Correlations and cause and effect relationships change, often with little notice.**

Decide

To illustrate this point, let's look at the San Juan Basin in New Mexico and Colorado.

During the mid-1990s the marginal natural gas supply outside this area usually came from the Opal gas plant in Wyoming. Generally, when demand for Opal gas went up, San Juan prices increased as well. However once Opal prices had increased beyond West Texas prices (adjusted for marginal transportation costs), the West Texas gas could then compete and be transported to the area. When this happened, the new marginal supply (West Texas) shifted the relationship. Now, when West Texas prices increased, San Juan prices increased. After reaching this inflection point, when Opal gas prices increased (within a certain band), San Juan prices were unaffected. So there was a cause-and-effect relationship *until there was a disconnect, shift, and inflection point.*

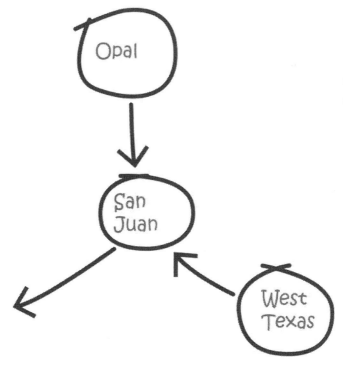

Let's say that Opal is the marginal supply into the San Juan Basin, and the two are moving hand in hand. Great, but one day, the pipeline between Opal and the San Juan Basin on the Northwest pipeline reaches full capacity. This new choke point causes a minor inflection point, and from that moment on, Opal prices can continue to drop without making one iota of difference in the San Juan Basin.

You need to understand the details and the flows in the circumstances to determine whether you have a correlation, and if that correlation is a cause-and-effect relationship. Unless you define the *why* in your models (mental and spreadsheet), apparent relationships may lead you astray. Or you may assume that the associations will hold true beyond that point (i.e. the switch from Opal to West Texas being the marginal supply) at which they will actually disengage.

Understanding the "why" (cause and effect) is the most valuable thing to figure out. When you can't quite understand the causal relationship but you have access to massive datasets, you can still benefit by learning the "what" (correlations) before anyone else does. Take what you can get when you can get it.

SOME THINGS ARE LESS PREDICTABLE THAN OTHERS

> "The future is an excellent topic for any author. By the time you realize I was wrong about everything I predicted, I will be dead."
> —Scott Adams,
> creator of the *Dilbert* comic strip

... In fact, things like what day the next big earthquake will hit Los Angeles cannot be predicted at all.

Consider this: If the best NFL team in the league plays the worst college team in the country, assuming that it's a fair and honest competition, I can predict with more than 99.99% certainty that the NFL team will prevail. Still, early in the college football season, it's not uncommon to see the number-one team in the country lose to an unranked team.

Decide

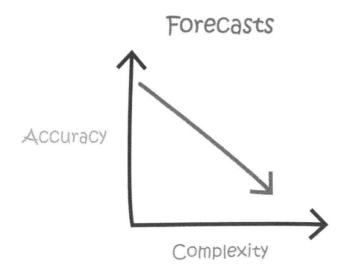

Likewise, if tomorrow's high daily temperature forecast from numerous weather services range from 92 to 94 degrees Fahrenheit, then I can bet with over a 90% confidence level that the high temperature will be at least 85 degrees F tomorrow. And yet, I have a better chance of predicting when Haley's comet will next come closest to Earth (the year 2061) than guessing whether the Dow Jones Industrial Average will close higher or lower on the next trading day. The Dow is a complex and dynamic system, whereas Haley's comet follows simpler (but not that simple) Newtonian physics. When the number of essential variables increases, the interaction of each variable with the others and the potential outcomes are harder to gauge.

TRADING WEATHER

In early 1996, I was spending time with Enron's weather forecasting group, part of the research team run by Vince Kaminski. He is a brilliant mathematician (with a PhD in theoretical economics) and student of trading, a very practical guy to have in your corner. Today, Vince is a professor at Rice University.

In many cases, estimating the direction of the near-term natural gas market came down to determining if it was going to get hotter than expected (during summer) or colder than estimated (during winter). We had a forecasting advantage on the weather dimension on the trading side because we had more smart people working the problem (not to mention Vince's insights). I also believed that, in some ways, we were already trading weather indirectly, given its cause-and-effect relationship on natural gas demand and prices. So, I thought, Why not start trading weather explicitly? After all, it was a dimension that affected so many industries and businesses that it could be huge. It had major impacts on the agriculture, construction, energy, and tourism industries, to name a few.

Estimates suggest that at least 20-30% of the US economy is sensitive to variations in weather. Some businesses make more money when it's hotter than normal (think Baskin Robbins ice cream shops or a packaged-ice company), and others lose money (like the corn farmers in the 2012 US summer drought). So, there were plenty of "natural longs" and "natural shorts" related to weather.

Creating the weather trading business involved thinking in multiple dimensions (Multiple Dimensions = Degrees of Freedom). We could expand from trading natural gas and electricity to trading weather. But first, we had to get over the hurdle that weather could not be traded physically (like oil, corn, copper and electricity).

Normally we entered a new market by trading a physical commodity. Obviously we could not physically deliver colder weather, more rainfall, or fewer hurricanes, but we could create a derivative in which two parties took opposite bets on one of these dimensions. Our first products allowed two parties to bet on whether it was going to be hotter or colder than expected (considering the bias of the media and regulators, we were careful never to use the word "bet"). In this way, the trade could be a hedge against the weather damaging the profitability of a customer's business.

The variable we envisioned trading was the "degree day," which measures the magnitude of the need for heating and cooling. I got the OK from my management (Kevin Hannon and Lou Pai) to take one of my traders, Chris Foster, and have him work part-time on developing the weather market. When I was transferred to London later that year, an energetic woman named Lynda Clemmons took on the project full time. It was not until August 1997 that Clemmons did the first weather derivatives deal, and by then, I had been riding the London Tube (subway) for nearly a year.

Today, weather is traded on the Chicago Mercantile Exchange (CME), which received permission from the Commodity and Futures Trading Commission to start trading weather derivatives in August 1999. There are now several variations of weather derivatives being traded, including heating and cooling degree days (and options on them), rainfall, and severity of the hurricane season. In Niall Ferguson's book *The Ascent of Money*, he reported that, in 2006, the total notional value of weather-risk derivatives was around $45 billion. But it is a very small market (from a trading perspective), and Enron made little or no money at the business.

In hindsight, I don't think the weather market was ever going to be significant for Enron, although we garnered quite a bit of favorable publicity. Our information advantage in predicting weather would not have given us enough confidence to correctly make a big bet and rake in the occasional windfall. It wasn't the absolute information that would have put us ahead, but the relative information advantage *over the rest of the ma*rket that would have mattered. This is a continuing theme of Champ versus Chump. And no matter how many PhDs and meteorologists we had on the job, we were unlikely to have developed a substantial forecasting advantage over the National Weather Service (NWS), which has an annual budget of about $740 million, and gives away its forecasts and data—information that everyone else uses as a starting point for their own proprietary forecasts. **The natural gas and electricity markets were better at managing risk directly rather than trying to add the complexity of weather derivatives.**

In Nate Silver's *The Signal and the Noise*, he describes how the weather forecasting business is one of the "success" stories in the prediction business—and that's not saying much. Get this: by simply averaging the historic high temperature for any day at a specific location, you will have an average forecasting error of about 7 degrees Fahrenheit. So, any success in the temperature-forecasting business only adds value to the extent that it beats the accuracy of the historical average.

Lucky And Good

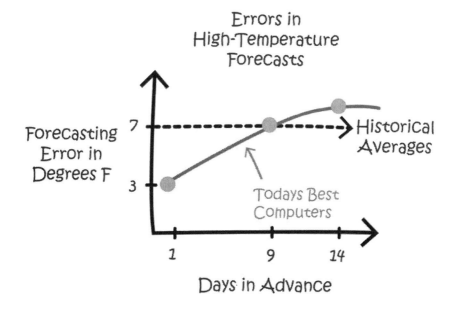

Today's sophisticated models still average an error of about 3 degrees just one day out. A 4-degree error three days out is still better than the 7-degree error using the historical average. But here is the curious part: currently, at about nine days out, the NWS's sophisticated weather models are no better at forecasting than simply using the historical averages. Even more surprising is that these models are *worse* than using the historical averages after just nine days.

MODELING HUMAN BEHAVIOR

Human behavior is sometimes difficult to predict and model. Managers at one natural gas utility may fill their storage at a predetermined amount per day regardless of daily price swings, while those at another may try to game their storage injection. This latter utility might delay filling their storage early on because they consider current prices above fair value, and believe that prices will soon drop. But a month later, having not bought any gas, their storage level may not seem prudent. The managers then decide to fill 'er up, immediately buying twice their usual amount for storage, and though local weather has not changed one iota, the market is surprised by an uptick in prices. This behavior is hard to model.

MARKET FORECASTS ARE IMPACTED BY:

- ❖ the number of major input variables that influence the price;
- ❖ the availability of accurate information about those variables;
- ❖ the complexity of the interactions of the various factors—especially exponential relationships (when factor X increases by 50%, then factor Y increases by 200%);
- ❖ the number of human decisions that are based on other human decisions; and
- ❖ the number of compound assumptions that must all come true in order for the primary forecast to come true.

Given all these interactions, the words of nineteenth-century writer William Gilmore Simms seem to apply: **"I believe that economists put decimal points in their forecasts to show they have a sense of humor."**

COMPOUND FORECASTS

The complexity of forecasting increases as the assumptions pile up. Here's an example of a compound forecast:

"A" (which has an 80% probability of happening), will happen, and

"B" will happen (which has a 75% probability); and

"C" will happen (which has a 70% probability).

In 2002, one might have forecast that:

a) national median housing prices would increase by at least 10% in the next year (80% probability);

b) interest rates would not increase by more than 0.5% on the typical 30-year mortgage (75% probability); and

c) unemployment would not increase by more than .5% (70% probability).

But the compound probability that *all three* of these assumptions would hold (making a very liberal and simplifying assumption that they are independent variables) was: 80% X 75% x 70% = 42%. Far from a sure thing.

In John Sandford's novel *Mad River*, detective Virgil Flowers was asked if he would "get" the murderer (convicted). Virgil thought about it, and then answered, "No. Not unless something weird happens. If I could find the guy who gave or sold the gun to Murphy, then I'd have a better chance. If I find that Murphy took the money out of the bank, one thousand dollars the day that Ag O'Leary was murdered, that'd help. If I got both of those things, and the right jury, then … maybe. But I don't think I'll get both of those things. I might not get either one."

Virgil Flowers understands compound assumptions!

On the evening of November 6, 2012 (election night), one newscaster stated that Republican presidential candidate Mitt Romney had a chance to win if he took Florida, Virginia, Ohio, North Carolina, and Nevada. Romney was obviously in trouble, because he was behind in all of these must-have states. If he had a 40% chance of winning each contest, and the results were likely to be independent (again a very simplistic assumption) of each other, his odds were approximately 0.4 to the fifth power, or slightly greater than a 1% chance. I went to bed early.

Some forecasts are simply harder to get right than others. Here is a typical caveat for a market forecast based on compound assumptions: "Of course, all of my projected trends are based on the economy healing itself in the coming year and no major economic catastrophes." Very big ifs! Do not buy into **contingent assumptions** without careful consideration. And never believe that every assumption is a given, even if it sounds quite plausible.

*****

In his 2010 book *The Age of Deleveraging*, Gary Shilling discusses seven great calls (code for "predictions") that he made during his first 47 years in the business of economics. His criteria for great calls are:

- ❖ they must predict an important change,
- ❖ the prediction must fly in the face of other economists' consensus, and
- ❖ the forecast can't ultimately be right only as a result of dumb luck (for example, a recession caused by a traumatic event such as 9/11 or a tsunami).

A couple of points: First, Shilling had more "great calls" than any other forecaster I have found. However, I don't have a complete list of his bad calls. And his great calls only came at a rate of about one every 6.7 years. It's impossible to generate a great call just because you really need one now to pay the mortgage.

Second, more money can usually be made with a correct forecast that goes against the grain (Think in Opposites). When everyone thinks that interest rates are on the rise, more money is to be made by being the only one who accurately predicts and bets that interest rates will drop.

When evaluating a bet, longer horizons require more skepticism. For instance, if a forecaster makes four sequential forecasts, each of which is twenty years out, you won't know the results for eighty years. If each forecast has a 50% probability of being correct, the forecaster still has a 6.25% chance of being right on all four of the predictions, through sheer luck. Nassim Nicholas Taleb discusses this phenomenon in substantial detail in his book *Fooled by Randomness*. And when Edmond Halley predicted back in 1705 that his namesake comet would reappear every 75 to 76 years, he would not live to see the day he would be proven right even once (slow feedback).

Shorter forecasts are more subject to noise and randomness. But the longer out your forecast, the more subject you are to black swan calamities, unanticipated inflection points, and complex interactions. Even a few decades from now, when our computers are exponentially faster and able to handle far more data, weather and climate forecasts will still be far from perfect because some changes can never be predicted. For example, what happens if Mount St. Helens erupts again? When that occurred in 1980, it released a plume of ash that eventually spread 15 miles above sea level, affecting the cloud cover and temperatures over a vast area. So, even far more sophisticated and accurate weather forecasts will always be at the mercy of such upheavals.

Success depends, too, on the variable that you are predicting. In weather, it's clearly easier to predict the temperature tomorrow than the temperature in 10 years. But for other factors, the story is different. I will give you much better odds that the world's population will be higher in 10 years than whether 10-year Treasury yields will be higher or lower in a week. On the other hand, company earnings forecasts are usually quite accurate for the current quarter or two; five-year earnings forecasts are virtually worthless.

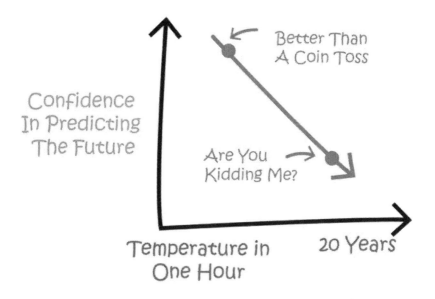

Please accept that random factors and events (storms, earthquakes, and terrorism) impact both short-term and long-run results. *Every* prediction is at the mercy of the unpredictable.

Let's consider: When you roll two dice, you know that you will only roll "craps" (2, 3 or 12) four out of 36 times, on average (11.11%). So, if I bet that you will *not* roll craps on the next roll, I have an 88.89% chance of being right. You might turn around and roll craps four times in a row, but your odds of doing this are only .0152%, and I will take my chances (every time) that you will fail in pulling off this feat (unless I'm at risk of running out of cash, and here I might even make an exception).

If you roll the dice once daily, I can more confidently predict that you will not roll craps for the next 300 consecutive days, than whether you will not roll craps on the next roll. The odds are in my favor, making it nearly (not *totally*) impossible for me to be wrong about the results of making money over a 300-day period.

*****

Events based on many occurrences may reveal opportunities that, with intelligent analysis, consistently offer bets that will win on average. If each and every day I make reasonably-sized bets (relative to the size of my bankroll) with a probabilistic advantage, over time and many bets, I will *probably* have won in both the short term and the long run. This is where we can think back to the roll of the dice, realizing that truly random dice rolling involves *independent* chances, whereas many variables in the business world are *dependent* and r*elated*. Remember, I never promised you a sure-fire way to succeed; I simply want to increase your chances.

Many investment advisors blame the random nature of markets to excuse their own inability to predict short-term changes, which is reasonable. However by the time their long-term forecasts (their bread and butter) either win or lose, many of their clients have forgotten their predictions. **If the investment advisor was right, he reminds his customers of his brilliant forecasts; if he is wrong, he quietly moves on to his next prediction.**

I COULD'VE GONE BAD (BEING AN ENRON EXECUTIVE DOESN'T QUALIFY)

Here's a little story of what might have been, and one of the reasons I asked you not to be too hard on the inventor of the Wake'N Bacon alarm clock. I am not embarrassed about anything I ever did or said at Enron, but I am uncomfortable with another business episode from over 30 years ago. You need to hear the dirt along with the triumphs.

In the late 1970s, it was still uncommon for a pregnant woman to get an ultrasound to reveal the sex of her unborn child; most of the time, the newborn's gender was a surprise to the parents until the birth. A friend and I hatched an idea.

We decided to run a $500 advertisement in a leading baby magazine: "Is it a boy or a girl? Send $19.95 and your birthday, the father's birthday, and the expected birth date, and we will let you know the sex of your baby. Money back guarantee if we're wrong." In advance of any responses, we pre-printed two types of certificates, one pink that said, "It's a Girl," and one blue, announcing "It's a Boy." We didn't have color laser printers at the time.

Using an early printer, we attached a two-dimensional curve (much more precise than the drawings in this book) to the certificates, to add a bit of credibility to these predictions (remember the saying: "If you can't be accurate, be precise"). We figured (we'll never know for sure) that we would be right about half the time—although, based on the small sample size, we may have gotten lucky and been right on all of these predictions. One of our business assumptions was that, if we were right, the parents would proudly put evidence of the prognostication in the baby's scrapbook. (It looked pretty cool.) We also assumed that, if the baby turned out as little Billy when we had predicted Suzie, the parents would also have fun putting the prediction in the baby's scrapbook to show the world how little Billy had fooled the "experts." (I hope we didn't put little Billy at any added risk of transgender issues.)

We were right—either in all of our "forecasts" or in assuming the desire of all of our customers to keep their certificates. We did not have a single request for a refund, and even had a letter from one happy customer singing our praises. As of this writing, I will still honor our guarantee to return the $19.95 to any unsatisfied patron who contacts me and returns the certificate (partly because I would love to have a copy). I have decided to make the guarantee a lifetime guarantee for as long as my client and I are both alive.

Satisfying customers, however, was not enough to make us profitable. We simply did not get enough bang for every advertising dollar we spent. We paid $500 for a single ad, and only got 13 orders for roughly $260 in total revenue. So the business was put on indefinite hold after our one and only venture into the market. This was a slow hunch that never came back from hibernation.

What I came to realize is that, unlike bluffing in poker or a misdirection play in football--both considered honorable and required to win--this kind of BS is bad business. We implied that we could predict the sex of the baby when we couldn't.

I was lucky. If my first foray into the "prediction business" had been profitable, I might today be marketing vitamin water, debt consolidation, or miracle health cures—or be looking for federal government loans for a solar panel manufacturing plant. This last case would require me to donate vast sums to non-Libertarian politicians, which would really annoy me.

BEWARE OF IDIOTIC LEVERAGE

"... Another day older and deeper in debt."
—Merle Travis

In 2012, it was revealed that Poway Unified, a California school district north of San Diego, had borrowed $105 million at a 12.6% interest rate over 40 years. But they didn't have to pay a dime on the bond for the first 20 years, with it all coming due in years 21 to 40. As a result they were able to go to their voters in a 2008 election and ask approval for the bond while explaining few of the details, except that property taxes would not be increased—for now. In two decades, the school district will have to pay almost $50 million per year for 20 years. Do you think property taxes might increase then? Or do you think this school district will simply declare bankruptcy?

Lucky And Good

Governments and public institutions do not use leverage to increase profits. Almost exclusively, they do it because they can borrow now and pay later, and therefore defer the pain and bring forward the love (votes).

I am not suggesting that you should avoid *all* leverage (or debt), simply avoid idiotic amounts. Reasonable debt allows capital that is sitting idle to be transferred into the hands of those who can put it to productive use. When managed well and within limits, lending is a real boost to economic growth.

But too much of a good thing is a real problem—think Lehman Brothers, Greece, Spain, Detroit, Stockton, Illinois, and California. Debt is the biggest risk that most individuals, businesses, and governments face. Once in debt, it's harder to stay solvent during financial emergencies—like when a bet goes bad, or a hurricane destroys your home. In considering leverage, please also take into account your unfunded liabilities (a promise you have made without putting aside the required funds) and contingent liabilities (a potential liability based on the outcome of a future event, such as ongoing litigation or a natural disaster). If the world were totally predictable, if relative values never changed, and there were no "Life Happens" events, you could count on leverage to increase your business profitably. Once again, that's far too many ifs.

Leverage can take many forms: for example, simple debt to buy assets, or borrowing to pay the bills. It can also mean that a company uses borrowed money to place a business bet (perhaps betting that interest rates will decline). In the last few decades, governments in the developed world have dramatically increased their leverage, possibly resulting in local and state government defaults, and chaos for sovereign nations. **The US government's unfunded liabilities represent leverage that is at least four to five times the recognized government debt**.

If you invest your entire net worth in a single stock without leverage and it loses half its value, then you've had a very bad day. But if you're leveraged at 30 to 1, then you're busted, even if the value of the stock drops by only 3.23% (you are a Chump).

However, that's exactly what the US government overlooked and what contributed to the US housing bubble. The government, and the housing and banking industries encouraged people to buy homes with small or zero down payments. It was a great free option for the home buyer (since these were usually non-recourse loans), but a horrible deal for the lender (or guarantor to the lender) which, in most cases, was the US government. There were many idiots and villains in this process, but the bottom line is, Freddie Mac and Fannie Mae were bludgeoned by Washington politicians, like now-retired Rep. Barney Frank, to lend, lend, lend—which they did, indirectly, by purchasing the loans made by the banks.

How about leverage at investment banks? This had the feel of crony socialism. (I refuse to use the term "crony capitalism.") By this I mean that these companies kept all the upside, and the government stepped in to absorb many of the losses (sometimes referred to as "moral hazard"). In 2004 the Securities and Exchange Commission changed the regulations so that the largest five investment banks—Goldman Sachs, Morgan Stanley, Lehman Brothers, Bear Stearns and Merrill Lynch—were allowed to increase their leverage from a maximum of about 12 to 1 (assets to net capital) to as much as 40 to 1. The ratios were reported end-of-quarter figures, and I suspect that they were much worse during the quarter. We saw what happened:

Lehman went bankrupt, and the others were either acquired or bailed out by the federal government at taxpayer expense. None of these five investment banks exist today in their old form as an independent investment bank. Goldman and Morgan Stanley converted into traditional (well, sort of) banks. Lehman went into bankruptcy. Bear Stearns was acquired by JPMorgan Chase, and Merrill Lynch was acquired by Bank of America.

In trading operations, leverage can be confused with the size of the total book. Does a Las Vegas sports book that accepts $10 million in bets that the 49ers will beat the Packers by three and a half points, and another $10 million that the Packers will beat the same spread against the 49ers, have $20 million in exposure? No; in reality, since the book is balanced, they have probably come close to locking in a profit, regardless of the final score. Remember, they don't have any credit risk because they already hold the cash for all of these bets.

If an investment bank took all of its "betting capacity" and placed it on the change of one variable (perhaps the relationship of the euro to the dollar), its risk of going bust would be tremendous. Even the most aggressive firms don't come close to doing this.

What they will do is place bets on many dimensions in a range of markets, with many of those bets self-cancelling. For example, if JP Morgan bought 10,000 MMBTUs per day of natural gas from Goldman Sachs in the Permian Basin (West Texas) for the year 2003 at $4.00 per MMBTU and then, a month later, sold the same volume of gas back to Goldman (after the market had moved up slightly) at $4.02 per MMBTU, what would J P Morgan's total exposure be?

In this case, JP Morgan's original purchase would have been $4.00/MMBTU * 10,000 MMBTUs per day, times 365 days per year = $14.6 million. When they turned around and sold the gas back to Goldman for $4.02 per MMBTU, that second transaction had a notional value of $14.673 million. At this point, JP Morgan's exposure is not $14.6 million plus $14.673 million (or $29.273 million). In this example, I assume that Goldman and JP Morgan have an "offset agreement" in place that offsets what each owed the other in the event of a bankruptcy. With such an offset agreement, JP Morgan has zero price exposure in the universe of these two transactions; JP Morgan has an asset of $14.673 million versus a liability of $14.6 million in a Goldman bankruptcy. JP Morgan's only exposure is the credit risk on the locked-in profit of $73,000 ($14.673 million minus $14.6 million) that Goldman ultimately owes them.

The truth is, we really don't know what the investment banks' positions actually were. (At least, I don't.) You can't simply add up all their individual bets and know their total net exposure. But we do know that Lehman Brothers, Bear Stearns, and a few others had bet heavily on the housing bubble continuing, and on the mortgage-backed securities paying off. Unfortunately, these bets were so highly leveraged, (the technical term is "betting the farm") that they either went bankrupt or had to be bailed out.

Leverage is such a wonderful tool when things are going your way and you are getting a percentage of the upside. On the other hand, it's very painful when events fall off the rails because of bad beats, black swans, or just poor bets.

There is a good reason that small tech start-ups usually begin with all equity and no debt. They have enough other risks and concerns to consider without having to worry about managing their debt. No one wants to lend to such speculative companies, anyway.

THE MANIA OF LEVERAGE

Excess leverage is treacherous, but even if a very large company like Enron is involved, the downside for the broader markets is fairly limited when a single company fails. When unrestrained leverage infects an entire industry or market, it will result eventually in systematic collapse. This is frightening when it happens in the country's financial sector.

In the 1920s, US stock investors were allowed to borrow on margin up to 90% of the value of their stock portfolios. In other words, if an investor wanted to buy a stock for $10, he could borrow $9 from the broker or bank, and only put up only $1 of his own money. Not a big deal if only one or two small investors took advantage of this "opportunity," and the market was moving up. The mid-1920s (until September 3, 1929) were great years to own US stocks, and buying on margin became widespread.

This additional leverage increases prices because more money is chasing a limited supply of assets (what law is that again?). The trend continues until there is no more leverage to be had, or until prices have gotten so crazy that a few rational investors start to have doubts.

The collapse never happens soon enough (Don't Jump the Gun). Word gets out that those who have been buying on margin have made much more money, so even more people buy on margin. Eventually, though, even the most optimistic investor starts to take money off of the table. And ultimately, it all comes crashing down. The investors lose everything, and the banks that lent them $9 for every $1 of stock they owned lose up to nine times as much. Is it any wonder that we had so many bank failures after the 1929 stock market crash? Of the more than 25,000 banks in business in 1929, fewer than 15,000 survived until 1933.

After the 1929 crash, legislators tightened the margin requirements and limited investors to buying with a maximum of 50% margin instead of 90%. But our government was not smart enough to avoid the same mistake in the mortgage market. In order to promote housing, our Chumps in Washington, D.C. allowed 100% margin. Then, they stepped in and guaranteed the loans—actually, they had the rest of us Chumps guarantee the loans.

When considering leverage, you will need to know how far to go. Remember our principle (Find Inflection Points), because crazy amounts of leverage will ultimately result in a price collapse. This is a cause-and-effect relationship that you can count on—eventually.

*****

Since the vast majority of governments in the developed world have gotten deeply leveraged with traditional debt, and unfunded pension and health care liabilities, the global economy faces new territory. Japan, the US, and Europe hold staggering liabilities. The developed world has done a great job at slowing birth rates, but we never stopped spending and promising. In 2004, the ratio of people younger than age 65 to those 65 and older in the EU was approximately 4:1. It is estimated that, by 2050, this will narrow to about 2:1.

Disinflation (a decline in the rate of inflation) drives interest rates down. This is great for paying off traditional debt but, ironically, a real challenge for our government's unfunded liabilities. In *Real-World Application Five* (Chapter Six), I address the problem of unfunded pension liabilities. These pensions are actually long inflation and higher interest rates because they simply can't make the required returns in a low-interest environment to meet their promises. If you are running CalPERS, the big California employee pension system, what are the odds of earning 7.5% on your capital if U.S. 30-year Treasuries are yielding only 3.75%? Slim to none, over the long run!

No computer model is going to tell us how this will all work out; I challenge you to find one time in history when we have been in such a grand pickle. Will the value of gold go through the roof (as of June 2013 the price had dropped by over 20% from recent highs but has partially recovered by late August, 2013)? Will we face hyper-inflation, or will we find ourselves (as Gary Shilling predicts) with deflation for years to come?

THINK ON THE MARGIN

"This ostrich-like behavior—selling the better assets and keeping the biggest losers—while less painful in the short term, is unlikely to be a winner in the long term."

—Warren Buffett

Intel was founded in 1968, and its early success was in random-access memories. While it created the first commercially available microprocessor in 1971, by the early 1980s their business was still dominated by the memory market. But that business was getting much more competition from Japan, dramatically reducing Intel's profitability, while at the same time the IBM personal computer (introduced in August 1981) was generating an enormous opportunity in microprocessors.

In a classic 1983 Harvard Business case study, Andy Grove (Intel's then President and future CEO) and Gordon Moore (then CEO) were grappling with their declining fortunes. Grove said:

> **I looked out the window at the Ferris wheel of the Great America amusement park revolving in the distance, then I turned back to Gordon and I asked, "If we got kicked out and the board brought in a new CEO, what do you think he would do?" Gordon answered without hesitation, "He would get us out of memories." I stared at him, numb, then said, "Why shouldn't you and I walk out the door, come back and do it ourselves?"**

And that decision to abandon the memory business and focus on microprocessors not only saved the company, but thrust it into a dominant position in the emerging personal computer business. It was a classic case of thinking on the margin.

This is Econ 101 again. **It doesn't matter if a trade is currently showing a profit or a loss, a trader, entrepreneur, or investor needs to forget about "sunk costs."** It is irrelevant, other than for tax planning. Frequently, just the fact that it lurks in the back of your mind can lead to bad decisions.

Don't dwell on sunk costs; don't allow them to influence your thoughts. **Perhaps a whole new specialty in psychotherapy will evolve to help patients forget sunk costs and gain the mindset that allows them to make decisions based on go-forward marginal economics.** The logic is easier than the practice.

A trader today keeps a balance sheet and income statement that he modifies daily. This "mark-to-market accounting," or fair-value accounting, refers to documenting the *current value* of an asset or liability—based on its present market price, that of similar assets or liabilities, or on another objectively assessed "fair" value. Fair-value accounting has been a part of Generally Accepted Accounting Principles (GAAP) in the United States since the early 1990s, but has been used in various forms since the early 20th century.

Here's an example: A trader starts day one with $50 in cash, and uses it to buy one share of Stock A for $50. He now has $50 in assets and no profit or loss. The next day, the price of Stock A goes from $50 per share to $51 per share. He now has $51 in assets and $1 in profit (we will ignore taxes and fees for this discussion). The next day, the price of Stock A drops by $3 to $48. He now has $48 in assets and $2 in cumulative losses.

The price of Stock A at any point in time—and the trader's view that it's going to go up or down from then on—drives the trader's decision to either keep the stock or sell it. The fact that he paid $50 for it should have nothing to do with his trading decision to either continue to own the stock, sell what he owns, or short the stock. This seems very basic, but it is hard to stick to this discipline.

Entrepreneurs, traders, and investors should start from a sunk cost or mark-to-market perspective each and every day. What you paid for something means nothing the next day, when you decide to keep or sell the asset. Your point of view going forward makes all the difference. This is mark-to-market accounting: Recognize your losses (and profits) at the end of each and every day, in both your electronic and mental spreadsheets, and then move on.

This mental posture puts you in the best position to see clearly today, because you took your lumps yesterday. Without this discipline, an investor who is used to only being long US equities for 10 years running has trouble ever unloading his position, let alone taking the opposite side of the bet.

 Look at it this way: a trader will ask you if you would buy your home if you didn't already own it. If you wouldn't buy it, why are you keeping it? A trader asks the entrepreneur if he would start the business if he were not already invested in it. A trader might ask Warren Buffett if he would buy part of Wells Fargo if he didn't

Lucky And Good

already own it. Do you rent out your home when you're moving because you're underwater, and don't want to sell it and take the loss?

Too many non-traders (and a few traders) avoid taking a loss, and this keeps them from benefiting from the next opportunity. And sometimes they avoid making the right decision because, even though they have made money on the purchase, the price of the home is lower than it was at its peak. They want to wait until price returns to its former glory—a costly way to operate.

Try changing the reference point. Consider the question: If we did not own it, how much would we think it was worth?

If you buy a home at market price on day one for $100,000, you should immediately mark the value of the home on your balance sheet at $94,000 (we're including a selling cost of 6%). Now, if the value goes up by 10% a year later, then your valuation should be $103,400 ($110,000 minus a 6% sales cost). So, you are finally "in the money."

Likewise, if an investor needs to raise cash from his portfolio to pay investors or pay bills, what does he sell? Let's say he owns two stocks: one stock that is worth more than he paid for it, and one stock that's underwater. Which one is he more likely to sell?

 A trader understands that what she paid for each of the two stocks is irrelevant. What matters is this: Which one is she is more bullish on? That's the one she holds, and she sells the other.

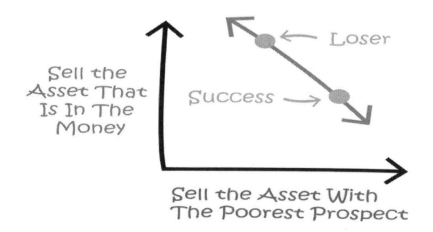

In reality, too many investors sell the stock on which they have made money, rather than the one they are more bullish on. They love the process of notching a victory, and hate to acknowledge a loss; they act like Chumps.

*****

Thinking on the margin means that you accept your profits and losses *each day* and move on. Let me provide another illustration, which is based on Daniel Kahneman's work.

You are watching Jack Bauer, the famous hero from the television series *24*.

At the beginning of the show (that I'd love to write, if they ever bring the series back), Jack has just learned about a terrorist plot to blow up Las Vegas. Based on the busy time of year, it will kill 600,000 people if the scheme is not thwarted. He has narrowed down his possible actions to two alternatives. In Jack's case, he makes these decisions in nanoseconds, but you know full well that he has analyzed all the odds carefully. The two choices are:

Alternative 1: Even with Jack's help, 300,000 people will be saved and 300,000 will die.

Alternative 2: There is a 33.3% probability that 600,000 will be saved and no one is murdered. There is a 66.7% probability that all 600,000 will die.

Here Jack Bauer, like most people, chooses the "riskier" gamble (Alternative 2), even though, on average, more people will be saved with Alternative 1. Although Jack is almost always a Champ—in this case, he's a Chump. On average, 300,000 will die with Alternative 1 compared to the average of 400,000 who will die with Alternative 2. There is clearly an element of perceived fairness in this decision, but even when the fairness dimension is removed, most folks (including hero Jack Bauer) will take risks to avoid losses.

 Most decision makers are risk takers when both outcomes are negative. On the other hand, decision makers prefer the sure thing when the outcome is good.

Clearly, you must understand this rule when presenting alternatives to others. You may play up the risks in some cases and the "sure thing" possibilities, when making a pitch. But be aware of this bias and adjust accordingly when making your own decisions and bets.

Here is a silly investing and trading quote: "Pigs get fat, hogs get slaughtered." What in the heck does this mean? Perhaps that it's OK to be greedy but not "too greedy." How do you know the difference? When the media discusses greed, they never miss a chance to conflate it with criminal behavior—the greedy Bernie Madoff and the latest inside trader being escorted via the perp-walk to jail.

You should always look at the numbers, and consistently make excellent decisions based on expected values and your best guess at the probabilistic outcomes. Some will call this greed; I call it making the planet a better, more efficient and less wasteful place. Understand the psychology of the decisions that you and others are making. This might sometimes involve giving up a little upside, in order to increase the odds that you will survive (Never Run Out of Cash). But, when running out of cash is not a factor, simply go with the decision that gives you the best expected value. **Ignore the probability that you will be notching a win or a loss on this one decision, because you are playing for the long run, and after thousands of decisions and outcomes, what matters is your cumulative profits—not your win-loss record.**

KNOW THE LONG AND SHORT OF IT

"Unhappiness is not knowing what we want
and killing ourselves to get it."
—Don Herold

THE INDUSTRIAL VALVE BUSINESS

I had an opportunity to invest in a small business that managed an inventory of such a broad selection of industrial valves that the company could meet almost any customer need within 24 hours. It seemed like a great niche, because time matters in replacing a defective industrial valve. If you have a big oil refinery or chemical plant and lose a major line due to a malfunctioning valve, the downtime costs are enormous.

The trouble was, the more I looked at the numbers, the more I was convinced that much of the company's recent profits came from their vast unsold inventory increasing in value. For a couple of years, copper prices drove up the value of industrial valves. The company made profits from buying a valve one year and having the wholesale price double while the inventory sat in the warehouse. It was, of course, easy to increase customer prices in line with the rising wholesale market prices. From February 2009 until early spring 2011, wholesale copper prices went from about $1.40 a pound to about $4.50. This company was "long" the price of industrial valves and, therefore, indirectly, long the price of copper.

Unfortunately, what goes up usually comes down (except public debt). Since the spring of 2011, copper prices have dropped to a level close to $3 a pound (as of June 2013). So, with the same business model, during this latest period, the company would have done well to break even. One had to separate the overall price movement from the value of the rest of the business. And it would have been much more profitable to buy that business when copper was $1.40 a pound rather than when the price was reaching historic highs.

When the broker pitching the deal couldn't separate the profits associated with the changing inventory value, I knew that it was time to move on.

*****

Every business or venture is "short" certain factors and "long" others. For some factors, you want the price or the number to increase. For other elements, you root for the opposite. While traders instinctively think in longs and shorts, this is not usually the case for entrepreneurs and investors. But the lesson of longs and shorts can be a critical factor for everyone.

Here are simple examples of companies and organizations that are both long and short. If you were considering investing in one of these businesses, it would make sense to understand and believe in these fundamental positions:

The Google Search Business. This internet business is short smart IT people (they can never have enough). They're also short the price of servers, the price of cloud storage, the price of electricity, and short Yahoo and Bing. Google wants the cost or influence of all of these things to go down. Conversely, Google is long their own advertising rates and revenue, which they want to increase.

A Local Vineyard. A grape-growing business is long Chardonnay grapes and short water, electricity, and labor. If it builds a winery for transforming the grapes into wine, it would then have the same shorts, but would be long wine rather than long grapes (whose prices are correlated, but not one for one). If grape prices subsequently fall but wine prices remain steady, the business would look even more attractive.

Coal Mines. A US coal-mining operation is obviously long the price of coal, but is also long natural gas prices. Recently, US natural gas prices have gotten so low that generation plants powered by natural gas have started to cannibalize the business of coal-fired power plants. In fact the US Department of Energy released data showing that natural gas use by power companies jumped 32% in the first half of 2012, while coal use dropped by 18 %.

Electricity Generation. Calpine Corporation was formed in 1984 in San Jose, California, and morphed over the years into a "merchant" power company (in other words, it generated power without having a long-term contract to sell it). This made Calpine short natural gas and long electricity. The company started to change this balance in 1997 when it began to buy natural gas production and reserves, and ended up long natural gas. It was still long electricity prices, and in 2001 was the world's ninth-largest electricity producer. A few years later, electricity prices started to drop across America, and their business went downhill; in 2005, Calpine declared bankruptcy. Many folks believed that, since Calpine was vertically integrating by buying up natural gas reserves, they were reducing their risk. But in reality, they were simply changing the nature of their bets, and the combination of the elements in which they were long or short. They were still long electricity, which headed south—and if they had not gone bankrupt, their natural gas investments would probably be losers today, as well.

Longs and shorts are fascinating elements of a fluctuating market, but that's not why you track them. Note that, in order to Think on the Margin, you first have to know where you are, to begin with. It sounds obvious to traders, but less so to those unaccustomed to managing a myriad of trading positions. **You need to know what you are rooting for and why you are rooting for it.**

WALNUTS, LABOR COSTS, AND CEMENT

Here are a few more examples of longs and shorts:

- A California walnut orchard owner is long wholesale walnut prices, and the weather; it is short water, electricity prices, diesel prices, California income tax rates, and labor costs.
- A specialty cement-blending company is short cement, specialty chemicals, trucking costs (for transporting to the market), and labor; it is long the US construction business.
- The State of California is short interest rates (based on having about $16 billion in debt, as I write this). But its big pension programs (CalPERS and CalSTRS) are long interest rates via their unfunded liabilities.
- Risky trades aren't the biggest risks that JPMorgan Chase faces. Chairman, President, and CEO Jamie Dimon told the Senate Banking Committee on June 12, 2012, "Dramatically rising interest rates and a global type of credit crisis—those are the two biggest risks we face." So, according to Dimon, JPMorgan is primarily long global credit quality and short interest rates.
- Public employee unions in the US are long the Democratic Party, long the prosperity of the country, and short government financial problems. These unions are also long the performance of many public pension programs because their members are frequently the beneficiaries.
- US presidential incumbents running for a second term are long the health of the US economy and short unemployment. Their November opponents tend to have exactly the opposite position.
- Private security companies are short the effectiveness of the local police, short labor costs, and long local burglary rates on properties they are not protecting.

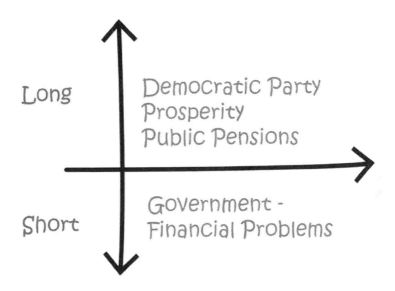

As a trader, I naturally think in the world of longs and shorts, and I could go on for hours with other examples. If you need a few more to help you understand this thinking, you will find additional examples in Exhibit D.

DO NOT IGNORE PRIDE OF OWNERSHIP

> "Riches are not fobidden, but the pride of them is."
> —John Chrysostom, c 347-407
> Archbishop of Constantinople

For more than 10 years, investor Ng Goon Lau made a specialty of buying haunted houses in Hong Kong (one where a prior occupant had died under mysterious circumstances), or *hongza*, in the Cantonese language. Ten years ago, he could buy a haunted house for up to a third less than a comparable non-hongza property. This discount exists partially because many banks won't issue a mortgage for a hongza home. But both the rental and purchase market for apartments have continued to boom during the last decade, (prices doubled during the last four years alone), and this markdown has shrunk to a mere 5%. Lau went short the ghost discount, long the underlying real estate, and made a fortune.

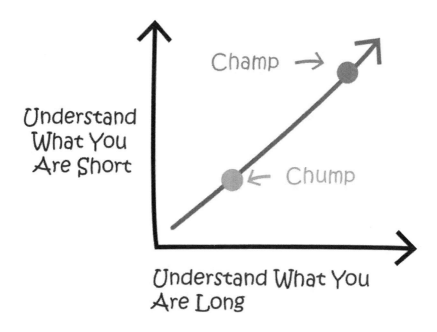

Investors and entrepreneurs take pride in owning the underlying asset, like the beautiful home they just purchased, the Paul Cezanne painting entitled *The Card Players* which sold in 2011 for $259 million, or the Los Angeles Dodgers, sold in 2012 for an astounding $2.15 billion. Ownership can be prestigious. A trader views the "pride of ownership" premium as just another variable that can increase or decrease over time. However, pride of ownership can also make it emotionally tough to unload an asset to which one is emotionally attached.

Decide

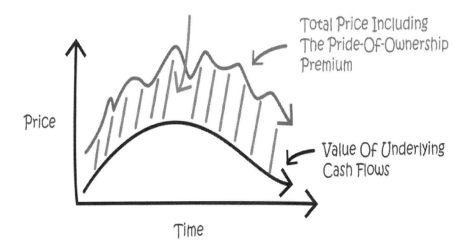

The pride-of-ownership premium can even be negative for the kind of business that you don't want to admit to your friends and family—say, organized crime, drug dealing, politics, or a legal Nevada brothel.

90% OF THE VALUE OF GOLD IS THE "PRIDE-OF-OWNERSHIP" PREMIUM

Worldwide, about 50% of gold is used in jewelry, 40% in investments like gold coins and bars, with only 10% left to make things (other than jewelry, gold bars and coins). This means that roughly 90% of gold's value is Pride-of-Ownership (jewelry plus investments). It's harder to predict the change in Pride-of-Ownership premiums than the underlying practical value.

Pride-of-Ownership premiums are based solely on people's cumulative beliefs, today and tomorrow. I can confidently predict that a doubling in the price of gold makes it less competitive versus other dental alternatives (amalgam, composite resin, and porcelain). But, when that price doubles, those who believe that gold is a wonderful investment will have their views (at least in the short term) reinforced, making them likely to buy even more, thereby further driving up the price.

Gold, as an investment (sitting in the world's safes), has the advantages of being liquid, compact (value/cubic inch), and transparent in value. Significantly, it has a seemingly unlimited shelf life (unlike food, medicine and machinery).

However, at a recent $1,400 per ounce, you are unlikely to eat it (it is actually edible because it is non-toxic, but provides zero nutritional value), plant it, build with it (other than jewelry), or fill a dental cavity with it.

India holds roughly 11% of the world's gold stock, and has until recently been gold's biggest importer. Virtually all of this is used in jewelry or held as an investment. Culturally, the Indian people have long believed in the investment value of gold, and as their economic fortunes have improved, much of that new wealth has been invested in the metal. In January 2013, the Indian government increased the import tax on gold (for the second time in 10 months) from 4% to 6%. Prior to March 2012, the tax had been only 2%. When these import taxes failed to discourage gold imports (which puts downward pressure on their currency), the Indian government prohibited gold imports altogether on August 14, 2013. Over time, higher friction costs tend to reduce value (discussed in the principle: Fight Friction Costs), and the recent all-time high for gold prices was at the end of August 2011.

Gold advocates believe that, when the consequences of massive government debt problems start to unfold, the yellow metal will retain and gain more value than anything else. Clearly, if the shitake hits the fan, the basics of food, water, and energy should have more trading value than a gold bracelet or a gold coin. On the other hand, you can only carry so much food and water on your back as you flee one country or region for another.

GARBAGE OR WINE BUSINESS?

My thesis is that it's easier to make money in the garbage business than it is owning a California vineyard. Why? Because of the pride-of-ownership differences between the two assets.

They both might have the same underlying cash flows (say $1 million per year), but with the garbage business, start-up costs might be $5 million, while the vineyard might require $10 million up front. Please bear with me: I know that vineyard economics are not nearly this attractive. Another way to put it is that, for the same $10 million investment, the garbage man can buy $2 million yearly in cash flows, and the vineyard buyer only $1 million.

Now, if the pride-of-ownership premium increases by 20% in the first year, then the vineyard buyer has made up for the smaller cash flow (20% * ($10 million - $5 million)= $1 million). Absent that boost, the vineyard owner will not do as well financially. Few prices go up forever (even in these less tangible dimensions) so what if, for unforeseen reasons, the pride-of-ownership premium actually drops? Suppose vineyards become the object of broad union strikes, and the union leaders consistently talk about the rich vineyard owners' exploitation of workers? Then the differences in the relative returns might be even more dramatic.

Another consideration in evaluating the garbage versus vineyard business is that it is tougher to make money competing against those who don't care about making money. The only reason that someone would go into the garbage business would be to make a buck, but there are plenty of pride-of-ownership motives for planting a California vineyard or building a winery. And every time one of your neighbors plants yet another vineyard, it increases the supply of grapes, and in some small increment drives down the price (another pesky reminder of the crucial Law of Supply and Demand). By the way, there are two beautiful vineyards adjacent to my California property and they are perfect—I get to enjoy their splendor and my neighbors foot the bill.

In my Chapter Six discussion of Sutton Bridge, I relate how, upon its sale, Enron Europe extracted hundreds of millions of dollars for what was essentially the pride-of-ownership premium. So, the principle applies beyond vineyards, fancy Malibu beach homes, and Major League baseball teams.

Another way to put it is that a trader tries to identify the current market value of the "sizzle" separately from the value of the "steak." If the supply of sizzle is growing faster than the demand, then—like anything else—its price is likely to drop. If the sizzle is gaining momentum and more attention, then perhaps the trader should scoop it up. In a more flexible world, you might find a way to go long the sizzle and short the steak, or vice versa. But I will need very imaginative readers to help me find a way to put this trade on. And, of course, the sizzle of the steak has a negative value to my vegetarian wife.

These premiums and discounts change over time—frequently in ways that are independent of the value of the underlying cash flows. The wealthier an investor is, the more willing she is to pay extra for this "pride-of-ownership" premium because she can afford the bragging rights. And the more superstitious a Hong Kong renter is, the more he will refuse to even consider renting a hongza.

However, when the economy turns south, we see more sellers, and the pride-of-ownership premium is likely to shrink. The only rational financial reason to pay up for pride of ownership is a belief that, later, someone will pay even more for it—or that your wealth renders the extra cost irrelevant. But most buyers of pride-of-ownership care less than the average trader about future cash flows.

Ignore the pride-of-ownership premium, like the ghost discount, at your financial peril.

DON'T JUMP THE GUN

"The market can stay irrational longer
than you can stay solvent."

—John Maynard Keynes

In her December 19, 2010, CBS *60 Minutes* interview, Wall Street banking analyst Meredith Whitney said, "There's not a doubt in my mind that you will see a spate of municipal bond defaults. You could see fifty sizable defaults…This will amount to hundreds of billions of dollars' worth of defaults."

In the year after her prediction, municipalities had few defaults, and muni bonds performed very well as a class because of dropping interest rates. About a year and a half later, the City of Stockton declared the biggest municipal bankruptcy in US history. And then, on July 18, 2013, Detroit declared bankruptcy, and crushed Stockton's record. Can Los Angeles, Baltimore, and Chicago be far behind?

Whitney may have been right—but early (my guess). If you had followed her advice immediately after hearing it, you would have been substantially poorer by the time she was finally proven to be right. As Terry Jones, the founder of Travelocity, says in his book *On Innovation*, "Sometimes you are just too early."

The usual cliché is: "We weren't wrong; we were just early." A critical part of analyzing an opportunity is considering whether the timing and momentum are right. And to profit from an inflection point, it rarely pays to be too far "ahead of the curve."

The old adage tells us the patient investor sacrifices immediate payoffs in favor of long-term growth. Granted, the trader's time frame is usually shorter than the investor's, but neither the investor nor the trader can schedule the next great opportunity. Therefore, they must both wait patiently until the time is right.

A good trader invests in the future by making money today and maybe, tomorrow. If you're a trader, try telling your boss, "I'm sorry—I'm going to lose five million dollars during the next month, but we'll come roaring back with a six million dollar profit during the next two years." You will be quickly shown the exit door marked *Chumps*.

A better trader considers how he can make five million as the market moves in one direction, how he might make another eleven million by reversing positions once the trend changes, earning a sixteen million dollar total profit. Frequently, the patient trader just waits until the time is right to bet along with the long-term trend (Start with the Big Picture and Macro Trends).

*****

Back in 2000, Bill Gates predicted a shift from PCs to tablets within five years. He was early, and Microsoft was not aggressive. By the time Apple released the iPad to rave consumer reviews (2010), Microsoft had surrendered its potential early-mover advantage. In mid-2012, Microsoft announced its new tablet product (The Surface), having already fallen behind the iPad and the Android tablets. Even

Lucky And Good

with the huge Apple/Android lead, it may be too early to pick the eventual winner, although today Microsoft has substantial ground to make up.

In January 2011, one analyst said: "I know pundits have been predicting this for the last three years, and if the economy remains moribund this year, then they will be wrong again. If, however, demand for credit escalates and corporations start to spend their $2 trillion hoard of cash, rates will climb to reflect higher demand for credit. Just make sure you are not in long-term bond funds, because they will suffer the biggest declines." In the year and a half after this prediction, 30-year Treasury yields dropped from about 4.5% to 2.5%. The analyst has since recovered some of his losses (assuming he stuck with his own advice), as the yield had swung back up to about 3.75% by late August 2013. His timing was definitely premature.

Gordon Chang, in his 2001 book *The Coming Collapse of China*, wrote: "How much time does China have? No one knows for sure, but China cannot continue to spend at the current pace for much longer. Beijing has about five years to put things right. No government, not even China's, can defy the laws of gravity forever." I suspect Chang will ultimately be proven right, but he was at least seven years early.

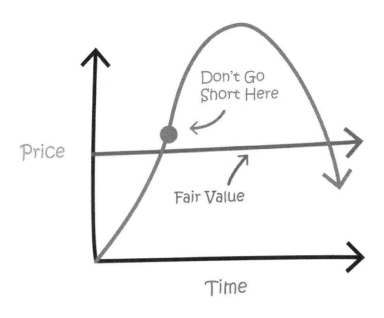

By 2003, there was an obvious housing bubble in the US. If you had started shorting the market then, you may have gone broke (Never Run Out of Cash) by the time the bubble began to burst. In fact, I have to admit that when I graduated from college in 1975 and moved to Newport Beach, California, I saw a housing bubble coming. At the time, real estate on Balboa Island and Laguna Beach was some of the most expensive in California. I did the calculations and determined that, relative to renting the same homes, housing prices were too high. (I wasn't considering the Pride-of-Ownership Premium). I was a bit early, but only by 30 years. Subsequently, I bought into the investment trend, first with an FHA-subsidized mortgage when I bought the smallest and cheapest new home in the San Francisco Bay Area a couple of years later, and a few more homes since.

As Sir Isaac Newton, an early nerd, said: "A body in motion tends to stay in motion." Just because a variable is overvalued or undervalued does not mean that it will be rectified tomorrow. In fact, it may take months, years, or decades to correct. Get ready, but don't pull the trigger too early. Patience! **You not only have to be right, but you have to be timely.**

Prepare for inflection points, but look for signs that the tide has actually started to turn. Getting it right but acting too early means getting it wrong.

FIGHT FRICTION COSTS

"Watch the costs and the profits will take care of themselves."
—Andrew Carnegie,
Scottish-American industrialist

All costs are your enemy. Friction costs are expenses that relate to buying or selling an asset, or putting on and unwinding a trading position. An important element of these costs relates to something called "liquidity." The term has two different but closely related meanings.

LIQUIDITY VERSUS "LIQUIDITY"

When it comes to potentially running out of cash, liquidity simply means that you have enough cash or access to cash to pay your current bills. "Enough" cash may mean having the money in the bank. For a large company, it may mean, short-term, using its bank credit lines. An individual might simply rely on a pre-approved home equity line of credit or even credit cards (at exorbitant interest rates). Illiquidity, or lack of liquidity, might come into play if you only have a single asset that cannot be converted partially or wholly into cash. For example, if you are the plaintiff in a lawsuit, you might anticipate collecting $10 million in three years. But no bank will lend you money based on this *speculative* asset, and in the meantime, you have to pay the rent and put gas in the tank. In this case, you are definitely illiquid, unless the lawsuit-funding industry steps in to help. (More about this later, in Chapter Six.)

Those who complain about a "lack of liquidity" imply that they have plenty of assets but are *temporarily* short of cash. But if a company is illiquid today, has no cash, and has no assets that can be converted into cash to pay the bills, it is also insolvent, bust, bankrupt, toast, and a Chump.

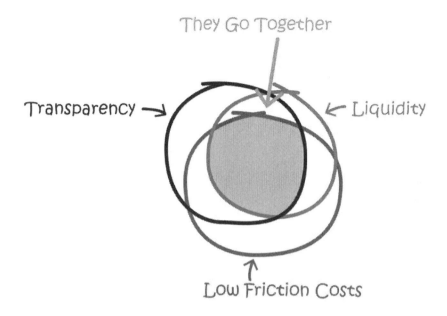

It was a lack of liquidity (cash) that forced Bernie Madoff to 'fess up about his Ponzi scheme.

An entrepreneur can retain more liquidity by:

- ❖ keeping costs down, or, as Mark Cuban puts it, "Recognize that it's OK to live like a student";
- ❖ generating real-world sales that can be evaluated by potential investors;
- ❖ generating a positive cash flow as early as possible;
- ❖ trying to secure flexible terms and conditions from suppliers; and
- ❖ keeping the customer offerings as narrow as possible.

The most flexible form of liquidity for any entrepreneur, though, is plenty of cash.

But when I discuss "liquidity" in terms of buying and selling assets, the term has another meaning. We use the term to describe the *friction costs* of buying an asset and then selling it. On the liquidity continuum, some assets can be converted into cash within seconds, while others might take years.

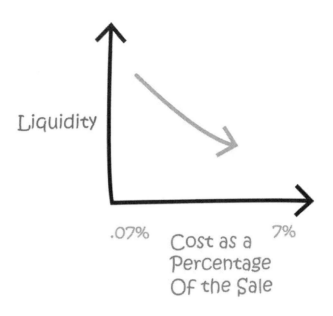

If I have a poker chip at a casino, I can convert it into 100% of its cash value simply by walking over to the cashier's cage and making the exchange. (If you put the chip in your pocket, and the casino goes bankrupt later that month, it is a different story.) The cage is open 24x7—meaning the friction cost is virtually zero. But if you own a multimillion-dollar rural home, it might take years to find a buyer and close on the transaction, thereby converting the asset into cash.

Better liquidity is seen in parallel with low transaction costs. Liquidity also goes hand in hand with transparency, which we'll consider in a moment.

Some positions are extremely illiquid, with high transaction costs, making them unlikely to be a profitable market for the trader. Traders prefer positions with greater liquidity and lower friction costs. Investors are less concerned about transaction costs, because they intend to own the investment for years, if not decades. Investors don't plan on transacting very often.

Decide

Most large-cap stocks on the New York Stock Exchange are very liquid, with the "bid-offer" spreads (the difference between the best posted sales price and the best price to buy) $.01 per share. So, if the market does not move, a trader can buy 10,000 shares of GE for $18.55 (a July 2011 price), then turn right around and sell the same 10,000 shares for $18.54. The bid-offer spread is only $.01, and the market is "liquid" enough to allow a trader to buy and sell a large number of shares without moving the market price. (Regardless of market liquidity, buying or selling 20% of outstanding shares in a single day would dramatically move the market.)

Brokerage fees of $7.95 per order to buy and $7.95 to sell 10,000 shares bring the total "friction cost," or transaction cost, to only $115.90 (10,000 shares * $.01 per share + $7.95 + $7.95). This is a $115.90 transaction cost on assets with a value of $185,545 (10,000 * $18.545). So, the *total friction cost* for buying and selling $185,545 of GE stock is .062% ($115.90/$185,545)—($6.20 on every $10,000).

Compare this to the friction cost of buying and selling a house with a market price of $185,545. The seller has to pay the realtor a 6% commission on the sales prices, and both buyer and seller must each pay closing costs of about $800 (typical).

Total in-and-out costs, then, are about $12,733 ((6% * $185,545) + $800 + $800). As a percentage of the value of the asset, this is 6.9%. So, for our purposes, we describe the .062% stock transaction as very liquid and the 6.9% house transaction as illiquid. However, other investments are still far less liquid than your average home. (For example, a small gold mine purchase, which we discuss a bit later.)

Time It Takes To Sell

Aside from the transaction costs for buying and selling illiquid assets, their sale takes more time than unloading liquid assets. As long as the stock market is open, the trader can buy or sell at any time. The sale of a home, though, might take weeks, months, or even years, during which time the price is likely to change. You probably won't notice the price movement when it goes your way, but you will be very annoyed when the price starts to fall.

Liquid markets are always more "transparent" than illiquid markets, making the current price obvious. Such transparency means that a buyer is unlikely to pay too much, and a seller is unlikely to settle for too little (based on the current market price).

Decide

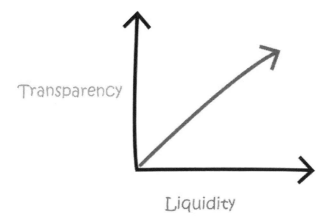

On May 1, 1975, Congress deregulated the stock market by removing the power of the New York Stock Exchange to set its members' commission rates. This opened the door for discount brokers like Charles Schwab to drive down the transaction costs for buying and selling equities in the US, thus creating both a negative inflection point for the old-style brokerage houses, and a huge opportunity for discount brokerage businesses. Combined with the subsequent advent of online trading and computerization of the entire value chain, the friction costs are now a small percentage of those prevalent in early 1975. The biggest winner, of course, has been the investing and trading public, a prime example of the benefits of deregulation, competition, and free markets.

PLAYING A LESS THAN ZERO-SUM GAME

In some games, bets, and businesses, more money is lost than is made; these are *Less than Zero-Sum Games.* Generally the difference between what is made and what is lost is spent on friction costs.

For poker, sports betting, horse race betting and some businesses, the following formula shows the sum total of the results:

Profits = Losses - Friction Costs

In the interest of simplicity, I ask purists and accountants to accept the above equation as representing absolute values (for each of the three elements).

Friction costs are transaction costs (fees, commissions, brokerage expenses charged by those administering or facilitating a market) plus the cost of your own due diligence and miscellaneous costs.

Before we get any further, let me start by defining a related gambling term: "vig"—short for "vigorish." It is simply the amount kept by the sports book in Vegas as gross profit, before paying operating expenses, out of the bets placed.

For a typical college football bet, one bettor puts down $110 on USC versus Notre Dame, and is giving up three and half points. He wins if the Trojans win by more than three and a half points. Since there are no half points in the game of football, we are assured that, in this example, there will be no tie on the bet. Another fan bets $110 on the Fighting Irish, and gets three and half points. This Notre Dame bettor wins the bet as long as USC does not win the game by more than three and a half points. The winner of the bet (the "better bettor") then collects the $110 that he gave to the sports book plus $100 out of the $110 that the other guy bet. The sports book keeps the remaining $10—the vig.

In the world of NBA and NFL sports betting, the total friction cost, or vig, is typically 4.45% ($10/$220). If the betting professional makes $100 (on his $110 bet), the Chump loses $110, and the house keeps the remaining $10 vig for administering the market.

$$\$100 = \$110 - \$10$$

In *Trading Bases: A Story About Wall Street, Gambling, and Baseball*, Joe Peta stresses that one of the benefits of betting on Major League Baseball versus football or basketball, is that the vig on a 50/50 bet is usually less. This is because it is a slow period for the sports books. Two bettors would each bet $105, and the winner would receive $205. In this case, the vig is only 2.38% ($5/$210), and the friction formula would be:

$$\$100 = \$105 - \$5$$

All things being equal, it is easier to beat a market with a 2.38% friction cost than one with a 4.45% vig. I'll discuss the horse betting business, in which the vig can approach 25% (ouch!) in Chapter Four.

There is no free lunch relative to friction costs, so you need to understand them before you decide to play any game. Only Chumps ignore them.

*****

An illiquid, nontransparent investment requires a judicious, well-informed investor to remain patient while waiting for a great deal. The buyer *might* be able to buy a $150 million Caravaggio masterpiece for $100 million. If she is not skillful and knowledgeable enough, she might also end up paying $200 million (Chumpdom), because the lack of transparency makes it tough to evaluate the value. Skill in price-assessment, coupled with the patience to wait for good value, is critical to an investor. Warren Buffett is the reigning Champ at this game.

Dominant players (the big dogs) in most markets usually prefer keeping things illiquid and nontransparent, because they then have a greater chance of taking the outsiders (Chumps) for a ride.

Other investments are illiquid based on their rarity and on the difficulty in comparing assets—they simply don't change hands very often. Let's say you're in the market to buy a small privately-owned gold mine located in the US. Hypothetically, it has proven reserves of 10,000 ounces of gold with a value of $450 per ounce (reserves are worth less than gold in hand). This mine is generating positive cash flow of $200,000 per month by producing $400,000 of gold per month (the difference being expenses). The amount of gold production is expected to remain flat in the foreseeable future, and you don't expect a change in price for refined gold (a major assumption).

The value of the private gold mine might be approximately (10,000 * $450) + 5-times ($200,000 * 12 months per year) = $16.5 million. (I have used the ratio of five-times the positive cash flow, which is representative of small-business valuations.) How liquid do you think this gold mine might be? Do you really think that you can buy the gold mine and then turn around and sell it the next day for the same .062% friction cost as a gold mining stock trading on the NYSE? ... **Fogetaboutit!**

Lucky And Good

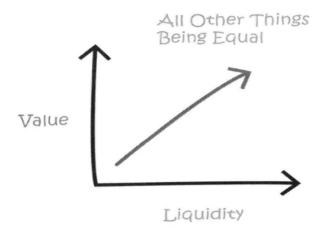

I have never bought or sold a gold mine. However, in May 2000 Enron purchased MG PLC (at the time, one of the largest metals traders in the world) for about $445 million (plus some acquired debt), making your humble author an indirect manager of the company for 18 months. Joe Gold (what a great name to have in the metals business) ran the business.

I recently investigated but did not purchase a small share of a private US gold mine. A reasonable amount of due diligence led me to believe that purchasing a gold mine might involve about a 10% transaction cost, with another 8% required to sell it (18% total, in and out!). This is the epitome of an illiquid investment.

Venture capital firms considering an investment in a new business always contemplate their exit strategy. An exit strategy is the timing and method by which they will convert an illiquid partial or full ownership in a small company into cash. It does them no good to have picked a winner without being able to ring the cash register—and make their next investment. Again, Warren Buffett is far more patient in delaying his opening of the cash drawer. He intends to buy and hold forever (he has no exit strategy), and he generates cash for his next investment by buying companies that will pay him regular and growing cash dividends—a different strategy entirely.

Sometimes the "liquidity dimension" is shown in reverse, as an "illiquidity discount" for investments (such as private equity) which are less liquid than publicly traded equities. For example, if the discounted cash flow estimates for a small private company looks like it's worth $500,000, an investor might knock down the value by 20% because ownership is illiquid, and selling it would be more costly than selling publicly-traded shares in the stock market. Nailing this illiquidity discount is an art more than an exact science, but it is clearly a factor in how many investors look at private equity investments.

Notably, the investing public faces a trade-off when investing in most publicly traded shares versus privately held companies, such as limited liability companies and S corporations. This comes down to a fundamental tradeoff: Stocks in publicly traded companies (usually C corporations) offer greater liquidity and transparency, but this advantage is offset by higher taxes (corporate taxes combined with the individual taxes paid on the dividends and capital gains). A few specialty securities, like master limited partnerships (MLPs) and real estate investment trusts (REITs), sometimes are structured to have both great liquidity and low combined tax rates.

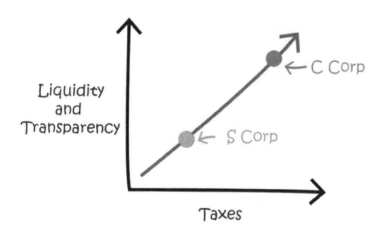

Investors would be well-served to think more about liquidity and transaction costs. You may very well intend to hold onto an investment forever, but the ability to change your mind is a valuable (but usually not free) option.

Entrepreneurs, of course, make some of the least liquid investments of all. Their product or service has virtually no buyer until they develop their business to a minimum threshold. Their debt and equity is illiquid and risky, and for all the reasons that we have discussed, the underlying investment usually fails.

Finally, it's critical to understand that value, prices, transparency, liquidity, friction costs, and volatility are all interrelated and ever-changing. When prices start moving quickly, some participants (buyers and sellers) eventually pull back. This results in less liquidity and hence less transparency—which affect all the other variables.

I COULD'VE BEEN A HEDGE FUND MANAGER

If I were unscrupulous and able to flim-flam like Allen Stanford and Bernie Madoff, I would have opened 16 separate hedge funds in late 2006, each with $1 billion in other people's money. My hedge funds, all totaled, would have given me assets to manage of $16 billion. **(Please don't take this example as a suggestion that I consider hedge fund managers unethical—I believe that most are quite ethical. I simply believe, and mean to illustrate, that they impose high friction costs.)**

I would have charged a typical 2% per year (others typically charge this as 0.5% each quarter, but that's too much work) of the value of the assets under management, at the beginning of the year. That would start me with a tidy $320 million (2% times 16 funds times $1 billion per fund). This $320 million would turn out to be slightly more than a quarter of all the money I would ever make running these funds over the next four years. I would also charge 20% of the profits, (a "performance fee"), but take none of the downside (a great gig if you can get it).

I would have told each fund's investors that if they ever had a losing year, I would shut down their fund and return their remaining capital. By the way, I wouldn't have bothered to inform each fund's

Decide

investors about the existence of the other funds, and how I planned to make money (it was a "proprietary" black box algorithm), no matter what happened in their fund.

On January 2, 2007 (markets are closed on January 1), I would have invested half (8) of all of these hedge funds in a *long* S&P 500 ETF (exchange-traded fund). We would have gotten the appreciation in the overall market during the year (which turned out to be 3.53%), plus we would have gotten the dividends earned by this asset over the year, about 2%; I also would have had to pay expenses of 0.1% to the company that managed the ETF. Investors' total return would've been 2.63% (after my fees). How impressive can you get? But after all, we are professionals.

On the same day, I would have invested the other half of these funds (8) in a *short* S&P 500 ETF. These would have made money if the value of the S&P 500 *decreased* during the year. As it turns out, we would have lost the same 3.53% in the first year and had to pay 2% for the dividends earned by these companies (just the opposite of had we owned them), and the ETF management fees of 0.9% rather than 0.1% for the long ETF. Therefore, all of the 8 short funds would have each lost 8.26% (including my fees) of their value in the first year, so, sadly, they were all shut down (which was a shame, since we would have loved to keep collecting that 2% per year).

In the discussion of less-than-zero-sum games, I gave you the formula:

Profits = Losses - Friction Costs

In this case, the results would've been:

2.63% = 8.26% - 5.63%

Notice the enormous friction costs (5.63%) in this example, compared to only 2.38% for betting on baseball games and 4.45% for football. Also note how much the friction costs exceed the profits.

At the end of the year, we would have sucked it up and moved on. I knew that I was going to lose half my funds after the first year; that gave me more time to drink beer, play poker, and watch baseball. This sure wasn't as hard as working on the farm.

Originally, I had to move this $16 billion into two different assets, then sit back and wait. At the end of every quarter and the end

Lucky And Good

of the year, I had to send statements to all investors (both winners and losers), a simple chore that would have been automated. And, finally, at the end of the first year, I had to shut down half of the funds and return the money to the investors who had lost money, with a sad commentary about how unlucky we had been. I definitely would have left this unpleasant work to a few trusted minions.

By the way, at the end of the first year, I would have made an additional $5.25 million incentive payment for the 20% profit that I had earned on the 8 long funds.

Starting the next year, 2008, I would have gone through the same process again: left half of the remaining funds (four) in the long S&P 500 ETF, and moved the other four funds into the short S&P 500 ETF. But before that, I would have collected my usual 2% on the remaining assets, which was $8.21 billion times 2%, or another tidy $164 million (a pleasant day, indeed).

It turns out that 2008 was a very bad year for owning stocks, and the S&P 500 declined in value by 38.49%. (Remember the banking crisis.) But at least they paid almost 1.5% in dividends. At the end of the year, I would have had to shut down half of my funds again. But it was a very good year for making money via my 20% of the profits on those that had gone short. My clients who were invested in the four funds that were short in the second year (and who by now really understood my wizardry) were up 30.6% (after my fees) on their investments after two years. Compared to their friends and neighbors, they had really done well. They were busy buying new private jets, but not me. I had already bought mine after collecting the first $320 million on day one. But, because of the big move in the market, my share of the profits was much bigger than the year before, and I earned another $280 million in performance bonuses for my 20% of the profits of the winners.

After four years, I would have been down to one, and only one, hedge fund, renamed the "Perfectus Fund." I had made about $1.15 billion (before taxes). In total, the original 16 funds had lost a combined $1.185 billion (a little more than I had made). But the Perfectus Fund had done extraordinarily well (one out of 16 ain't bad), and made me a superstar after plenty of self-promotion. So naturally, I shut it down. Then, I would have opened another 16 funds

(Perfectus 1 through Perfectus 16), this time with $2 billion in each of them.

The reality is that it ain't that easy to get billions of dollars to start your hedge fund (and for good reason). Investors, such as pension funds, want you, the hedge fund manager, to put most of your own money into the fund, plus demonstrate an impressive track record, before giving you a penny. So, it would be impossible to start 16 different hedge funds of a billion dollars each unless they were all comprised of your own money to begin with—and then, why bother?

Nevertheless, I have three reasons for never investing in a hedge fund:

1) friction costs are high,
2) past performance does not necessarily predict future performance, and
3) most of them won't share (in any meaningful detail) their secret sauce for profiting in their chosen markets.

The friction costs are so high that they have to be unbelievably lucky or amazingly skillful investors and traders to overcome the huge fees that they charge. This may seem strange, coming from a trader, but that's the way I see it. In all fairness, I know of some hedge funds that have been tremendous investments. Former Enron trader John Arnold did extraordinarily well for his investors in the Centaurus Energy Master Fund. The March 2013 Forbes "World's Billionaires" estimated his net worth at $2.3 billion, at the ripe old age of 39. He shut down the fund in 2012.

Former New Jersey governor Jon Corzine, who took MF Global (a virtual hedge fund) into bankruptcy in 2011, announced on August 16, 2012, that he was considering starting a hedge fund. Perhaps he had gotten an early copy of this book, and is going to use the Perfectus "strategy" to make his move before we make the *New York Times* bestseller list. Maybe he thinks that his past performance really won't impact his ability to raise money.

Warren Buffet essentially manages Berkshire Hathaway (BERK) as a hedge fund for a salary of only $100,000 a year (plus a few perks and benefits). His hedge fund has some extra friction costs because of double and triple taxation. It would, for example, be triple taxation for the shares of Coca Cola that he owns: Coke first pays a corporate income tax on their income, then, when they pay Berkshire a dividend, BERK pays income tax on the dividend income, then—and finally, when an individual makes a capital gain on the appreciation in the price of the Berkshire shares (they don't pay dividends), the individual investor ultimately pays a capital gains tax on the increase in their value.

But Buffett is quite frugal with corporate expenses, and the total management friction cost has been one of the greatest bargains in history for the average BERK shareholder. I have yet to find any other "hedge fund" managers who have been nearly as thrifty with their fees and expenses (especially as a percentage of the value of the assets).

DECIDE TO DECIDE

> "I define fear as standing across the ring from Joe Louis and knowing he wants to go home early."
> —Max Baer

GOLD VERSUS SILVER

Let's consider a common bias in decision-making. If you recognize this natural obstacle to taking action, you can work to overcome it (perhaps you should discuss it at your next psychotherapy session—I'm making these shrinks rich!). This is another example inspired by Daniel Kahneman's book *Thinking Fast and Slow*.

Paul owns $2,000 of gold. During the past year, he considered selling the gold and buying silver instead, but then decided against it. He now learns that he would have been better off by $500 had he sold his gold and bought silver.

George owned $2,000 of silver. During the past year he sold his silver, and used the money to buy gold. He now learns that he would have been better off by $500 had he kept his silver rather than selling it and buying gold.

How much did Paul and George each lose, based on their decisions? They both would have been better off by $500 owning silver.

Who feels the greater regret?

Most folks answer that George feels more remorse.

The only difference in their circumstances is that George got to where he is by acting, whereas Paul got to the same place by doing nothing. **People tend to have stronger emotional reactions (especially regret) to an outcome produced by their action, rather than to the same outcome produced by inaction. In other words, the average person feels better about sitting on his keister and failing, as opposed to making a decision that ends up wrong.**

However, winning entrepreneurs, traders, and investors are proactive. Therefore, they make more decisions and take more actions that result in bad outcomes than those who are passive. But they also have more chances to get it right. You need to understand the psychology of regret over taking an action that may turn out poorly—then cast aside the emotional bias, and make the smart move.

This is an advantage of a sunk cost or mark-to-market mentality, because every day, the trader is making the conscious choice to stay put or not (Think on the Margin).

We've seen how the media treats mistakes made via action versus those made by inaction: in 2012, JPMorgan lost $6 billion during a three-month period. While legislative hearings investigated this "calamity," the US government debt continued to increase by $4 billion per day. So, folks will not only beat up on themselves for making the bad call, but the media and Congress will hound them, as well (while lawmakers hypocritically fail to make the tough decisions that might reduce the deficit). It is easy for politicians to kick the can down the road, but entrepreneurs, traders, and investors can't afford to delay the pain—or their businesses might not make it until next year, let alone the next election.

♦♦♦
♦♦♦

CHAPTER FOUR: GO FOR IT

> "If I bring in Tippy Martinez to face Graig Nettles and Nettles homers, that's not a mistake. Those are moves that didn't work."
>
> —Earl Weaver, manager of the Baltimore Orioles for 17 years

OK: You've done the analysis and decided to go for it. Do it quickly, with full force and absolute focus.

This stage of business opportunity is the easiest part for a trader, and the hardest for an entrepreneur. This is where the rubber meets the road.

We are talking about the execution of your idea, trade, investment, or new business. This entails more decision making, risk taking, risk mitigation, and bets that you'll have to make. If you are an entrepreneur, you will also worry about accounting, taxes, hiring, firing, managing, and leading...but, most of all, selling. These tasks require long hours and hard work. But you'll never get to those aspects if you don't make smart decisions—and that is the essence of this book.

STRIKE WHILE THE IRON IS HOT

> "If everything seems under control, you're just not going fast enough."
>
> —Mario Andretti

My cousin has been a professional horse race bettor since 2004. Beginning in 1992, he studied the odds, developing computer models that allowed him to regularly predict horse race results, which he sold in daily racing sheets. But a couple of inflection points changed the magnitude of the opportunity. In 2003, he discovered "rebate betting"—in which large bettors could receive as much as a 15% rebate on their total bets if they went through certain wholesale betting brokers. Since the track cut (or "rake") on most betting operations is usually 25%, this reduced his friction costs dramatically, from 25% to 10% (Fight Friction Costs). The second factor was that he could place his bets via a phone call from his home for almost every track in the country, rather than having to actually travel to the track to make a bet. These two dynamics resulted in him transitioning, in 2004, from selling his picks to the betting public to becoming a professional gambler.

Because of the politics and economic structure of horse betting versus online poker, online poker has been made virtually illegal in most of the US (although the laws are not consistently enforced), while online horse betting is not only allowed, but encouraged via rebate betting. Nevada and New Jersey recently enacted laws that legalized internet poker among players within their states. Just as—according to the US tax code—owning an investment for 364 days is evil and 365 days is golden (think capital gains taxes), playing online poker is wicked, and making an online horse bet is noble. Go figure!

In 2005, my cousin's betting business hit another fortunate inflection point. In that year, his broker allowed him to start downloading his bets online via computer, rather than via telephone. This allowed him to massively scale up the business, and make more wagers every day. 2006 ended up being his busiest and most profitable year. He placed about 15 million horse wagers that year (yes, *15 million*), and was one of the largest horse bettors in the country, all as a one-man show—programmer, mathematician, accountant, risk manager, owner, CFO and CEO.

But that year was as good as it got. Others have since come into the "market," and today, there are probably one or two dozen companies (they don't tend to advertise, so this is a guesstimate) that bet professionally on horses. Their models do not predict radically different race results (if they did, they would quickly go out of business). So, over time, the "juice" (profit) has gradually been squeezed out of the opportunity. In 2012, my cousin only made about

1.9 million wagers, and his profits dropped to about 7% of his peak. Don't feel sorry for him, though; his good years were very, very good. As of 2013, the profitability appears to have bottomed out, but the enterprise is still worthwhile since it is almost completely automated.

Understand that every opportunity has a limited shelf life. The expression "strike while the iron is hot" harkens back to a time when a blacksmith would remove a piece of iron from the fire, wanting to quickly strike and mold it before the iron cooled off. Once cool, it became brittle, and the opportunity to hammer it into shape was gone. Likewise, virtually no good opportunity will last very long, whether a trade, specific investment category, a technique for professional gambling, an opportunity for an entrepreneur—or the chance to hammer a piece of iron into shape.

A great period for opening new coffee shops in downtown areas may exist, but once the market is saturated, opening yet another one is unlikely to pay dividends.

Wayne Huizenga made a fortune by consolidating independent video stores into the Blockbuster chain, and he was either brilliant or lucky in selling it off before the video store business model became antiquated and, eventually, went kaput. Either way, having the guts to make the moves (the creation of the business and then the sale of it) is what paid off.

THEN AND NOW

The truth of this principle is as evident today as it was in ancient times.

The Spice Trade. Spices such as cinnamon and ginger were used for trading and storing value as early as 10,000 BC. Traders who moved spices from Asia to the Middle East and eventually to Europe were some of the world's earliest entrepreneurs. They were motivated to be flexible and ready to move when the time was right, because the opportunity was always changing (although over decades rather than months). Early on, for instance, spices were transported via overland routes, but eventually sea routes became advantageous.

As far back as 3000 BC, the Egyptians traded with northeast Africa (now Somalia and Eritrea). By 80 BC, Alexandria had become the dominant trading center for Indian spices entering the Greco-

Roman world. These trade routes were early "trade secrets." However, since Gutenberg had not yet invented movable type, retired spice traders did not share these secrets via their memoirs. As a result, those secrets remained secret longer than they do today. At times, black pepper traded for as much per ounce as gold. If you had the staying power (many centuries), it would have been a great spread trade to have shorted black pepper and gone long gold. Nevertheless, savvy traders knew how to optimize the value of the spices they found in exchange for value back home.

SAN JUAN OPTIONALITY

From 1994 through 1996, I managed the Natural Gas West Desk for Enron. In those years, we knew more than anyone else about moving gas around different pipelines and optimizing our profits, including producers, utilities, marketers, pipeline companies, and other traders (in my opinion).

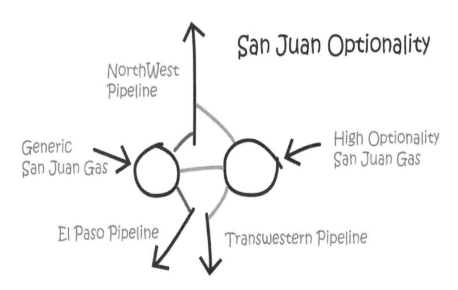

In order to understand how the system worked, you had to know:

- ❖ how the pipelines scheduled gas,
- ❖ which plants' gas was given priority,

- how El Paso Pipeline's pooling system worked, and
- where gas was trying to move.

In general, traders try to move their natural gas to the most expensive market while incurring the lowest marginal transportation costs. As gas tries to move, it comes across constraint points, with some gas getting through and some, blocked. Depending on a company's transportation rights, they might get all of their gas through a constraint point, or very little.

We could bring Canadian gas to the San Juan Basin via the Northwest Pipeline. We could bring domestic gas down from the Opal gas plant using the Northwest Pipeline. And we could use two sources of San Juan gas—the gas that came through the Bondad constraint point (a compressor station on the El Paso system) and gas that didn't move through Bondad. Buying gas at the Williams San Juan Plant had the greatest flexibility. We could send this gas directly into the Northwest Pipeline going north or to El Paso (bypassing the Bondad constraint point), or we could nominate into the Transwestern Pipeline.

In the El Paso system, gas coming through Bondad would get prorated, and only some of it would flow. This gas would initially be scheduled two days out, and so the next day, you had to figure out what to do with the gas that didn't get confirmed.

When gas was not confirmed two days out on the El Paso system, most of the time it would not flow at all on that pipeline. So we could send it north on the Northwest System or send it on the Transwestern Pipeline (usually receiving a lower price). Or we could not flow it at all (like most of the other traders did), which usually meant that the remaining gas was shut in.

Having all the options in your toolbox allowed the game to be played like a Champ. The primary tools were transportation rights on Northwest, El Paso, and Transwestern pipelines. **We created optionality by selling generic pool gas in the El Paso system (which could be supplied from any source) while specifically buying Williams Plant gas that we knew had the most optionality.**

Depending on whether prices were increasing or decreasing, we used our optionality to play the San Juan game more profitably than anyone else (Find Free Options). The problem was that many of our traders and all of our schedulers knew the game, and our competitors were always trying to hire our crew. Over time, our information advantage started to fade. In fact, I myself had taken some of these San Juan tricks of the trade from American Hunter to Enron when I changed teams in 1994. That is simply the way many ideas flow back and forth in a competitive market.

No opportunity lasts forever—in this case, I suspect that at least six other trading companies began to use the same methodologies within a couple of years.

DIAMONDS AND THE GRIDIRON

I was upset when the book *Moneyball* was published. It laid bare the way the Oakland A's evaluated baseball talent. I was troubled because as an A's fan, I hated the idea of every other team in the league being embarrassed into adopting some of the A's advantageous strategies (except the Giants, who are also my team). I would have been thrilled to read the story if instead I were rooting for the Boston Red Sox. The book focuses on the 2002 year, when the Oakland A's had the third-lowest payroll in Major League Baseball ($45 million versus $125 million for the New York Yankees). And yet, Oakland managed to have an outstanding 103-59 record.

It was a great story, but I would have preferred they had guarded their secrets more closely. The A's' cooperation with author Michael Lewis helped spread the word a little faster—now almost all teams have taken another look at how they appraise talent.

Alas, word was going to get out anyway. Bill James, the original Sabermetrics guru, was hired by the Boston Red Sox in 2003. In 2004, Billy Beane's assistant general manager, Paul DePodesta, was hired as the GM of the Los Angeles Dodgers (the book made DePodesta look pretty smart). In 2010, the New York Mets hired Beane's predecessor, Sandy Alderson, and Alderson hired some of Beane's former associates. It's tough to hide a good idea. Yet the A's repeated this *Moneyball* magic in 2012, when they again won the American League West, this time with the second-lowest payroll in the Major Leagues.

Go For It

It also turns out that the *Moneyball* strategy wasn't all that new after all. Earl Weaver, the long-time manager of the Baltimore Orioles, had long used and described most of the same tactics.

Weaver's four books, which all preceded *Moneyball,* (1972's *Winning!,* 1982's *It's What You Learn After You Know It All That Counts,* 1984's *Weaver on Strategy: A Guide for Armchair Managers by Baseball's Master Tactician,* and 1996's *Together We Were Eleven*) describe *Moneyball* tactics (without using the term) up to 30 years before Michael Lewis started to write about the Oakland A's.

Weaver's teams won six Eastern Davison titles, four American League Championships, and one World Series over his 17-year Major League career. But evidently not enough of the sport's competing management ever bothered to read and adopt Weaver's approach. He suggested, just as *Moneyball* does, that:

❖ the sacrifice bunt should be used only sparingly because it gives up a precious out;

❖ stealing bases is usually a loser, unless the runner has a greater than 75% chance of success (*Moneyball* and Sabermetrics tend to use the figure 70%);

❖ getting to first base with a walk is almost as valuable as a single; and

❖ the homerun has more value than most baseball management realized.

WEST COAST OFFENSE

Bill Walsh first implemented an early version of what would become known as the West Coast Offense in 1968, while an assistant coach with the Cincinnati (a famous West Coast city) Bengals. Walsh didn't have much talent on the Bengals, a team in their third year as a franchise. He was looking for a way to get the most from his quarterback Vince Carter, an accurate short thrower who lacked enough arm strength for the long bomb.

Out of necessity, Walsh knew that he had to reinvent his offense if his team was to have any chance of winning with the players that he had. His strategy was based on spreading his offense horizontally, and then using short, high-percentage timed passes. He passed first and occasionally ran the ball, rather than the conventional approach of running first and passing only occasionally (Think in Opposites).

When Walsh became the head coach of the San Francisco 49ers in 1979, the team was coming off a season with the worst record in the League. He continued to refine his offense. Two years after the 49ers' dismal 2-14 season, and with the lowest payroll in the NFL, his team won the Super Bowl. He was wildly successful (three Super Bowl championships, and elected to the Professional Football Hall of Fame), and this resulted in other teams copying his offense.

Many of Bill Walsh's assistant coaches ended up as NFL head coaches. Soon, his "secret sauce" wasn't secret at all. Walsh had eight assistant coaches (including Mike Holmgren, Ray Rhodes, and Dennis Green), as well as at least 20 assistants to assistants (from Andy Reid to Mike Shanahan and Tony Dungy) who went on to become NFL head coaches. The nature of the business made it impossible to protect the innovations of the man who the sporting press called "The Genius."

*****

There is, of course, a tension between the principles Don't Jump the Gun and Striking While the Iron is Hot. Not jumping the gun means anticipating but not acting on the reversal of a long-term trend before you have evidence that it has actually started to turn. If you jump the gun by a couple of years, you may be out of ammo when the opportunity is ripe.

"Strike While the Iron is Hot" applies best when you have tried something that actually works. You have a competitive advantage—for now. Don't waste your lead by bragging about it. Instead, step on the pedal, and take maximum advantage for as long as it lasts.

DON'T PICK UP DIMES IN FRONT OF STEAMROLLERS

For years, Enron completed several project financings, representing billions of dollars, for energy projects around the world. This was a positive development and, when all went well, resulted in a stronger corporate balance sheet. Unfortunately, a little-known provision in many of the financing documents held that, if Enron Corp's credit rating ever dropped below investment grade, the loan immediately came due. I am sure that we got a slightly better interest rate for giving this "protection" to lenders. But when Enron's credit rating was downgraded on November 28, 2001, the company was obliterated. I doubt that the provision helped the lenders either, as it guaranteed the company's bankruptcy.

Problematically, this pricing system also distorted our perceived cost of borrowing. Most of the company's executives thought that Enron's borrowing costs were lower than they actually were, because these financings had picked up a few dimes along the way.

In a related factor, Enron consistently discounted its trading positions at the Libor curve (the London Interbank Offered Rate), the rate at which banks normally lend to one another. But Enron was only BBB+ and didn't have the de facto government guarantees that serve to keep borrowing costs lower for banks than for most nonbanks. At the time, I never even gave this disparity a moment's thought, but in hindsight, it dramatically distorted our cash management practices. It favored positions where we put out cash early and received it later, rather than the other way around.

"Don't Pick up Dimes in front of Steamrollers" is a long-held trading maxim that refers to a practice of consistently collecting a small and regular profit for taking on a risk that can eventually crush you. It's especially dangerous if you are oblivious to the chance that the steamroller is right around the corner. The steamroller can be a black swan, or it can be a calamity that everyone knows is going to happen sooner or later, but hasn't recently occurred.

The dimes that you collect can lull you into having more confidence than is warranted. The longer the dimes keep coming, the more that overconfidence builds.

Those who don't know what they're doing (but think they do) could sell "far out of the money" options (i.e. selling an option for two years to buy AAPL for $1,000), or write credit default swaps on Stockton municipal debt for small gains, or sell California earthquake insurance, consistently booking profits until they have a really bad day. These long-shot risks might make sense to Champs from time to time, if they're getting paid enough dimes to justify the risk. But, by the very nature of the small sample size of experiences, Chumps might be in a danger zone without even knowing it.

*****

Increasing your leverage via excess debt and contingent liabilities is another violation of the principle (Beware of Idiotic Leverage). It may improve your financial results today, but put you at the mercy of uncontrollable Life Happens events tomorrow.

Canceling your insurance policies will improve your short-term cash flow and profits, but if you cannot survive the loss of your car or office building, you're bringing the steamroller into play. If you can afford the downside of losing your car or your home, that's a different story, and falls under a different principle (Play the Odds). I'll bet that Warren Buffett self-insures his buildings against fires and theft because for him, these are minor threats.

One challenge in reviewing the performance of any company or trading system is to understand the "steamroller exposure." By simply looking at the returns over a short time, one can miss the fact that easy dimes came at the expense of a looming risk. Only by digging into the details (usually difficult for an outsider) can you make that assessment.

Investment advisors were comparing government bonds at 2012's low interest rates (end of July) as akin to picking up dimes in front of a steamroller. As of mid-2013, it turned out that they were right. (Hindsight brings such clarity.) Although, many of these same advisors were saying the same thing in the preceding two years and not only missed dimes but substantial gains. Thinking that 30-year Treasury yields would drop all the way down to 2% from 2.7%, however, still gave you the chance to make an additional 20% on your money—not exactly dimes (as of this writing, they are back up to about 3.75% and the momentum is higher). On the other hand, buying a stock that has an annual dividend of 2% (compared to earning .01% on a Fidelity money market account) is close to picking up dimes (if that is the logic for the purchase). You might, in fact, earn the 2%, but if the stock declines in value by 20% during the next year, you have taken it on the chin.

To a private lender, offering small-business loans can be similar to picking up dimes. If you make five successful $10,000 one-year loans at 15% annual interest and things go well, you will have made $7,500 in interest. If the sixth borrower stiffs you...you just had an up-close and personal steamroller encounter.

A common tactic used by some in no-limit Texas Hold 'em poker is to wait until there are a few chips in the pot, and then go "all in." A player might bet $5,000 for the chance to pick up $200 in the pot. It can work several times in a row—until it doesn't. Then the culprit finds that someone is sitting back quietly, (pleased as punch but looking quite stoic), holding a pair of aces. Unless he gets lucky, the all-in bettor is usually busted.

A betting system that typifies "picking up dimes" is the Martingale strategy that originated in France in the 18th century. Players make a bet that has close to a 50% chance of winning (for example, if you play the pass line in craps, you will lose on average 1.41% on every dollar bet). Under the Martingale system, after each loss, you increase the size of your next bet enough to make up for your cumulative losses. When you win, you reduce the size of your wager to the original small bet. Losing several times in a row would require larger and larger bets, until one of two bad things happens: a) the player runs out of money to bet; or b) the casino or regulator limits the amount that can be bet to an amount smaller than that needed to get even.

It is not unusual to hear an undisciplined trader boast: "We are going to double up and make all the money back." So, unfortunately, the Martingale strategy is not confined to casinos.

This system frequently wins, providing plenty of warm, fuzzy feelings—until it loses huge amounts and usually all your money. "Traders" who resort to this system tend to end up in other lines of work before long.

DON'T RUN OUT OF CASH

"Dear Lord, help me to break even. I need the money."
—Author Unknown

In his book *IWoz,* Steve Wozniak tells the story about Apple's first order for the Apple I computer. It came from Paul Terrell, who had opened one of the country's first personal computer stores, The Byte Shop, in Mountain View, California.

Terrell gave Apple their first order for 50 computers. The question was, how would Apple pay for the parts to make the computers? First, Woz's friends loaned him $1,200. Then, they found a chip distributor, Cramer Electronics, who, after confirming the order with Terrell, would give them 30 days' credit. The credit worked out, with Terrell agreeing to pay cash on delivery for the computers, which meant that they could pay Cramer Electronics on time.

But it was a bit more complicated than that, according to Woz: "The distributor gave us the parts, which went into a sealed closet at the Santa Clara company that was manufacturing the boards. On the day that they were ready for them, the parts came out of the closet, were accounted for and soldered on, and then we had thirty days to pay."

This is the kind of hustle and support that entrepreneurs need every bit as much today as Steve Jobs and Steve Wozniak required, back in 1975. An entrepreneur lives or dies by having enough cash and liquidity. It is the oxygen of business. And guess what? This applies to big businesses big as well as small.

This is a warning to the poker player, trader, investor, or anyone starting or running a business: no cash, no business. When we talk later about taking chances, always start and finish with this principle. There may be a great bet or opportunity out there, but you need to consider whether you have enough cash to play the game and to withstand the worst-case scenario. If you take a risk and lose it all, how will you keep on keeping on?

The concept is described as "risk of ruin" in gambling and finance vernacular. To avoid running out of cash, you must play "the game" so that you minimize (there is no 100% certain antidote) the chance of losing it all.

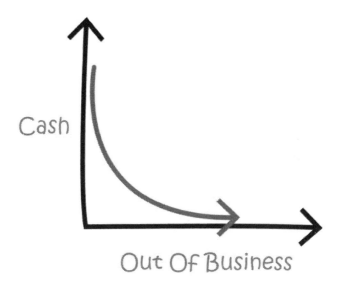

This starts with being cheap and never, ever wasting money. Live frugally and keep enough money in the bank to get you to the point where your business is generating cash. You can produce cash in lots of ways (working a side job, customer advances, or family loans)—but if you can't get lean enough to pay your car insurance, rent, food, and cell phone, as well as the cost of doing business, you are doomed.

To play within these boundaries, you must choose a game in which you can afford setbacks, and not enter a game that you cannot afford to lose. For example, if you're the best poker player in the world but only have starting capital of $500, you don't have enough to play in a game where players routinely win or lose $2,500. Champs know that, to make $10,000, they may very well first lose $2,500. Unless you get lucky early, you will not have a big enough sample size to allow your probabilistic advantage to pay dividends. You have too great a chance of going bust.

To keep the dream alive, an entrepreneur has to be realistic about incoming cash. When anticipating payments, optimistic entrepreneurs frequently count on the average (sometimes even the best) case and don't plan for the "real world." They have made an agreement with a customer for payment within 30 days; the customer might pay 10 days late. Then the bank doesn't credit their account for another 10 days until after the check clears. Sluggish and uneven cash flow is the norm, not the exception.

Despite the myth of the entrepreneur or trader winning an all-or-nothing wager, an all-in bet violates the principle of not running out of cash. Can you get away with it? Sometimes. The younger you are, the more sensible it is to bet it all. (You may be so poor, there is no alternative.) If you have laid aside enough money to get you to your next gig if you fail, you are taking a bet that is close to all or nothing. Just out of college, even Warren Buffet had two-thirds of his net worth in a single stock (Geico).

Mark Cuban is the owner of the Dallas Mavericks and an entrepreneur who developed Broadcast.com with his partner, Todd Wagner. At the peak of the dot-com bubble, they sold the company to Yahoo for $5.9 billion in Yahoo stock. In his blog and book, Cuban talks about an advantage that entrepreneurs have—they only have to succeed once. Unlike an NFL quarterback or an investor, you can fail many times. But you have to have a means to get back on your feet (to reset), and not be homeless if your new business goes bust. It is very tough to get restarted from the payphone at the homeless shelter.

The thing that takes down most new ventures (and a few older ones) is simply a lack of cash. You need to pay great attention to cash flow, and be reasonable about your assumptions. "Hope" is a four letter word that the Urban Dictionary defines as "mankind's greatest weakness and greatest strength." Hope kills a lot of promising businesses because life happens, customers pay late, and suppliers want to be paid up front.

Going bust is the ultimate dream killer. **If you go bust, you lose your ability to evolve, to learn, to win, and to apply your skill set.** All the hope in the world can't turn that equation around.

CREDIT AND THE ENTREPENEUR

As a kid, my parents took me to Shakey's Pizza Parlor, a West Coast franchise. They had humorous signs on the walls, and the sign that I still remember said: "We made a deal with the bank—they wouldn't make pizzas and we wouldn't cash checks."

If only it was still so simple. It would be great if you could stick to making pizza, and leave the credit business to the banks. Starting with that assumption takes down many a new venture.

If your suppliers grant you 180 days to pay your bills and your customers prepay, cash flow is a breeze. Guess what? It usually works in reverse. Your customers want to pay you in 180 days, and your big, established suppliers want to be prepaid when you place an order, because you're a start-up with no credit history and a small balance sheet.

Today's small business can't succeed by simply focusing on a product or service without facing the realities of obtaining credit (especially from suppliers) and granting trade credit to customers.

For many start-ups, handling cash flow is the key to getting the company on a solid footing.

This part of the business plan is often ignored by new entrepreneurs, until it is too late.

Here's a paradox: the bigger your customer, the slower they pay. Their Accounts Payable Department is run by accountants, and it is "safer" for them to pay slowly than to pay fast. It is also less work, because they don't have to make as many adjustments. The irony is, this destroys overall value. The big company is going to make perhaps 1% per year on the funds they pay later (as of 2013), but the cost to the entrepreneur for getting paid late might be as much as 20% per year (on a credit card). So, in this typical example, for every month that the big company pays the small company late, the total lost value is (20% - 1%) / 12 months = 1.58%.

Sometimes, the slow pay can cost the entrepreneur far more than 1.58% per month; for example, in instances when the small-business owner simply does not have enough cash to fill an order. This entrepreneur works her butt off to make a sale to a new customer, and then can't fill the new order because her suppliers want the money up front and she doesn't have it.

Cash flow problems are a sad story, but that doesn't mean that anyone will cut you any slack. I have had a variation of the following conversation with several entrepreneurs:

Entrepreneur: I have a fantastic new product called the Whizblast, with patents granted by the US Patent and Trademark Office. We had great interest in our product at the last trade show, and I just got my first order for 100 units. The $100,000 order is only going to cost me $75,000 to have manufactured in China and shipped to my customer.

Me: Great—so what's the problem? (knowing full well what I'm about to hear...).

Entrepreneur: I don't have the $75,000 to pay my supplier to manufacture and ship them. I need a loan to fill the order.

Me: So, who's going to lend you the money? (I can see what's coming next a mile away.)

Entrepreneur: Well, how about you?

Me: Hell No! (Unless you're a close friend or blood relation—and even then, the answer is probably, no.) Do you have any friends or family who will loan you the money?

Entrepreneur: No, they're just as broke as I am.

Me: So, how are you going to fill your first order?

Entrepreneur: Well, that's what I was hoping you could tell me. I keep hearing advertisements for factoring and invoice financing for small businesses, and I was hoping they would lend me the money.

Me: Are you kidding? Even though they help small businesses, they never provide finance for first-time orders with businesses that have no track record. You're addressing this problem too late in the game. This should have been a critical part of your pre-startup business planning. You never gave this any thought, and now you're toast.

And the poor guy crawls away. These newbies don't need me: they need to stop and press "Reset." Let's think about it: What are some creative ways to get the necessary credit?

If you find yourself in this situation, go to the company that wants to buy from you, and also to your suppliers, and see how you can massage the cash flow of the business. Can you pay later? Can you get paid earlier? Can you pay your supplier only half when the order is placed and the other half 90 days after you receive the product? Can your buyer pay half of the order price when he places the order, and is he willing to pay the remainder 10 days after receipt via wire transfer? Can your buyer wire you the funds on the day of the delivery, and will your suppliers give you additional time if you pay by wire transfer (so they don't have to wait for your check to clear)?

As a small business with a tiny balance sheet, your bank will put a long hold on your deposited checks at exactly the time you need immediate access to the cash.

 Be humble and don't try to pretend that cash flow is not a challenge. Look at this problem from a hundred different angles. If you can't solve it, you're dead in the water. Even if you have to sell your Whizblasts to the customer for a lower price, or buy the materials at a slightly higher price, you need to make sure that you can get through the cycle without running out of cash.

THE COUNTERINTUITIVE CREDIT GAME

To get established, the entrepreneur may need to start slower, with smaller customers. The adage about getting credit from the "big players" is that sometimes their pockets are deep, but their arms are short. Smaller customers know the challenges of new company cash flow, and they're used to paying at least partially up front. When Mark Cuban started MicroSolutions, he received a $500 advance from his first customer.

Too many entrepreneurs start selling to Walmart and Home Depot before they have anything near the capital required. Cuban says, "It's OK to start slow. It's OK to grow slow."

Remember: This discussion only covers bankrolling the first order. It doesn't reflect many of the other start-up and development costs, or filling the second and third orders.

For example, an entrepreneur needs $75,000 to generate revenue of $100,000 and a profit of $25,000, assuming that nothing goes wrong and the entrepreneur is doing all the other work. What if you get a *second* order for another 100 Whizblasts before collecting on the first order? Now, instead of needing $75,000 to get the company started, you need $150,000.

And what happens if your hustle pays off and you get a *third* order for 100 more Whizblasts before receiving payment for the first? Now you need $225,000 of up-front capital to get the job done. This is exactly the "success" you were hoping for. If you have a product that nobody wants—then you're going to fail anyway, and this discussion is moot.

Amazon Lending to Partners. In September 2012, word got out that Amazon had quietly started a lending program for their third-party vendors (those that fill orders on the Amazon platform and ship directly to the Amazon customer). In 2011, these suppliers represented about 40% of Amazon's total sales of $48 billion. Amazon usually charges a commission of 6-15% of the gross as a servicing fee. The higher the volume, the bigger Amazon's profits. Amazon already has an incentive to find ways to increase this third-party business—and many of their suppliers are constrained by cash, as small businesses usually can't simply go to the bank and get another loan. Amazon created a subsidiary, Amazon Capital Services Inc., to manage their lending business.

I know from first-hand experience that Amazon will find incredible red tape in the myriad state lending laws across the country. But they can manage that bureaucracy because of their size. However, if they had asked me, instead of offering outright loans, I would have instituted a program for approved suppliers in which Amazon paid them earlier via wire transfer, and deducted an agreed-to discount. This would have gotten the cash to their partners faster while still bringing in a tidy profit. But traditional finance/lending/accounting people don't think this way. My approach would have avoided the need for new state licenses and other legal hassles. And it wouldn't have been subject to nearly the same credit evaluation system, since the product would have already been delivered.

Other smaller parties—such as Kabbage, which extends cash advances to sellers on Amazon, Yahoo, and Ebay—were already lending to Amazon's partners. Although Kabbage stated: "We're flattered that Amazon is building a business model on ours," this new Amazon service is probably *not* good news for Kabbage. Bluffing is not confined to the poker game. They don't have access to the contact details of Amazon's suppliers, hence their cost of sales and credit evaluation might be substantially higher. On the other hand, they do have a system that is agnostic to the sales platform, so a retailer on several different online markets might find the Kabbage system more convenient.

Elance. I am a big fan of Elance.com for a number of reasons. They are a global online independent contractor platform that allows users to request bids, and work with entrepreneurial suppliers from all over the world. I have procured artwork, editing, research, video production, and even legal services through them.

Elance has a major advantage in managing cash flow and credit risk for entrepreneurs. If I post a job for legal research and accept one of the bids, I am normally required to put the funds in an Elance escrow account up front, before the work starts. After the work is done and I have accepted it, I release the escrow funds to the service provider. So, in addition to being a great networking platform, Elance has provided a couple of features that help the service provider get the cash earlier and manage credit risk: 1) the funds are already on deposit, so there is little doubt that, if the work is completed, the entrepreneur will get paid (a dispute process settles the matter, if buyer and service provider disagree over the quality of the work); and 2) once the work is done and accepted, there is no incentive for the buyer to mess around and delay paying, since the amount has already been charged to his credit card when the funds were originally placed in escrow.

When the funds have been released to the service provider, that contractor can either have a check sent via the US mail, get paid via PayPal, or receive a direct bank deposit. If the supplier is in a crunch; he can pay Elance an expedited wire transfer fee (in addition to his own bank) to get the funds transferred and available in his own checking account on the same business day.

Elance charges the service provider an 8.75% fee for jobs of up to $10,000, and 6.75% for jobs bigger than that. It also charges a wire transfer fee after the first wire transfer of the month. It beats the hell out of getting stiffed by a customer. And, if cash is low, having the funds available today rather than after 10 to14 days might mean keeping the lights on.

BIG COMPANY CASH FLOW

You may have read about Enron's huge bankruptcy in late 2001. Well, I was there to experience it firsthand.

There are plenty of explanations for why Enron went under, but I will tell you, the final blow was that we simply ran out of cash. Enron was using huge amounts of short-term credit via commercial paper, and even larger amounts of trade credit extended by our suppliers when we purchased a commodity. (We still weren't leveraged anywhere nearly as aggressively as investment banks were in 2008.) Our options to use commercial paper (short-term unsecured promissory notes) disappeared first. But I have heard little discussion about our reliance on trade credit.

Enron was trading in commodity markets all over the world. In a typical physical trading market (as opposed to futures exchanges and derivatives), this is how the cash worked on the transactions: For US natural gas, in September we would deliver $1.21 million of physical natural gas to a buyer. That company would pay us via wire transfer on October 23. We would simultaneously purchase $1.2 million of physical natural gas. If everything went smoothly, we would earn $10,000 (gross) during the month on these two transactions.

Notice that we were granting our September buyer "trade credit" of $1.21 million, and we were receiving $1.2 of trade credit from our supplier. As long as we got paid on or before the day we paid our supplier, we had enough cash.

But we were doing a massive amount of business. In September 2001, Enron had global revenues of about $17 billion—more than ExxonMobil. So, when Enron's credit quality came into question (we were BBB+ at the beginning of that month), many of our suppliers declined to sell us gas in September and accept payment on October 23. They wanted to get paid upfront on September 1. The problem was that we were not going to get paid by our customers until Oct. 23.

I don't know exactly how many suppliers suddenly demanded up-front payment, but it soon became a daily occurrence for Enron Europe. If we assume that one-fifth of Enron's suppliers now wanted up-front payment, we needed roughly $6 billion in additional cash ($17 billion * 1/5 * (23 days + 30 days)). That was $6 billion in cash that no one would lend us. Game over.

*****

Exceptions to this rule (Don't Run Out of Cash) seems to have been big US banks, and the insurance giant AIG. After making huge concentrated bets that went bad (i.e. the 2008 US banking crisis), they were bailed out by the US government.

This rule also applies to governments. If a country finds itself short of cash, unable to borrow, and controlling its own currency, it can simply print more money (at the risk of eventually creating inflation). As I write this, though, we are seeing the challenges faced by Eurozone countries running out of cash (Greece, Spain, Italy, Crete, Slovenia, and Portugal) with no ability to print more. It's a mess.

Some have come roaring back from bankruptcy, including Henry Ford, Walt Disney, and P.T. Barnum. But the investors who backed them on the first go-round typically lost every penny.

There are plenty of ways to run out of cash. The most common route for entrepreneurs is not having enough to begin with. Even when you start with enough (a rarity indeed), your suppliers will still want to get paid early, and your customers will still want to pay late. Do whatever it takes ethically to stay solvent.

AVOID GAMBLER'S RUIN

"My ventures are not in one bottom trusted,
Nor to one place; nor is my whole estate
Upon the fortune of this present year;
Therefore, my merchandise makes me not sad."

—Antonio, *The Merchant of Venice*,
William Shakespeare

Managing the size of your bets is summarized in a concept called "Gambler's Ruin."

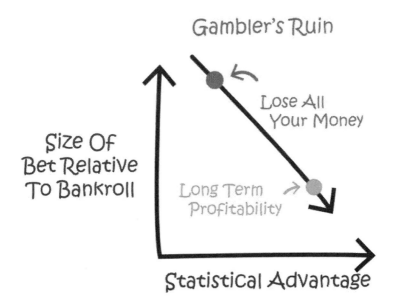

Expressed in several forms and variations, Gambler's Ruin has three major themes:

1) If you consistently bet when the odds are against you, you will eventually lose all your money, whether or not you hit an early lucky streak.

2) If you have an even bet (50% chance of winning and a 50% chance of losing), and you keep making bigger bets when you win and don't make smaller bets when you lose, you will eventually lose all your money.

3) If you have a statistical advantage and consistently bet too much relative to your advantage, you will also lose all of your money. The most basic example is when you go "all in" on a single bet. Putting all your money on the line with an 80%/20% advantage still gives you a 20% chance of losing it all after just one bet.

What if you have a 60%/40% advantage and repeatedly let it all ride on five independent (uncorrelated) bets in a row? In this instance, you have a 92.2% chance of losing all your money before you have completed those five bets. On the other hand, if you get lucky enough to win all-in five times in a row, your bankroll is now worth 32 times as much and the financial media will understand your "genius."

In my lawsuit business, Job One is avoiding Gambler's Ruin. Naturally, the more I like a case, the more money I want to invest in it—to a point. There is no way that I will invest so much in a single case that a single "Life Happens" event would cripple me.

KELLY CRITERION

One formula that helps avoid Gambler's Ruin, while betting the optimum amount, is the Kelly Criterion, first described in 1956 by J.L. Kelly. It is used by some traders and professional gamblers, and I consider it when deciding the right amount to bet on any single lawsuit.

This formula, unlike any of mine, comes complete with a mathematical proof, conveying the optimal betting decision to a trader, gambler, or investor. This is based on the probability of winning the bet and the winning payoff amount. The formula assumes no ties.

The formula is:

Kelly Criterion

f = fraction of current bankroll to bet

b = net odds: you could win $b (plus $1 bet) for a $1 bet

p = probability of winning

$$f = \frac{bp - (1-p)}{b}$$

Let's review an example with a chance to bet $1, and a chance to collect $2 on a winning bet, ($1 original bet plus the $1 profit [the variable labeled "b" in the formula]). I call this a "2X" bet.

Kelly Criterion Example

$b = \$1$ (to win a total of $2 for a $1 bet)

$p = 60\%$

$$f = \frac{1 \times 60\% - (1-60\%)}{1} = 20\%$$

Here, you have a 60% probability of doubling your money. The Kelly Criterion says that you should bet 20% of your bankroll (or your entire net worth, if your net worth is all in the form of cash).

This formula demonstrates quite logically that:

1) For a 2X bet you should *only* bet if the probability of winning is above 50%. In fact, if the probability is below 50%, you should try to find a way to take the other side of the bet or trade (go short).
2) At a 51% probability of winning, Kelly suggests that you should bet 2% of your bankroll.
3) At an 80% probability of winning, Kelly suggests that you should bet 60% of your bankroll.

Lucky And Good

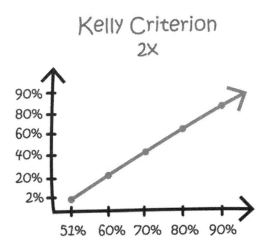

Kelly's original paper made the point that the criterion is only valid when a large series of bets are made. Even though the formula says that one should bet 98% of your bankroll when you have a 99% chance of winning a 2X bet, that still leaves you with a 1% chance of going broke—too high for me, at this stage in my life.

Although I am comfortable taking risks and making substantial bets, the Kelly Formula *feels* more aggressive than my inner voice approves. Obviously, for a lawsuit investment, I have to adjust the formula based on the probabilistic estimate of when the bet will pay off, and then adjust it based on my assumed discount rate (the amount that reflects the discount for getting paid later). And a minor detail is that I never know the *exact* odds. But even if I did know the exact odds, and expected an immediate payoff, I can't conceive of putting 60% of my net worth on the line, even if I had a marvelous 80% probability of winning. So maybe I need to take my own advice and get a little specialized psychotherapy—so I can de-wussify, and get on board with making bigger bets.

As an alternative to getting psychotherapy, when I have trouble "manning-up" to make a big enough bet, I remind myself of my poker-playing friend Luther's quote: **"The less I bet, the more I lose when I win."**

ALL-IN

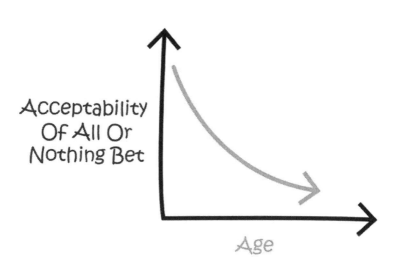

Many successful entrepreneurs, traders, and investors take measured and intelligent risks, while trying to avoid at almost any cost the all-or-nothing bet. This is, after all, the ultimate hazard of Gambler's Ruin. But the younger you are, the less reckless it is to violate this principle because you have, on average, a smaller bankroll and more time to recover, if you lose it all.

If you are poor, you are likely to have no alternative to the all-in bet. This is why I encourage young people to get started on their entrepreneurial ventures sooner rather than later. You have to love it when a 14-year-old puts every last dollar he owns into a lawn mower to start his landscaping business—so long as he keeps enough capital to fill up the gas tank.

AND THE SURVEY SAYS...

I wanted to know how my friends and family would answer questions related to the Kelly Criterion. I asked them to complete the following survey on SurveyMonkey.com:

> **I have three questions regarding the level of risk you would take, with your own assets, under three different conditions. This involves the amount of money you would wager in each circumstance.**

The premise is, you are playing an absolutely fair, honest, and random game, similar to picking a chip out of a hat. Some of the chips say "win," and the rest say "you lose." If you win, you double the amount wagered; a loss means, you lose the amount of the bet.

You know in advance exactly your chances of winning. In every case, you are 30 years old. (Please try to adjust your thinking to how you would have played or will play this game at this age.) You have a bankroll of $100,000 which is the entirety of the assets that you have in this world, and is all you have to work with. You have no home, no IRA, no retirement, no job. This contest is always in your favor, sometimes more than others. The three conditions we will consider are 60%, 75%, and 90%. In other words, you have a 60%, 75%, or 90% chance of doubling the money you bet. Another way of looking at it is that you have a 40%, 25%, or 10% chance of losing your bet.

Under each of these conditions, what percentage of your bankroll would you bet? (The choices are between 0% and 100%, in 10% increments.) Let's go.

Question 1) At a 60% probability of winning, what percentage of your bankroll would you bet?

Question 2) At a 75% probability of winning, what percentage of your bankroll would you bet?

Question 3) At a 90% probability of winning, what percentage of your bankroll would you bet?

THE ENVELOPE PLEASE...

❖ I asked everyone to imagine that they were 30 years old, with a $100,000 cash bankroll, constituting their entire net worth. I wanted to minimize the age bias; as people get older, they generally shy away from bigger risks. The questions were intentionally silent about the number of children and other "big responsibilities" the participant had. The survey was also intentionally mute about the prospects of the participant landing a job, in the event she lost everything.

- Sometimes, when people consider an *imagined* scenario, what they **say** they will do differs from what they will ***actually do***, when the rubber meets the road. In this case, if I had about $5-10 million dollars that I was willing to invest in a real live experiment, I am sure I could have found 50 30-year-olds willing to take the test with real money. But it was not quite that important to me. I also suspect that people, on average, are more aggressive when facing a conceptual question rather than a real life choice.

- For each of these questions, the Kelly Criterion calculates the optimum answer (based on one in a long series of bets). If you know exactly your probability of winning and the exact amount of the payoff, "Kelly" calculates the optimum bet. Theoretically, if you always bet this amount, after many bets, you have the greatest chance of ending up with the biggest bankroll.

- If you bet less than the Kelly amount, you are "risk averse," to your detriment. Bets larger than the recommended size require too much risk; also detrimental, on average, in the long run. If you bet zero, when Kelly says you have a 90% chance of doubling your bet, you are "ultra-risk-averse." If you won't take this bet for at least some of your bankroll, you are going to miss most of life's great opportunities. If you bet 100% of your stack, you are going "all-in," at risk of going bust.

- The survey results surprised me, in that my friends and family were more willing to take risk than I had expected. Maybe I hang around some "weird" folks.

- The survey results do, however, reflect the "Wisdom of Crowds." While the responses varied greatly, each question's average results were reasonably close to the Kelly Criterion—however, some participants were very risk averse, and others quite willing to lay it all on the line. I "declare" the aggregate results rational, although I might be saying this because my answers were close to the average.

- ❖ On average, as the bet approached "all-in" or 100% of one's bankroll, responses became more conservative, relative to the Kelly Criterion. This is reasonable, because the questions, as framed, never promised that the participant was going to have the chance to make the same bet thousands of times.
- ❖ The third question brought the biggest swings. Three respondents said they would not bet a penny (even with a 90% chance of doubling their money), and four would bet their entire bankroll. Slightly different risk tolerances.

Probability of Win	60%	75%	90%	Total
Kelly Criterion Percentage	20%	50%	80%	
Survey Average Amount Bet	25.8%	39.26%	59.26%	
# of Risk Averse (bet less than Kelly Criterion)	28	49	56	133
# @ Kelly Percentage	15	14	9	38
# Greater than Kelly Percentage (bet more than Kelly Criterion)	38	18	16	72

FIND FREE OPTIONS

"The best things in life are free."
—American Proverb

Before the 2012 season, the Oakland A's signed designated hitter Manny Ramirez, giving Oakland the chance—without the financial obligation—to add a big hitter to their roster at a very low salary.

Go For It

While Oakland clearly hoped that Manny would get his hitting mojo back, critics worried that the deal made GM Billy Beane "look desperate" because Ramirez, who would turn 40 that year, was clearly a long-shot to contribute.

The detractors just didn't understand the value of free options. *Sports Illustrated's* Ann Killion lambasted the deal: "The Oakland A's are the clown car of baseball, a small-market team crammed with weird ideas. Just when you think they've all emerged, another one pops out. This week's floppy-shoed, red-nosed development is Manny Ramirez, an almost 40-year-old, two-time drug violator whose last good year was in 2008."

The A's signed Ramirez, number 14 on the all-time Major League home run list, to a one-year $500,000 deal. But the $500,000 would only be paid if Ramirez actually played for the A's. Ramirez ended up having mediocre results during the pre-season, instead starting the regular season for the A's Minor League team. The club never exercised its option to promote him to the Majors, and eventually released him.

The Ramirez free option was clearly for a volatile talent at a low strike price ($500,000 per year)—which sounds great to aspiring athletes, but is very inexpensive for a proven designated hitter in Major League Baseball.

Having plenty of low- or no-cost long shots pays off when one or more of them works. This free option didn't pay off (as most don't), but that doesn't mean that you should stop gathering them. It was an excellent *Moneyball* move by Billy Beane, despite what the idiot reporter in the clown suit reported.

*****

Here's how free options work: The market for next month's San Juan Basin natural gas is $5.00 per MMBTU. But a producer wants to sell it to you for $5.01. So you ask very simply, "Can you hold that price for me for the next hour?" If the answer is "yes," the producer is giving you a free option.

Virtually any free option has value, especially in a nonlinear world with exponential dynamics, sudden changes, and Life

Happens events. So it's great to receive them, and a poor idea to give them away!

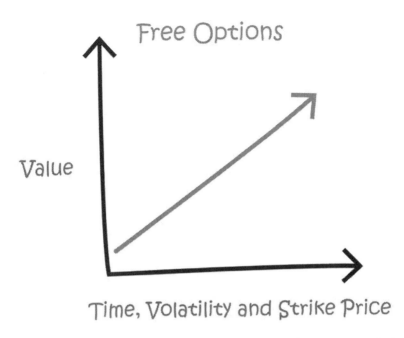

The value of the free option (like those you have to pay for) is a function of a few variables. While Taleb criticizes the accuracy and assumptions of conventional option pricing, please note, I am not trying to convey an exact formula nor adherence to a dataset that fits the bell curve. Nevertheless, the major levers in the value of an option are:

Time. The longer the option extends, the more valuable it is. (The value of time probably increases disproportionately the more of it you have, because the amount of change in the world seems to be accelerating.)

Volatility. An option such as a rental agreement with an option to buy at a fixed price—is more valuable in a fluctuating market than it is in a flat one. Interestingly, and ironically, the more stable the price has recently been, the more likely that the world will assume an extension of the current trend, and give you a free (or inexpensively priced) option. It's dangerous for the giver, but great for the receiver.

Remember, it's the future, not historic volatility that determines the value of an option.

Certainty of the Bargain. Will the other side honor the deal? You would rather get a free option in a written contract (in exchange for some minor consideration, a requirement for a binding contract) from a creditworthy counterpart. However, you might not get the free option in writing, and the giver of the free option might not have AAA credit quality today, or, more critically, when you want to exercise your option. (Think AIG.)

Usually free options are doled out because the giver simply undervalues them, or would be so pleased with the option being exercised (as he views the world when he offers them) that he's willing to give up some potential value. When he gives the free option, he's thinking that he would be quite satisfied with that price and that he would be greedy asking for more. Beware, though: Getting a free option from someone unlikely to honor the commitment has little value.

Strike Price. If you're buying, the lower the price at which you can buy (the strike price), the greater the value of the option. If you're selling, the higher the price at which you can sell, the greater the value. If I get a free option to buy San Juan natural gas next month for $5.00 per MMBTU when that is the current market price, then I'm getting a heck of a deal. If the free option is for $10.00 per MMBTU while today's price is $5.00, then the free option is a very long putt. Always remember that you can get a free option to buy or a free option to sell.

The art of getting free options is a critical skill for an entrepreneur trying to bootstrap a business. Her conversation might follow like this: "I have a great movie script. If I can get Tom Cruise to play the lead role, will you finance the movie for $100 million?" Or "I have a great movie script, Mr. Cruise. If I get Steven Spielberg to produce it, will you play the lead?"

RECOGNIZE FREE OPTIONS

Don't wait for free options to fall in your lap. Keep your eyes open, so that you'll know them when you see them, and ask for them if they're not offered first.

Reservations. Reservations in the restaurant, car rental, and hotel business have historically involved free options. I make a reservation for three nights at a hotel for $149 per night and, as long as I cancel within 48 hours, I have the right—but not the obligation—to use that reservation at that price. Restaurants normally don't even require a credit card in order to secure a reservation.

Priceline.com was the first to break apart this value proposition of free options for hotels and car reservations. I can use their system to reserve a midsize car from Avis without cancellation or a no-show penalty (perhaps for $75 a day). Alternatively, I can use their auction process, "Name Your Own Price," and bid for a midsize car, and then maybe get a reservation for $60 per day. But in the latter case, I must prepay for reservations, cancellations are not allowed, and if I don't show up, the rental company won't have any incremental wear and tear on the vehicle.

Apple Computer Shares. In his book *IWoz*, Steve Wozniak, the co-founder of Apple Computer, describes how, in the early years of Apple (prior to it being publicly traded), an English venture capitalist called him up and offered to buy some of Wozniak's stock at the current price. Woz said yes, but the Brit didn't follow through.

Then the guy called Woz back at a "slightly later date" and again asked him if he would still sell him the Apple stock at the same price. By then, the market price had risen 10 fold above the price they had discussed. The guy told Woz, "You promised to sell me some at this price. Will you?" Woz actually honored the deal and later lamented, "So I kept my word, and the English guy made a ton of money."

Woz had given a free option. And a very poorly defined one at that. If the value of Apple shares had dropped, he never would have heard from the investor again. Woz didn't put any conditions (like a time limit) on the free option, and it cost him. I am not suggesting that you take advantage of people like this venture capital guy did, but never forget the lesson.

Real Estate. Some industries are built on free options. The real estate business comes to mind. Typically, once a contract for sale of a property is signed, the buyer has a couple of weeks to inspect the property, secure a mortgage, and sometimes even close on the sale of the buyer's existing home. I once put an offer on a house with the contingency that it was subject to the approval of my mother (an obvious free option and a decision I never discussed with her).

It would be hard to turn around the free option business practice in this industry, because of collective ingrained habits, but don't give away any more than you have to.

Market Makers. In the principle Think in Opposites, I discussed how Enron had done very well by operating as a market maker. One downside to this model was that, by offering both competitive buy and sell prices, we were always giving free options to the rest of the market—although we never promised that a price was good for even a few seconds into the future. The price was what it was *now*, and if you wanted that price, then you had to take it *now*. In exchange for this service, every time a transaction was completed, we knew who had bought from us or sold to us, so we were gaining an information advantage in exchange for giving the options.

On the other hand, in many electronic markets today, market makers don't know who is on the other side of a transaction. So they have the downside of providing free options without the upside of gaining compensating information. As a result, exchanges in lightly-traded or newly-established markets have trouble finding anyone willing to be a market maker, and it is hard to get these markets off the ground.

Canadian Gas. Dave Pope was a pioneer in the Canadian natural gas market as it started to deregulate in the late 1980s. In 1992, he sold his company to Enron, and it ended up being the foundation for what would become Enron Canada, one of Enron's most profitable units.

Not long before Pope sold his company, he negotiated a free option that, more than two decades later, he still remembers fondly. Pope bought 10,000 MMBTUs of gas per day, at $1.02 Canadian per MMBTU, under a one year term contract, backing a commercial market he had at $1.04. (Today, gas in Canada is sold in gigajoules.) His gross profit on the year-long deal was $72,000 Canadian. As the negotiations with the producer were closing, he asked for one more feature: He wanted the right to buy the same amount of gas the following year at a price to be negotiated, but with a cap of $1.14. At the time, the producer would have been thrilled to be getting that higher price, and quickly agreed.

After Dave subsequently sold his company to Enron, and still during the first year of this gas contract, the price of Canadian gas more than doubled. So by buying Dave's company, Enron had lucked into this free option. Obviously, Enron exercised this option in the second year, since by then prices were $2.40. The value of this option alone was worth almost $4.6 million Canadian. When Dave cut the deal, he didn't understand (as he does today) the Black-Scholes option pricing model, but with an engineering degree and a great business sense, he correctly figured that he could never lose by asking for this free option.

PUT YOUR SOCKS ON RIGHT

> "Wrinkles can lead to blisters."
> —John Wooden, Hall of Fame
> UCLA basketball coach and
> winner of 10 NCAA titles

John Wooden is famous for spending the first hour of practice of every season teaching his team how to put their sweat socks on properly. This was one of those details that he decided to conquer rather than lose a player to a painful blister in a critical game. This principle involves finding the opportunity in the details, and not getting waylaid because you ignored them.

*****

Prior to late 1992, when the Federal Energy Regulatory Commission (FERC) issued FERC Order 636, companies owning US interstate natural gas capacity had to either use their capacity or lose it; they were prohibited from reselling or subleasing it. Although FERC Order 436 (1985) had made the unbundling of pipeline services theoretically possible, it never happened. FERC Order 636 did plenty to open the market up, and the following year, allowed pipeline capacity to be sliced, diced, and resold.

I am proud to say that, while still working for American Hunter, I completed the very first capacity release transaction in the country.

We bought 5,000 MMBTU's of Transwestern Pipeline daily capacity from the San Juan Basin (Four Corners area) to the California border from one of the long-term owners of this transportation. The first contract was a month-long fixed-price deal that didn't require competitive bidding.

One FERC limitation was, shippers who released capacity at less than the full published tariff price for longer periods were required to put the capacity up for competitive bid. This allowed others a chance to obtain the capacity by outbidding the original deal.

I soon reached a longer term agreement to purchase that same capacity. Although my counterpart was satisfied with the price, it was subject to competitive bidding, giving me only downside. I could match any higher bids but doing so would add to the cost. Looking for alternatives, I dug more deeply into both the FERC and Transwestern rules, and learned that Transwestern allowed formulas to be used on these transactions.

I dragged out my dictionary (they were printed on paper, back then) and started to write. By the time I finished, I had a two-page formula, referencing, among other things, the average natural gas price at the Henry Hub in Louisiana, the oil price, the Consumer Price Index, and average interest rates. The first paragraph stated that the *minimum* price was $.05 per MMBTU per day; later, at the end of page two, it said the *maximum* price was $.05 per MMBTU per day. It did not take a brain surgeon to figure out that the price would be exactly $.05. An equivalent example is a teacher who administers a test, several pages long, the first instruction saying: "Read the entire test first before answering any questions"; and the final line on the test is: "Do not answer any questions; return the test to the teacher."

I received several phone calls from fellow West Coast traders asking what the heck I was up to, and in-house we had many laughs over the move, which never faced any alternative bids and held up as originally negotiated.

We found an opportunity in the details of Transwestern's rules and procedures, and assumed that few of our competitors would bother reading the minutiae of our formula.

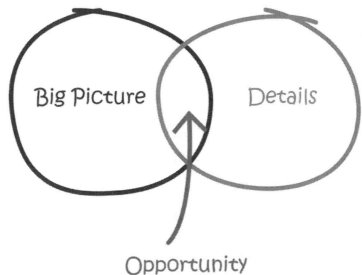

Over time, entrepreneurs catch on to these tricks of the trade, and the opportunities fade away (Strike While the Iron is Hot). In this case, the "pricing formula" worked once and only once. If I'd had the chance to use the technique over and over again, you can be sure that, before long, my competitors would have figured it out and eliminated the advantage.

*****

Scrutinizing the details is both a defensive and offensive skill—increase revenues *and* reduce expenses. This is the study of the microscopic organisms in the trees, as opposed to Starting with the Big Picture and Macro Trends, which look first at the overall health and ecosystem of the forest. You have to pay attention to the "nitty gritty" (per Urbandictionary.com, "To get down and dirty, get in the muck of things") in every contract you sign. Attending to details can differentiate your product or provide an overall competitive advantage.

Steve Jobs was a master of the details. He was famous for getting into every aspect of the design of the iPod, iPhone, and other new products created during his revival of Apple Computer. A typical story about Jobs' attention relates to his conversation with Vic Gundotra, a Google senior executive.

Jobs called Gundotra on a Sunday and said, "So Vic, we have an urgent issue, one that I need addressed right away. I've already assigned someone from my team to help you, and I hope you can fix this tomorrow. I've been looking at the Google logo on the iPhone and I'm not happy with the icon. The second "O" in Google doesn't have the right yellow gradient. It's just wrong, and I'm going to have Greg fix it tomorrow. Is this okay with you?"

In contrast, former Arkansas head football coach John L. Smith displayed an attention deficit for details. He declared bankruptcy in September 2012, with liabilities of over $40 million from his real estate endeavors. Earlier, in 2011, Smith was sued for breach of contract, and told the court that he was being unfairly punished. But the judge on the case, Audra Eckerle, corrected him: "Smith was not duped into signing the notes, but instead had sufficient time to read the agreements, ask questions, and/or seek legal counsel regarding the documents' terms. Having failed to either read or comprehend the significance of the...provisions, he may not now assert that he was fraudulently induced to sign."

You may think that this kind of sloppiness is uncommon in the business world. But after reviewing thousands of legal disputes in my legal funding business, I can assure you: this was not a rare instance.

I always read contracts carefully, and always write (at least initially) my own contracts. I will sometimes use an attorney to review them if I'm not familiar with the area or subject matter, because composing effective contracts involves understanding what each and every sentence and word is *meant* to convey, and actually *does* convey. These contracts are written with far more seriousness than the copyright warning I wrote at the end of this book.

Details provide an opportunity in any endeavor. Since I pride myself on looking for the opportunity in the details, I tend to migrate to propositions with greater complexity. Greater complexity means that many other people will gloss over the details, and this can create opportunity.

NATURAL GAS STORAGE

In 1991, just after I started to work for American Hunter Energy, my boss, Bob Shiring, made a trade that I admired. Our small company consisted of an office in Irvine, California, comprised of Shiring, a gas controller, and a secretary. I worked out of my home office in Northern California.

It was the first time SoCal Gas had offered natural gas storage to third parties. Prior to this, SoCal had controlled all their capacity, and used the stored natural gas to balance their system between incoming supplies and on-system demand. The move to offer storage capacity was driven by the California Public Utility Commission's (CPUC), efforts to further deregulate and create more competition in the state's natural gas market. The CPUC ordered Pacific Gas & Electric Company (PG&E) and SoCal Gas Company (SoCal) to offer some of their storage capacity on the open market.

Shiring had bought and sold physical natural gas in the western US, including California, and was quite knowledgeable about the SoCal and PG&E systems. He knew that SoCal had pipeline capacity constraints that restricted natural gas flows into Southern California from the interstate pipelines (El Paso and Transwestern), and that, in high-demand periods, SoCal would supplement their supply using gas from their storage fields.

As part of the negotiations involving storage capacity unbundling, the CPUC stopped requiring utilities to use gas from storage to serve large commercial and industrial customers. Under the new program, the large companies were being opened to competition, and storage capacity retained by the utility would be reserved only for small customers (residential and small commercial) buying gas on a bundled basis. Big users wanting the security of gas storage would have to successfully bid for it in the utility auction. If a large industrial or power customer couldn't bring in enough natural gas on a high-demand day via the interstate/intrastate pipelines or acquired gas storage, it would have to switch to another fuel, or shut down.

Based on this understanding of the details, Shiring thought that, during the high-demand winter season, with SoCal's limited ability to bring natural gas supplies via interstate pipelines, demand would outstrip supply. This would make natural gas in storage worth far more than the cost of the storage capacity, including the commodity cost of gas injected and carrying costs.

SoCal held their first storage capacity auction in the spring, to allow storage holders enough time to inject the natural gas. Shiring wanted to bid for one billion cubic feet (BCF) of storage capacity. Before selling gas during the next winter, American Hunter would probably have invested about $4 million in getting the gas into storage, plus payments to SoCal for the storage rights.

When Shiring explained the plan to his boss, John Schissel, headquartered in Calgary, Alberta, Schissel commented, "Bob, this better work, or you're driving a cab!"

Finally, (with Schissel's approval), Shiring submitted a very competitive bid and won.

Now, Shiring had one BCF of storage capacity and was thinking, "OK, I've got to fill this capacity, wait, and hope this winter is cold as heck." (He was "long" a cold winter, "short" summer gas prices, "long" winter gas prices, and "long" California gas price volatility.)

```
                |
        Long    |   Cold Winter
                |   Winter Gas Prices
                |   California Gas Price Volatility
    _____|_____
                |
        Short   |   Summer Gas Prices
                |
```

But before he started filling the storage, Shiring spoke to the Los Angeles Department of Water and Power (LADWP), a large buyer of natural gas for their own power plants. The LADWP buyer stated that they had not been awarded any storage capacity in the auction, and were going to conduct their own auction to buy storage capacity on the SoCal system. Obviously, you had to have been awarded storage capacity from SoCal to bid to LADWP. So Shiring investigated, discovering that only three other companies had been awarded SoCal storage: Chevron, Occidental Petroleum, and Berry Petroleum. This was a very positive development as Shiring expected that the other three storage holders had bought it for their own needs, not to profit from serving other customers.

At the time, LADWP could still burn low-sulfur fuel oil in their power plants, so the cost of burning fuel oil served as a ceiling on what they would be willing to pay for natural gas via storage. The bid that Shiring eventually submitted was calculated such that the combined cost of the storage capacity, plus the natural gas, was just slightly less than using low-sulfur fuel oil. He felt his bid was high, but believed that, if he didn't win the contract, he would just go ahead with his original plan.

LADWP awarded the contract to American Hunter—Shiring had won. It helped that he was the only one who even bid. As expected, his potential competitors wanted the storage capacity for their own security of supply, and were not interested in selling it to LADWP.

As it turned out, he held 1 BCF of storage capacity for approximately two months, never had to buy or inject a molecule of natural gas, and made $1 million. Outstanding return on investment!

SoCal held the auction again the next year, but by then the market understood the game, and Shiring never ended up with SoCal storage again (Strike While the Iron is Hot). Shiring followed a few principles, including Multiple Dimensions = Degrees of Freedom, Think in Opposites, and Think on the Margin. Most importantly, he understood the full scope of the opportunity by digging into the details.

INTERNET HOTEL RESERVATIONS

Lorraine and I love to go to Las Vegas a couple of times a year, and the Venetian is our favorite hangout. (They have a great poker room.) We usually wait for a special rate and then fly down for three to four days.

Several months ago, I made a reservation based on an internet offer. A few days before heading down, I got another email telling me about a new offer that covered the same time period as my scheduled trip.

But wait! I already had a reservation at a higher rate. So, of course, I called up and got the lower rate (a savings of about $20 per night). It took 10 minutes to get a total $80 (plus tax) in savings. At a normal annual work rate of 2,000 hours, this is the equivalent of earning an additional $960,000 per year (after tax).

Is it really so difficult to send the new offer only to those who don't already have room reservations at a higher rate? Maybe this will take a few more rocket scientists to solve.

When you combine attention to details with an understanding of the big picture, you will find yourself in a small minority.

THINK AND ACT WITH THE BIG PICTURE AND THE LONG RUN IN MIND

"I don't gamble, because winning a hundred dollars doesn't give me great pleasure. But losing a hundred dollars pisses me off."

—Alex Trebek, long-time host of *Jeopardy*

If your psyche demands that you win every time, and you can never accept some random bad luck, many of life's opportunities will pass you by. This principle is a reminder to bite the bullet and focus on making good decisions and bets that will pay off over the long run. Learn to get past your psychological baggage by stepping back and looking at the big picture.

The following two scenarios, derived from the research of Daniel Kahneman, illustrate the hows and whys of using this wide-angle vision.

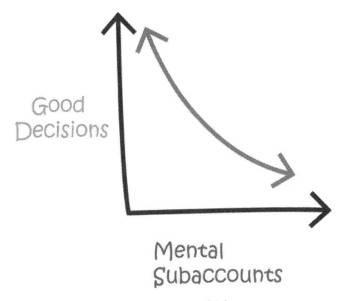

BET YOUR BROTHER

As you're walking along, your brother gives you a chance to bet $1 on the results of flipping a lop-sided coin. You have a 52% chance of winning with heads, and a 48% chance of losing if the underdog tails appears. (My brother wouldn't do this.)

 Even though the odds are in their favor and they can afford the worst-case financial loss, many people (including Alex Trebek) will decline the bet. Why? Because they hate to lose, and because they focus too much on the outcome of this single bet. They draw a circle around this one small "mental subaccount," rather than considering this one decision in the universe of thousands of similar decisions they will make over their lifetimes—situations in which they might have only a small advantage.

BLACKJACK INSURANCE

The decision about taking blackjack insurance combines this with two prior principles: Think on the Margin and Play the Odds.

A blackjack player has the option of making an insurance bet whenever the dealer has an ace showing. The player can "take insurance" by betting up to half the amount of his original bet. If the dealer has a 10, Jack, Queen, or King (all counting for 10) as his down card and therefore a total of 21, the player wins two to one on the insurance bet. Otherwise, his insurance bet loses.

Player does not have BlackJack

		Dealer Has BlackJack	Dealer does not have BlackJack		
			Tie	Player Wins	Dealer Wins
Does Player Take Insurance?	Yes	Break-even	-50%	+50%	-150%
	No	-100%	Break-even	+100%	-100%

If the player does not have a blackjack himself, and takes and wins the insurance bet, he ends up breaking even (losing the original bet, but making it up on the insurance bet). Of course, this player without a blackjack can also lose both bets (lose one-and-a-half times his original bet) or win the original bet and lose the insurance bet, in which case he ends up earning a profit of one-half of his original bet. Or finally, just to cover all the bases, the player could tie on the original bet and lose the insurance bet.

Here's the rub: By taking insurance, the player has a higher probability that he will not lose (when combining the results of the original bet and the insurance bet). But, unfortunately, this bet is frequently made when the odds do not favor the bet, and is usually a violation of these principles, Think on the Margin and Play the Odds.

The outlook is brighter for the player with a blackjack who is considering whether or not to take the insurance bet, because there are no bad outcomes. If this player does not take insurance, at worst he breaks even (the dealer also has a blackjack and they tie on the original bet) or wins one and a half times his original bet if the dealer does not have a blackjack.

Player has BlackJack

Dealer

Does Player Take Insurance?		Has BlackJack	Has No BlackJack
	Yes	+100%	+100%
	No	Break-even	+150%

But if the player has a blackjack and makes the insurance bet, he is guaranteed to win an amount equal to the amount of his original bet, whether the dealer has a blackjack or not.

So what could possibly be wrong with the approach that guarantees a win? The answer is: The player should not focus exclusively on this one outcome, but should play for the long run.

Let's start with a reminder: you should not be playing this game if you cannot afford the stakes. This analysis assumes that you can handle the loss.

Once you have made your original bet and the dealer is showing an ace, how should you make the insurance decision? Originally, the "10" and the other face cards (J, Q, K) represent 4/13 (about 31%) of the total cards. This ratio changes as cards are played. So, if you're not counting cards and calculating the percentage of unseen cards with a value of 10, the default probability that the card below is a 10 is about 31%, and you would never take the insurance bet.

But, if you are counting cards (the habit of the Champ), what is the threshold for taking insurance? If you win, you're getting paid back two dollars for every dollar you bet. The insurance bet makes sense when the odds are greater than what? 50%! So, if you're counting cards and there are 20 unseen cards, and 11 or more of them are 10s, the insurance bet is in your favor—take it. If there are 20 unseen cards and nine or fewer of them are 10s, the bet is not in your favor—decline insurance.

Does it matter if you have a blackjack when you decide on the insurance bet? Absolutely not! It doesn't matter one iota what your hand is, and it doesn't matter what your momentum is. Again, we rely on the principles: Think on the Margin; Play the Odds; and, of course, Think and Act with the Long Run in Mind. The only question in deciding whether or not to take blackjack insurance is the probability of a 10 being the down card for the dealer. If you have been paying attention, you will know the odds.

Here's a *faulty* pearl of wisdom about trading and investing: "You never lose by taking a profit." This classic adage promotes the losing blackjack insurance strategy (take insurance because it guarantees a win on this one hand), and violates the entire philosophy of this book. Hopefully this blackjack insurance example convinces you to set aside this stupidity.

♦♦♦
♦♦♦

CHAPTER FIVE: FIX IT

"Boy, was that a wrong mistake."
—Yogi Berra

In early 1991, Dave Pope (who we mentioned earlier in the Free Options story) was completing his first year as an independent marketer in the newly deregulated Canadian gas market.

By this time, even with very low natural gas prices, his monthly revenues were about $15 million Canadian, but he was operating on small gross margins (perhaps 2-3%). His biggest worry had always been that one of his big aggregating customers (they would sign up, and later resell to commercial and industrial customers) might go under, almost guaranteeing that Dave would also go bust.

He solved that by requiring his customers to pre-pay. Because Dave was offering a great price, they agreed; they were new to this market and were used to pre-paying. Dave, however, had worked in the industry for 11 years. Remarkably (as Dave would admit), Canada's biggest producers were willing to give him trade credit, allowing him to pay for the deliveries *after* the end of the month. (Today, after many a bankruptcy in the industry, these same producers would be unlikely to offer those liberal credit terms to a small start-up like Dave's.)

When Murphy reared his ugly head, the problem was not what Dave had worried about and anticipated (customers going bust)—rather, his big suppliers let him down.

Nova, the major pipeline operator, experienced mainline compressor problems, causing several of Pope's largest suppliers to either stop delivering to their customers, or meet customer demands by going to the open market and buying at a much higher price. Choosing the easier, less-costly way out, it was Dave who was cut.

Dave had a binding contract, and he probably would have prevailed in court—but against the big guys, he would have lost his business long before he got any legal or financial compensation.

Instead, over a weekend of frenzied buying, he paid much higher prices. Dave figured that he could last five days; any longer and he would be ruined. Luckily, the compressor problems were solved in a few days, and the producers started performing again. Interestingly, over the next few years, those same gas producers made it up to Dave with a few good deals (having jokingly acknowledged that they had shorted his life expectancy). But if Dave had not scrambled that weekend, he wouldn't have been in business long enough to receive the payback.

You have made the bet, taken a position, started the business; now the fun begins. You have to solve problems, adjust, tinker...and sometimes, cut and run.

The goal of decision-making in this stage of business is adapting the theories we have talked about to the real world. Making the right choices will involve hustle, street smarts, and absolute pragmatism.

LIFE HAPPENS

"Anything that can go wrong will go wrong."
—Murphy's Law

In *The Black Swan*, Nassim Nicholas Taleb relates how uncontrollable events (black swans) affect decisions. A "black swan" is a severe case of Life Happens; in contrast, a "bad beat" is a relatively minor variation. When poker players talk about "bad beats," they've lost despite very favorable odds, managing to snatch defeat from the jaws of victory. Taleb applies the term "black swan" to both unexpected *positive* events as well as surprising *negative* ones. The common denominator is that they seem to occur out of the blue.

When future Hall of Fame quarterback Peyton Manning underwent neck surgery in May 2011, he was sidelined for the entire season. It was a negative black swan for Manning and die-hard Indianapolis Colts fans, and a fortunate one for all the other fans in the South Division of the American Football Conference. But in this chapter, I will focus on the negatives.

Black swans can put you out of business, overthrow a government, or get you killed. A bad beat means only that you lose money you expected to collect from the poker pot. The poker loss is annoying but not life-threatening—so long as you don't have all of your money in that pot.

Black swans can emerge from what former Secretary of Defense Donald Rumsfeld would describe as things "we know we don't know," as well as the "unknown unknowns."

JPMorgan Chase's 2012 London trading losses of over $6 billion would be a black swan for most companies, but were probably only a bad beat for a bank the size of JPM, which, as I write this, has a market cap over $200 billion. In the Dave Pope example where his producers cut off his natural gas supply, he managed to avert a black swan and keep it to a mere "bad beat." It's all relative.

Significant black swans from history include the 9/11 terrorist attacks, the 1906 San Francisco earthquake, and the 2011 Tohoku earthquake and tsunami. All were totally unforeseen, and had serious consequences.

John Mauldin refers to a variation of black swans that he calls "lions in the grass." These are events as significant as black swans, but ones that have been foreseen and prepared for by a few keen observers. A lion in the grass was someone who anticipated World War II a few years before Hitler invaded Poland. Those who took action mitigated their risk, perhaps by emigrating to the US or Australia. Or, one who foresaw the approaching financial collapse that came as a result of the US housing bubble, and placed the right bets. Taleb refers to these lions in the grass as "gray swans." Some events are black swans to everyone. Some are black swans to most of us, but lions in the grass or gray swans for a few.

I'm sorry to be so pessimistic, but whether you call them black swans, bad beats, or simply random bad luck, some type of adversity is coming your way. Get ready! If you stick your head in the sand and remain oblivious to the possibilities of black swans and bad beats—and, therefore, have no backup plans—you are totally unprepared when life inevitably happens. If you miss the signs of lions in the grass, you miss the chance to be well positioned when they occur.

The most straightforward way to protect your back is to diversify your risks on uncorrelated bets, which is much easier said than done. It's not enough to have your eggs in dozens of baskets if those baskets are all sitting close together on the freeway, about to be run over by the next Mack truck. We discussed correlation in the principle, Correlation Is Not Causation. People err by ignoring the fact that correlations change, thus leaving their financial future locked into limited outcomes or a few rolls of the dice. Having your entire net worth tied up in ten uncorrelated US equities does *not* constitute diversification.

Risks go beyond simply the assets you own. If you were making a great living at Lehman Brothers in 2008 when it went bankrupt, and also had much of your nest egg in Lehman stock, you lost both your job and your major asset. If you owned a home in Stockton, California, and also worked for the city when it declared bankruptcy, you took a quadruple whammy: the value of your home dropped, your job was at risk, and your pension plan and retiree health care benefits were imperiled.

On August 1, 2012, market maker Knight Capital experienced a computer glitch that resulted in millions of shares of equities being automatically bought and sold. For a period of 45 minutes they lost about $10 million per minute. The next day, their stock (KCG) had dropped more than 80% to about $2.60, and the company was fighting for survival. This was a nasty black swan for Knight's major owners, senior managers, and the head of IT, but it was only a bad beat if, the day before, you had bought shares that represented just a few percent of your net worth. I doubt it was a lion in the grass for anyone. Knight was later acquired by Getco LLC, and the merged company is named KCG Holdings.

Let's look at the worst possible bad beat in Texas Hold 'em. You might have Ace-Ace (the best two down cards possible to start with). Another player has the 7 and 8 of clubs. The flop comes up Ace-Ace, 4 of clubs. You now have four aces, and the other player has nothing. You are sitting fat and happy (not necessarily "dumb"). But the next two cards are 5 and 6 of clubs, and you are busted, because his straight flush beats your four of a kind. When the flop is revealed (the first three shared cards), the only way you could lose is if these exact two cards came up. The odds of your losing after the flop were (2/45 * 1/44), which is approximately a .101% chance of losing—about one in a thousand. Life is hard!

Hours at the poker table can condition you to the emotions of getting beat by a highly improbable card or set of cards (and, by the way, despite playing for over 35 years, I have never seen a bad beat quite as horrific as the example above). It doesn't make the experience any more fun, but you soon realize that life happens, and great poker hands can lose. If you can't emotionally handle losing to a long shot, you'd better find another way to spend your free time.

How do you prepare for the bad beat? I hate to say it, but "practice, practice, practice." If you've never been beaten by some cruel twist of fate, the first time it occurs, you might think that you've been singled out. The longer you play, the more hardened you become. It's possible that you may have better or worse luck than the average Joe, but everyone faces some of the downsides in life.

Sometimes, simply focusing on the *process* of making great decisions rather than the results can make it easier to make good decisions. I find this most natural when I count cards in blackjack. I am absorbed entirely in the card count (the number of face cards relative to other cards), and based on that ratio, the dealer's up card and my cards, I make a decision. This requires enough of my mental horsepower (limited indeed) that it is easy to simply put aside whether or not I've won or lost the last hand. In blackjack, over thousands of hands, the significance of one hand is trivial. I completely concentrate on the process, not the outcome, until the end of each session.

Playing poker is a slightly different matter because the rest of the table's perception of my style of play—whether I have the hot hand or not, and how many chips I have relative to the other players—will impact my optimum strategy. For example, if I am perceived as a "tight," or conservative, player, I can bluff a little more. If I am perceived as loose, I can bet a little bigger than normal and expect more calls.

Suppose I have been playing with strangers for the last hour, had bad hands, and therefore played very little. In this instance, I will be perceived as a tighter player than I actually am. On the other hand, when sitting down at a new table and immediately getting great cards and playing many hands, I will be perceived as looser than I really am. And so I need to adjust my subsequent play accordingly.

In business, bad luck takes many forms. Maybe a deal falls apart at the end because the other side has a last minute management change, or the person you're negotiating with gets seriously ill. Perhaps you have an information technology meltdown (hopefully not as bad as Knight Capital's), or your broker goes bankrupt (think MF global) and locks up most of your cash for several years. Life does happen, so get ready. Be prepared, be paranoid, understand how to "go to ground," be optimally pessimistic, and, as the first part of Warren Buffett's famous saying goes, "Be fearful when others are greedy."

Both Taleb and Warren Buffett discuss black swans in their businesses (in Taleb's books, and Buffett in his annual letters to his shareholders), but the two men have totally different value propositions related to these Life Happens events.

Taleb prefers the slow and regular loss over time, offset when he comes roaring back with profits after a black swan hits. He consistently pays premiums for far-out-of-the-money options, betting on the rare occurrence. (This is my interpretation of his strategy upon reading his books, but he is a little vague, so please bear with me.)

Buffett has just the opposite approach with his reinsurance business. He takes in premiums up front, and makes money when black swans are eluded. When something hits like 9/11, Katrina, Sandy, or another big Los Angeles earthquake, Buffett takes it on the chin. Even with this "betting style," no member of the business media would dare refer to Buffet as a "gambler," but he is.

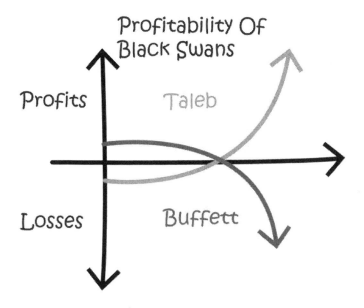

It's interesting that both value propositions have been profitable. Neither ignores the possibility of the "Life Happens" event. Denial or ignorance of these events is what's really dangerous. Taleb's value proposition can be copied with less capital, although picking the right black swan to bet on is no sure thing. Buffett's approach requires billions of dollars. In any case, investors who build these two methods into their repertoires have more ways to win.

I believe in the random nature of the world. As the German proverb states, **"Luck sometimes visits a fool, but it never sits down with him."** Sometimes luck works in your favor, sometimes it works against you. The key is to take advantage of it when it goes your way, and adapt and move on when it goes against you.

Lucky And Good

GET LUCKY

"If I never took a bad beat, I'd be playing some really terrible games. I want bad beats. I adore bad beats. Every time someone puts a bad beat on me, it means they got their money into the pot with the worst of it."

—Annie Duke, professional poker player, *Decide to Play Great Poker*

I mentioned earlier that, in the early 1990s, I worked for a small natural gas trading company, American Hunter. Like traders at other small shops, I also sometimes scheduled gas. It was in this role that I made a mistake while scheduling natural gas to flow from the Northwest Pipeline into the El Paso system. The gas never showed up on the Northwest Pipeline as we had intended, but Northwest delivered our scheduled gas to El Paso anyway. Thus, we now owed gas to Northwest Pipeline, but were able to pay it back via Canadian supplies over the next weekend, and at a much lower price than originally expected. **We were lucky to have initially been unlucky. From then on, I played this game like a Champ, first making the sale, then buying gas to fill the need.**

Fix It

But if I couldn't find the gas that day at a "reasonable price," I knew in the back of my mind that, over the weekend, I could buy the gas at the Canadian border. And gas that might cost $1.50 during the work week might be available for $1.20 later that weekend. This was a great free option (Find Free Options).

Aspartame, the artificial sweetener known as NutraSweet, was discovered in 1965 by James M Sclatter, a chemist working for the G.D. Searle & Company. He had created aspartame as an intermediate step in trying to produce an anti-ulcer drug. Sclatter discovered the substance's sweet taste when he accidentally licked his finger.

I have four main strategies about how to best take advantage of any luck that comes your way:

1. When you're lucky, acknowledge it, think about it, and separate (at least, mentally) the results due to luck from those you attribute to skill and hard work.
2. When you're unlucky, dig through the muddle and find the opportunity that others miss.
3. Take advantage of chance occurrences that others ignore. This is serendipity—the art of finding something useful while looking for something else—common among successful entrepreneurs.
4. Defend against and prepare for black swans, bad beats, and general bad luck.

Anticipate life's uncertainties. When things go your way, analyze whether you outplayed the other team or whether you won because the referee made a bad call. Most outcomes result from some combination of both luck and skill.

 Were you right for the wrong reasons? Did you get lucky because you were asleep at the wheel and didn't listen to the great advice that turned sour after a random event? If you are having trouble with this one, pull out a copy of *Forrest Gump* and watch it one more time.

Lucky And Good

Did you (like Forrest Gump) end up with the only functioning shrimp boat after the big hurricane?

Did you get a great price for your orange crop in California because they had a terrible freeze in Florida?

Did you get promoted because your primary competition left the company for another job?

The expert stock picker might correctly forecast the stock market's direction for six years in a row just as easily as picking heads or tails on a coin six times in a row. In the latter case, it's clearly luck. In the former case, it might be luck to a greater extent than an observer recognizes. In such a small sample size, we really don't know (The Numbers May Be Hazardous to Your Health). If we're honest in our assessment, the more we record our decision-making processes, sub-forecasts, and the actions we took as a result, the better we can differentiate (after the heat of the battle) between luck and skill.

I eat my own cooking (although, fortunately, not in the kitchen). Since last year, I have recorded my evaluation (and scoring) of every lawsuit investment I make. My plan is to review that sheet whenever an investment is resolved, and I have either made money or lost it. This will help me to determine which results were due to luck and which were due to skill when I originally made the bet.

Shorting an industry that has recently been lucky is not a bad rule of thumb. For example, the gold mining business was relatively lucky during the first decade of the 21st century, while the PC industry was relatively lucky during the 1980s and 1990s. If a company's success was the consequence of a random event, the business now probably has the same odds as other businesses do of winning when the next random event occurs. **And hubris is more likely to infect a lucky company than an unlucky one.**

Dealing with adversity helps you see the world from another angle (often from the ground looking up) and collect information that was not apparent before.

*****

If I could make a billion simultaneous, uncorrelated bets, each worth $1 million, and each with only a1% advantage, then I can be confident that I will notch about $10 trillion in profits on that lucky day. On the other hand, if I make a single bet with my one and only trillion dollars (a Ben Bernanke-size bet), and if I have an 80% chance of doubling my money and a 20% chance of losing, I have reasonable odds (20%) of going bust.

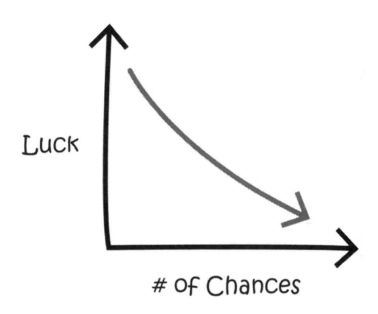

Part of being lucky is taking lots of independent, and uncorrelated, bets—each with an advantage, and each of which you can afford to lose. I wish I could claim that this concept is original, but Frenchman Antoine Gombaud, Chevalier de Méré, wrote virtually the same thing in what is known as Chevalier's Strategy, back in the 17th century.

*****

Chumps miss chance opportunities. They don't exactly miss them; they simply pass them by. **They miss the business opportunity because they are intent on complaining rather than learning, or are simply so focused on their next task that they**

can't broaden their peripheral vision. They don't take the initiative to follow up with the right person they may have met by happenstance. They miss the chance to talk to an irate customer or a worried supplier. They won't hang around to interview yet one more candidate who is interested in working for their company. And they stop observing and thinking when they're on vacation or on weekends.

Be open and aware of chance opportunities. Follow up with people you meet accidentally, and strengthen the ties from one-time to long-term friendships. This is one of the ways Champs "get lucky."

VINEGAR IS SO SWEET

Vinegar and water have been used for decades as an eco-friendly cleaning solution—but the vinegar industry was slow to promote this use. More recently, vinegar has been highly touted not only for its cleaning benefits, but also for its lack of risks compared to other cleaning products. It is non-toxic, leaves little or no residue, and if for some reason a bit of this cleaning solution is left on any cooking or food surface, it is harmless.

H J Heinz Company, in business since 1869, has been producing and selling vinegar for years. However, only recently has the company recognized the market's appreciation of its cleaning characteristics.

This serendipitous occurrence led Heinz to announce, in 2012, a "brand new" product: "Heinz All Natural Cleaning Vinegar," a vinegar product that is 20% stronger than traditional distilled white vinegar (they had to change something to gain any press coverage).

And if you happen to run out of salad dressing at home, you can still use this cleaning vinegar along with a little olive oil to flavor your salad. It may be the best-tasting cleaning product you've ever had.

BE OPTIMALLY PERSISTENT

"At some point, and that point should come quickly, you have to move on."

—Mark Cuban

As a kid, I loved watching the television program *Candid Camera*. Woody Allen, virtually unknown at the time, wrote many of the shows during the 1960s. The show utilized hidden cameras to record actors subjecting their "victims" to a variety of pranks.

The setting for my favorite episode was a bank with two open teller lines. When the victim got in one line, she would quickly move to the front, the next customer to be served. Things would then come to a screeching halt. The customer ahead of her would experience endless problems, leaving the target cooling her heels, seemingly "forever." Meanwhile, customers in the other line were whizzing through. Finally exasperated, the victim would give up and switch lines.

Here was the fun part. All of a sudden, the line she had just abandoned started moving rapidly. And her new line also moved fine *until* she was next in line to be served. Just like her experience with the first line, things then came to a grinding halt. The pranksters made sure that there was no way for the poor woman to ever reach the finish line. Have you ever have been in a line somewhere where you thought the *Candid Camera* crew was playing the same joke on you? The question is always: do I change lines or not?

It sometimes pays to "quit" one line and try another—sometimes, it doesn't. Knowing the difference is a discipline that marks a Champ.

Don't be a stubborn fisherman with a poor yield. Know when to reel in your line and try elsewhere. Entrepreneur Carson McComas, *Workhappy.net* blog, says, "I've had the chance to associate with some top anglers, and I've noticed something about them; they don't waste time in an unproductive location. If the fish aren't biting, they quickly move to a new spot."

The cliché "Failure is not an option" does not apply in business, nor anywhere else, for that matter. If you are a trader, you will debunk this myth within your first week. But the more important part of navigating the waters is knowing when to persist, when to pivot slightly, when to take a radically different direction, and when to abandon ship. There is a time for patience and a time to cut your losses, but there is no exact formula to tell you when to throw in the towel. It is based on experience, gut feeling, knowing your own tendencies, and looking at the situation objectively.

If you have a history of changing your mind often, you probably need a dose of stick-to-itiveness. But if you are an ultra-marathon runner, you may have the opposite predisposition.

The entrepreneur or inventor who sticks with one idea for decades, against the odds, makes a great story when he occasionally prevails. Think about the movie *Flash of Genius,* the story of Robert Kearns, who invented the intermittent windshield wiper system. He eventually triumphed over Ford Motor and Chrysler for infringement of his patents. He first came up with the idea in 1963 and filed three patents, in 1964, 1967, and 1982. He sued Ford in 1978 and Chrysler in 1982, but did not settle the Ford case until 1990 (for $10.1 million). He didn't see a penny from Chrysler until 1995 (29 years after filing his first patent), after the appeals had run their course, and then collected about $30 million. This, after having spent $10 million in legal fees. Had the case taken another 14 years, he may have collected zippo from Chrysler following the car company's 2009 bankruptcy.

Kearns was ultimately successful, but there are dozens of other inventors who ended up broke.

I know of no traders with experiences comparable to Kearns's. If a trader sticks with a position while it goes against him for even a moderate period of time, he is out of business—period. A poker player who can never fold a hand, or a general who insists on winning every skirmish may win more battles but lose the war.

*****

Experience helps to sharpen your instincts, and tells you when to pull the ejection handle. Sully Sullenberger, the heroic US Airways pilot, managed to land his airliner in the Hudson Bay after a flock of birds took out both of his engines soon after takeoff. In his book *Highest Duty: My Search for What Really Matters*, he discusses the decision that fighter pilots (his earlier career) sometimes are faced with: whether to eject or not eject from a fighter plane.

The decision comes down to when and if to "give up the ship." Passengers on Sullenberger's US Airways Flight 1549 on January 15, 2009, surely didn't want him ever to give up on getting the airplane down safely (the equivalent of surrendering in war). Of course, he had no ejection seat, and even if he did, he had a crew and passengers that were his primary concern.

But likewise, if you were sitting in the back seat of an F4 Phantom fighter piloted by Sullenberger during his Air Force career, you wouldn't have wanted him to dilly dally (a technical flying term) in pulling the ejection handle that would set you both free. You would have been rooting for "optimum persistence"—sticking with it as long as it made sense. In other words, don't give up the ship too early; don't give it up too late. When the time is right (or perhaps, in this circumstance, it is better described as very wrong), you want Sully to quickly and ruthlessly pull the ejection handle. Accept the loss (of the multimillion-dollar aircraft, not your lives) and move on.

As Sully explained in his book, *Highest Duty*:

> **There was an aircrew ejection study conducted years ago which tried to determine why pilots wait too long before ejecting from planes that were about to crash. These pilots waited extra seconds, and when they finally pulled the handle to eject, it was too late. They either ejected at too low an altitude and hit the ground before their parachutes could open, or went down with their planes.**
>
> **What made these men wait? The data indicated that if the plane was in distress because of a pilot's error in judgment, he often put off the decision to eject. He'd spend more precious time trying to fix an unfixable problem or salvage an unsalvageable situation, because he feared retribution if he lost a multimillion-dollar jet. If the problem was a more clear-cut mechanical issue beyond the pilot's control, he was more likely to abandon his aircraft and survive by ejecting at a higher, safer altitude.**

First, I want to remind you that ejecting from a jet aircraft is not risk free, but neither is flying a fighter jet to begin with. Think back to the scene in the movie *Top Gun,* when Tom Cruise's backseat radar intercept officer, Goose, was killed while ejecting. The decision involves many factors and must be evaluated in split seconds.

We don't know what those who ejected too late were thinking. I have not found the relevant study (despite spending substantial time looking), but it is possible that the situation looked like a cause-and-effect but wasn't (Correlation Is Not Causation). It is also conceivable that the group of pilots who faced an equipment failure were, on average, more experienced than those who had gotten into the fix through their own flying skills. Perhaps the subset of pilots that faced danger because of a mistake in judgment was less proficient. The opposite is also possible—more experienced pilots were slower to pull the ejection handle because they had a history of successfully working through predicaments.

So there is evidence here of correlation, but it is possible that it is not a cause-and-effect relationship.

Did these pilots spend extra seconds trying to fix the unfixable? One other factor in the decision may have been the career implications of crashing a multimillion-dollar jet (an F-22 Raptor had a price tag of about $150 million).

Or, possibly, when the trouble was someone else's fault, or the result of a mechanical problem for which the pilots had no responsibility, it was slightly easier to be objective (in a few split seconds) and timely in pulling the handle. It is also possible that, if it was pilot error, the cost of the jet gets put on your record in bold print. If it was a mechanical problem with no pilot error, it might show up on your record, but is probably more of a "war story" to tell at the local watering hole than a career ender.

Sully's conclusions apply to business. **Military, political, and business decision-makers take longer to abandon their own decisions and investments than those decisions made by others or prompted by events out of their control.**

*****

It has been said that the two greatest predictors of success are: 1) intelligence; and 2) discipline.

Raw intelligence is a great start, but all of us can upgrade our "smarts" to some extent through education and experience.

Discipline involves consistently doing the right thing even when you'd prefer not to. It means not having another dessert when you are fighting a weight problem, or going to the gym when you would rather go to the movies. It dictates doing the most pressing things first, even though you would rather start with something less significant and more entertaining.

Making the tough choices, and acting on the best data you've got is how you show discipline in the world of business decisions. Often (but not always) this entails refusing to quit as the situation changes, a theme voiced with enough admiration by the media that it is the most popular narrative.

Being disciplined, however, sometimes means cutting your losses and moving on—especially after you have gathered new information that contradicts your original hypothesis (Think on the Margin). You may need to discard your current business idea, trade, or investment despite the pangs of regret and loss. For many achievers it is harder to quit than to persist, even when the current evidence suggests that quitting is the right move.

In poker, the art of folding the hand is perhaps the toughest and most important skill of all. Most poor players will tell you their goal is to "win the pot." Wrong! Their goal should be to make the most money playing tens of thousands of hands. This means playing the hand in a way that the expected profits from any action minus the expected losses from that same action together are the most positive. Sometimes the most positive outcome (expected profit minus expected loss) is simply to throw in the hand. If your goal were just to win the most hands, then you might employ some very basic (albeit Neanderthal) tactic like raising "all-in" on every hand, and you might win the highest number of pots in the short term. But it wouldn't be long before you were broke. As professional poker player Annie Duke says: **"Set yourself free from the toxic notion that winning the pot equals proper play and losing the pot equals mistake."**

A single hand of poker is the equivalent of a single trade, a single investment, or one skirmish in a long war. **Your goal is to win the war, win the game of business, and be profitable in poker in the**

long run, based on making excellent decisions consistently in the short term.

In *The Start-Up of You* by Reid Hoffman (co-founder of LinkedIn) and Ben Casnocha, the authors discuss having a Plan A, Plan B, and Plan Z. Plan A is your original direction. After getting real-world feedback on your idea or trade, you will frequently "pivot" or adjust it by going in another direction—Plan B. Plan Z involves dumping the entire thing and moving on to the next opportunity. I would add a Plan P, for "pause." Sometimes to reach the right decision, you need to slow down and collect more information or cogitate on your slow hunch.

Being objective and persisting when you should—and quitting when it is demanded—requires equal and opposite kinds of discipline.

Being optimally persistent is clearly an art, not a science. Quitting before that one final sales call that would have revived your struggling company, or settling too early on a lawsuit, would be a real shame. But not pulling the ejection handle because you "never give up" will take you and your navigator down in flames. This principle requires objectivity and *discipline*. Once you develop those traits, you are well on your way to being a Champ.

♦♦♦
♦♦♦

CHAPTER SIX: REAL-WORLD APPLICATIONS

"I'm interested in the real world."
—Edward Bond, author

Lots of theories look great on paper (or your Kindle). You'll need to amass your own experiences as a trader, investor, or entrepreneur to realize how and why these business principles work for you. That is the essence of being lucky *and* good.

Let's see how these concepts have applied in eight real world business situations.

♦♦♦
♦♦♦

APPLICATION ONE
THE LITIGATION FUNDING BUSINESS

What is the litigation funding business? My clients tend to be entrepreneurs and businesspeople who are plaintiffs in a commercial lawsuit, trying to collect something from a defendant. Typically, they have lost everything and are trying to hang on until they collect on a settlement or judgment. These cases can take years (usually much longer than most plaintiffs realize), and frequently take a big chunk of the participants' time to assist in the litigation. I have had clients who worked on their lawsuits full-time for a year or two, cases in which the stakes were big and the details, complex.

While the legal system takes its sweet time to resolve the issue, the plaintiffs still need to pay their bills. To raise cash, they sell my company part of the anticipated proceeds. Months or years later, if the case is decided against the plaintiff, there are no proceeds and we lose our investment. As I have mentioned, I lose my entire investment about one out of four times. **This relatively high chance of losing, combined with the slow feedback to potential new competitors, is what helps sustain the opportunity for above-average returns.**

My company's investments are a "purchase of proceeds" from the plaintiff's share of a lawsuit. We are very careful to make sure that these transactions are not structured as loans, subject to state usury laws.

My very first case was a tortious interference lawsuit in Texas, against Halliburton. The plaintiff eventually settled for about $40 million, who then decided to stiff the 30 investors who had advanced him a total of about $2 million. This scum bag (my attorney friends have advised me to state that this is an opinion based only on my keen perception of the man) claimed that the transactions were usurious loans. About a quarter of the investors (including me) sued this jerk (according to the Urban Dictionary, "an insensitive, selfish, ignorant, cocky person who is inconsiderate and does stupid things"—again an opinion), and won.

As a result of our lawsuit against the scum bag, very strong law exists in Texas enforcing the legality of these agreements. But a few states, such as Kentucky, have quite questionable laws on the books. Even though my agreements usually state that Texas law prevails, if another presiding state court intervenes in my transaction, it can cost us extra legal fees to protect our investment. I know this now, and have adjusted my strategy so that I rarely have to litigate today in order to collect—only in about one in every one hundred cases.

We usually get paid after the contingency attorney's fees and expenses. A contingency fee applies when the law firm is not paid by the hour, but instead, gets a percentage of the eventual proceeds of the case. A lawyer will only take a case on contingency if she really believes in it, because she stands to lose her entire investment of time and expenses if she loses the case. All other things being equal, since the lawyers usually get paid before we do, we would prefer a 33% contingency fee to a 50% contingency fee.

We always interview the plaintiff's attorney (by phone). We want a well-established lawyer with plenty of trial experience, who knows the specialty involved in the case, with adequate resources to finish the job. The legal team generally cooperates with us so that their client is more patient about settling; hence the attorney has a better chance of receiving a higher contingency fee. (Yes, these attorneys are greedy capitalists, too.) But the lead attorney understands that, if the case ends up less profitable than expected, she may have to negotiate with us, as well as the client, and everyone may have to take a "haircut" to get the case settled.

Keep in mind that, even though our lien gets paid before our client's, the priority is usually a moot point. If the client does not sign-off on the settlement, no one ever collects anything. So, if we are due $300,000 and, according to the terms of the settlement, the client would end up with only $20,000, we might end up reducing our share just to get the deal settled and paid. In these cases, I usually ask the attorneys to take a reduction in fees as well, because we are all in the same boat.

If nothing is ever collected on the case, we lose our entire investment. My company collects either after a pretrial settlement, after a trial judgment has been collected, or after an appeal has been lost and the defendant's bond is forfeited.

Our only expenses (besides our time) tend to be for legal review. For larger cases, or ones that involve an unusual law, I sometimes have an attorney review the case.

The majority of our income is in the form of capital gains and losses. If we are paid off within a year, it's a short-term capital gain; if it takes over a year, it's a long-term capital gain. The sweet spot for us is a case that pays off after a year and a day, because of the tax savings.

HOW DO I FIND THE CASES?

I hear about plaintiffs in need through a broker network, from attorneys with whom I've worked before, my website Fundinglawsuits.com, and occasionally via client referrals. The typical brokerage fee is 10% of the amount advanced to the client, and this is rolled into the total amount due upon settlement. For larger investments, above $400,000, the brokerage fee decreases from 8% to about 3% (for investments above $2 million). We capitalize the brokerage costs along with payments to the client.

WHICH CASES DO I FUND?

Most of the cases I review are commercial: breach of contract, partnership disputes, tortious interference, fraud, patent and trademark infringement, and false claims (*qui tam*). I really like lawsuits currently under appeal, meaning that my clients (the plaintiffs) have already won at the lower court. In these cases, the defendant has usually posted a bond, so it removes the collection risk.

I do not take medical malpractice cases because the courts and state laws have made it very tough to get them settled. The growing limitation on punitive damages makes defendants less likely to settle, so malpractice suits take longer to bring to conclusion.

Here are my general criteria for a lawsuit investment:

- ❖ The defendant has deep enough pockets to pay a potential judgment.
- ❖ The plaintiff's attorney has taken the case on contingency.

Real-World Applications

- ❖ I expect at least enough of a settlement to pay me and leave plenty for my client.
- ❖ The plaintiff (my client) is articulate, appears to be good with details, and sounds reasonable (not irrational or vindictive).
- ❖ Liability in the case is obvious (the myth that these transactions increase the number of frivolous lawsuits is nonsensical).
- ❖ The plaintiff will appear sympathetic to a jury.
- ❖ My client has the home field advantage. Ideally, the case is being heard in the plaintiff's state, and the defendant is from out of state.
- ❖ I understand the facts and the law in the case, and believe that my client can prevail.
- ❖ The defendant may not want to go to trial because it would embarrass his company.
- ❖ The discovery is complete, and the trial is scheduled to begin soon.
- ❖ The attorney has significant trial experience in the subject of the lawsuit.
- ❖ The attorney's record shows that he settles some cases, but takes many of them to trial (see below).
- ❖ There are only one or two defendants (see below).

After looking at the nature of the liability, I size up the plaintiff, defendants, and attorneys in order to estimate the risk/reward in this opportunity. An open-and-shut case, for example, is obviously a good bet. One such instance occurred during the 2007 San Diego fires, when we had numerous government reports blaming the fires on downed power lines owned by San Diego Gas & Electric. Legal action against the company had a high probability of success. Likewise, I prefer to step into cases in which the attorneys' discovery is complete, rather than pending. This way, I have a better chance of seeing an unfavorable smoking gun that might affect the verdict and my investment.

I am more apt to bet on a client who comes across as knowledgeable about the lawsuit. She understands the details of the case and is practical about the potential outcomes of the litigation. She seems like someone who is willing to settle the case for a reasonable figure if and when that opportunity arises.

The chances for success increase when the plaintiff's attorney has a favorable track record in the relevant area of law. I prefer an attorney who has a solid trial reputation but who will settle if the offer is realistic. Some attorneys push for settlement because they dislike going to trial, and the word gets out. A plaintiff attorney who always settles is less likely to be taken seriously in any mediation or settlement discussions.

What about the other side of the argument? Defendants who are "loaded for bear" or who are taking an irrational stance to the proceedings raise red flags. If I get the sense that a defendant is dead set against settling, I am less inclined to invest because the case is more likely to drag on for years. The same goes for litigation involving multiple defendants. Even a clear-cut case requires more time, money, and emotional resources to resolve, with multiple defendants, so I shy away from them. If there are four different defendants, each represented by a different law firm, the time it takes to resolve the matter goes up dramatically.

WHAT CAN GO WRONG? PLENTY!

Since things tend to go right about 75% of the time, litigation funding is a decent bet. But things also go wrong about 25% of the time. The case can go south at many junctures and for a variety of reasons. I might never have a payday if:

The plaintiff loses the case. We spend considerable time reviewing the complaint and the responses from the defendant, and talking to the plaintiff's counsel. We only invest in cases where the attorney is on contingency; the fact that he only gets paid with a win is our first (but not only) criterion. Sometimes, though, the judge or jury makes a bad call. Sometimes a key witness changes his story at the last minute. (He was lying before, but now remembers the truth.)

The plaintiff wins the case but does not collect on the judgment. The second major question we investigate is the ability of the defendant to pay. If it's a publicly-traded company or insurance company, this is easy. Sometimes we just can't determine what the defendant is worth, so we won't invest. If it's a privately-held company and the case is under appeal, the defendant will typically have to put up a bond, so we are covered relative to collection risk. 90% of judgments in the US go uncollected (this stat is greatly influenced by small-claims judgments), but the collectability is a critical part of our evaluation.

The plaintiff dies. For cases that rely on the credibility of the plaintiff (like fraud and breach of contract), a death weakens the case.

The plaintiff goes to jail. Again, if you're relying on his credibility and if he is, for example, convicted of passing bad checks, your case goes down the drain.

The attorney refuses to pay us (at the client's request) when the judgment is paid. This is why we prefer larger law firms and require them to acknowledge our lien in writing.

The plaintiff declares bankruptcy. When this happens, the beneficiary of the lawsuit (besides the attorney and me) becomes the bankruptcy estate. If the money is collected and turned over to the bankruptcy estate, we're now dealing with a federal bankruptcy judge, who sometimes makes up the rules as he goes. (The 2009 General Motors bankruptcy is the poster child for this statement.) Bankruptcy decisions are unlikely to be appealed successfully, even when the judge blatantly ignores the law. So, we talk to the client about how they're going to survive until the case is settled. Keep in mind that most of them don't want to declare bankruptcy because then they lose control (and most if not all of the benefits) of their lawsuit.

The client has been lying to his attorney and me about the facts of the case. When evidence of this dishonesty comes out *after* we have invested, we're sunk. This is one scenario that is hard to protect against, and it has only happened to me a couple of times. It's also why I would prefer to invest after rather than before the discovery is complete.

The plaintiff is awarded a judgment, the defendant pays, but the plaintiff refuses to sign off on the disbursement. Sometimes clients feel wronged by the process and don't consider the award adequate, so they refuse to release any funds. This happened on a small case I had in New York, and the lawyer was still trying to get a signature years later. In the meantime, the plaintiff (an elderly lady) passed away, and so the complexity of the negotiations increased far beyond the money at stake.

The attorney forgets to pay my lien and pays all the funds (other than keeping his own fees, which he never forgets) to the plaintiff. This has happened a couple of times. Usually I strike a deal with the lawyer to get paid back over time. Larger firms don't seem to make this mistake, and I now use a more binding attorney agreement than I have in years past. I also require a higher standard for the attorneys representing the client for cases that I fund. In addition to having the attorney acknowledge my lien in writing, I remind her a couple of times a year of my lien. In most states, the state bar considers failing to honor a valid lien as a substantial ethics violation for attorneys.

The client has undisclosed liens. Plaintiffs may lie or simply be mistaken about the existence of other liens against the case, and counsel might not be aware of them or have forgotten about them. I have had one such case. When I make larger investments, I file a UCC financing statement with the secretary of state to record and perfect my lien. This does nothing to get an attorney to pay me if he forgets about my lien, but if we end up in an interpleader (the funds are turned over to the court to decide who gets what), this establishes the priority date of my lien. I can also file a notice to the court to officially notify the defendant of my lien. This has some downside, so I generally only do this when the client's attorney becomes uncooperative (a synonym for "schmuck" or "jerk").

The client fires the attorney. I had one case where the client fired three law firms in a row, and eventually tried to represent himself. Needless to say, this investment was a write-off. One challenge is that the second or third attorney has never signed my attorney agreement. I notify the new law firm of my lien, but I'm on weaker ground than I was with the original lawyer.

WHICH PRINCIPLES APPLY TO THE LITIGATION-FUNDING BUSINESS?

Nothing Is Risk Free. That reality is obvious in this business, and I price the transactions so that I can still make a nice living even if my losses exceed my historical 25%. I also diversify my risk by putting only a limited percentage of capital in any single lawsuit, in any one type of case, with any one law firm, or finally, in any single state. From my perspective, this portfolio of investments has much greater diversity than a typical stock and bond portfolio.

Start with the Big Picture and Macro Trends. This is important from a number of perspectives. For example, the growing public disdain for medical malpractice lawsuits and the restriction on punitive damages have combined to create a longer resolution period for these cases. Defendants have therefore become more unwilling to settle, so I no longer fund them.

Fight for Fast Feedback. This is another reason I shy away from cases that will need several years to resolve. I have found that attorney predictions routinely underestimate the likely time required to resolve the case. These cases rarely, if ever, conclude faster than originally anticipated. So I push hard to find cases that can settle early—13 months is my target.

Play the Odds. Assume that my funding contract gives me 2.5 times my initial investment plus 1.5% of the proceeds. I predict a 60% chance of prevailing, and an expected total settlement or judgment of $10 million on my $100,000 investment. In this case, the expected value of my investment is 60% times ((2.5 times $100k) plus (.015% times $10 million)) = 60% X ($250k + $150k) = $240k. My annual pre-tax rate of return on the investment depends on whether I get paid in six months or five years.

Beware of Idiotic Leverage. This business is both volatile and unpredictable, so I have chosen not to use leverage on any of these investments. If an investment is too big for my company, I sometimes bring in a single partner to co-invest; by doing so, I bring in additional equity, not debt. Others in my industry obtain loans based on a percentage of the value of their portfolio—not me. This is an interesting juxtaposition of being conservative on my capital structure, but deeply invested in "risky" bets. The dangerous mix that I avoid, of course, is a highly leveraged capital structure combined with high-volatile and uncertain bets.

Find Free Options. The principle says to look for free options, and be careful about giving them away. Frequently when I invest in a lawsuit funding, the client wants a guarantee that he can come back later and get a second transaction with the same terms. The answer is always "no"—unless he is willing to pay a substantial option premium for the right, but not the obligation, to do a later transaction. At the end of this discussion, the clients generally decide to simply cross that bridge when they come to it. If the case is going well, I will usually want to make another investment, anyway.

Put Your Socks on Right. The details are critical in this business. If the case is breach of contract, I spend considerable time reviewing the contracts, reading the emails, and understanding what actually went wrong. Likewise, I'll want a client who understands the details and recalls them from memory, with precision. And most important of all, I want an attorney who already understands the specifics of the case and the likely evolution of the litigation.

Life Happens. It happens to my clients and it can happen in a case that "can't lose." So I study the possible outcomes and make a bet, but totally understand that no investment is a sure thing.

♦♦♦
♦♦♦

APPLICATION TWO
ENRON ONLINE

While running Enron's Western US Natural Gas desk in late 1995, I was asked to study the impact of a new electronic trading system introduced by Williams Pipeline called "Streamline." Streamline was meant to replace natural gas market transactions that were typically made "over the counter" via telephone with an electronic trading platform. "Streamline" would provide a small incentive for market makers to post electronic buy prices ("bids") and sell prices ("offers") for natural gas across the country, at the most common trading points, from New York and Florida to the California border.

Enron's initial thinking was that we could:

a) create our own competing system using the same model as "Streamline,"
b) become an active market maker on the "Streamline" system,
c) use the prices and system on "Streamline" *without* being a market maker, or
d) ignore this new trading platform.

A "market maker" is a trader who will post a competitive "bid" price at which it will buy a commodity or asset, and simultaneously post a competitive "offer" price at which it will sell the commodity or asset. The less liquid the market, the more vital the role of market maker. Once a publicly traded stock is broadly traded (like GOOG, AAPL or FB), the large number of buyers and sellers reduce the importance of a market maker. But in new markets, they are critical. **The market maker maintains liquidity and transparency in the market—valuable functions.**

The Streamline venture never gained much steam. Williams had trouble getting market makers to provide "tight" (a very small difference between the selling and buying price) two-way markets. If the traditional phone-traded market's best offer was $4.02 and the best bid was at $4.01, Streamline might be showing an offer of $4.03 and a bid at $4.00. So, who would ever bother even checking Streamline? Most of the time, Enron was offering a tighter two-way market in the existing phone-traded natural gas and electricity sectors.

After mulling over the opportunity for some time, I came up with another alternative: creating our own electronic trading platform, with Enron as the market maker on every transaction. Both my boss, Kevin Hannon, and our managing director, Lou Pai (I was only a director at the time) quickly agreed.

Teammate David Grevelle proposed that we use the internet to deliver our electronic system, rather than a private network like Williams was using. It seems obvious today, but this was 1995, and the question of internet security was a real concern. We concluded that we would eventually build a platform where our counterparties could transact online, but to get started, we would just provide a system in which our traders could show two-way prices online, and then our customers would phone in (remember when we used land lines?) to actually transact.

We dabbled at this for a few years with little impact. Then, in the spring of 1999, Greg Whalley, Enron's head trader at the time, proposed expanding the system. The dot-com boom was in full swing, and we realized that we needed to get on with it, or we were going to miss the opportunity. To run the project, we tapped Louise Kitchen, a bright and aggressive 29-year-old woman who was then managing the UK natural gas trading desk for me. Within six months she had over 250 people working on the project, some full-time, others part-time (like the credit, payment processing, and accounting groups, along with the attorneys evaluating the law in 22 countries).

Of course, a critical group was our Information Technology Department, led by Philippe Bibi. Whalley, who was headquartered in Houston, was backing the project with incredible drive, and we both provided many of the employees who worked on the project. I had no role in the execution of this idea other than cheerleading, covering some of the costs from my budget, and providing key manpower.

A few business writers have questioned how Whalley and I could simply authorize this project without anyone else's approval. At the time, we managed 100% of the trading at Enron (by then we were both managing directors), and were funding the project from our own budgets. It never really crossed our minds to ask anyone else for approval. In September of that year, Greg and I decided to tell Jeff Skilling, Enron's president, about it. Once he got into the details, he quickly turned into a huge supporter. Skilling's general philosophy was, if it was worth doing, it was worth doing big and fast, which was great when things worked out, and costly when they didn't. By the way, the "go-big-or-go-home" approach was widespread in the business world in 1999, with the dot-com revolution leading the charge. Enron Online (EOL) launched on November 29, 1999, and within three months, it was processing a thousand transactions worth approximately $450 million every day. Before Enron came crashing down, (our computers never did), the system was routinely processing 5,000 transactions worth close to $6 billion daily. This was no mirage or figment of anyone's imagination; this system was changing the way that the commodity trading industry operated.

Many of these transactions were derivatives, so a $10,000 transaction would only have revenue equal to the eventual settlement on the transaction, which might be quite small. But when we sold $10,000 of physical natural gas, this resulted in the same amount of revenue. By September 2001, Enron was doing about $17 billion in revenue *per month* from all of its businesses, with its trading business producing the vast majority of it.

WHICH PRINCIPLES APPLY TO ENRON ONLINE?

Think in Opposites. We did the *opposite* of what the Williams Streamline system was trying to achieve. Their platform was based on multiple market makers, and the last thing they envisioned was one company being involved in every trade. Our value proposition was that we would provide outstanding liquidity and transparency in exchange for a big market share (we were on one side of every single transaction, so it didn't get any bigger), and in return, we knew who was buying and selling. At Enron, we wanted a system that enhanced our position as the leading market maker. If we had asked most of the trading world if they preferred a many-to-many market or a many-to-one market, they would have unanimously voted (with the exception of our one vote) for the first option.

Combine an Information Advantage with Volatility. We were providing transparency and liquidity to the market in exchange for knowing who was on the other side of every trade.

Welcome Forks in the Road. The first fork in the road was the threat that Williams' Streamline system presented to Enron's market dominance. The second fork was in early 1999, at the height of the dot-com excitement, when new entrants were using the internet to radically change the way business was done.

Think on the Margin. Once we established EOL, there were hundreds of potential enhancements that could have made the system marginally more valuable. For example, we might have opened the platform to third-party market makers, in markets where Enron did not want that role. This would have made the system slightly more "sticky," and helped to keep our trading partners glued to their EOL screen.

Don't Jump the Gun, and Strike While the Iron is Hot. When we first started looking at creating an online trading platform in late 1995, it really didn't feel to me like the right time to make a massive investment, no one else suggested it, and I didn't have much clout in the company yet. We didn't know what our trading partners would think, how reliable the internet would be, and how much it would cost to build. By 1999, it was a brave new world. Dot-com mania was at its peak, and it quickly became obvious to several of us that the time had arrived to stop messing around.

Fight Friction Costs. Once Louise Kitchen took over the project, she immediately emphasized a design that would improve the front-office/back-office flow. Prior to EOL, traders had to manually record and enter every transaction into a computer database. Forgotten transactions, transposed numbers, and other "creative" data-entry errors could be costly and waste time. The EOL system had the benefit that a completed trade was automatically recorded, perfectly, and everyone from the back office to the schedulers had access to this real-time information.

My goal was always to develop our system such that we could adjust our prices, counterpart by counterpart, in real time. This practice would manage our risk based on each company's ever-changing credit quality, and our exact credit exposure to that company. This is discussed in the Application Six, "Enron Credit."

Never Run Out of Cash. This was a challenge with this business model. We were totally reliant on the trade credit that our counterparts granted us. As a result of the convenience and value that this system offered to the commodity trading world, Enron was given far more trade credit than it would have otherwise received. Ultimately, we may have had an opportunity via EOL to radically change the payment timing on commodities (this was not in the works when we went out of business). For natural gas delivered during September, the seller did not get paid until about October 23. This lag time added to the credit risk and cash flow constraints in the industry as a whole. The history of this provision reflected the way utilities had always designed their payment terms, early on when they were the dominant customers.

But we might have had an opportunity to create a two-tiered system, offering a second payment option, where the seller was paid every 10 days. For example, in a new and improved system, the seller might get paid on the 11th for gas delivered between September 1 and September 10, and on the 21st for gas delivered between September 11 and September 20. We would then display two different prices, with the price for the commodity with the earlier payment being lower than the latter.

Find Free Options. We were giving free options (which I usually discourage), although our free options had no time value, because they always expired as the prices changed in real time. We charged nothing for having an EOL screen. This information was extremely valuable, and we might have started charging some or all of our counterparts for each screen they used—especially those entities that did not transact often.

Put Your Socks on Right. Prior to providing an online market-making function, the trader on our desk could intuitively adjust the price depending on who was calling (a buyer or a seller). EOL showed the same prices to everyone. We might have adjusted for customers in real time such that we displayed a slightly lower bid (or buy) price to natural gas producers, and a slightly higher ask (or sell) price for those counterparts that were always buyers (like utilities).

Be Optimally Persistent. In 1995, the time was not right from a technology perspective to have pulled off Enron Online with nearly the same success. But we kept the idea alive until the time was right. Three and a half years after our initial consideration, lower-cost technology (both software and hardware) made the project more feasible.

♦♦♦
♦♦♦

APPLICATION THREE
SUTTON BRIDGE POWER PLANT

In discussing this application, my thanks go to Dale Surbey (head of Enron Europe's structuring group) who knew, and still remembers, the details of this transaction amazingly well. This story also appeared as a *Harvard Business Review* Case Study. As you can imagine, if Enron ever hoped to repeat the deal with Eastern or another party, we needed to withhold many of the specifics. We did a reasonably good job of keeping our mouths closed, and finally you can read here about "the rest of the story."

In late 1996, Enron Europe signed a huge deal with the Eastern Group for a 15-year natural gas power plant tolling agreement. I want to walk you through this transaction, and review how some of the ideas discussed in this book applied. For those unfamiliar with the lingo, a "tolling agreement" is a deal between the provider of a finished product (such as electricity) and the supplier of raw materials (i.e. natural gas or fuel oil) to process the raw material for a specified fee ("toll") into a finished product. The tolling party also usually pays a fee or lease payment for the right to have the raw materials converted into a finished product.

The Sutton Bridge transaction was a totally new way of financing a power plant. The IPP (independent power producer) was developed by a company "independent" from the usual monopoly utility that used to build and operate all of the power plants in their service area.

Historically, the way independent power producers (IPPs) had been structured around the world was:

- ❖ the IPP developer signed a 15-year fuel contract to supply the new power plant;
- ❖ the IPP developer simultaneously signed a 15-year off-take agreement for the electricity generated by the new plant (almost always with a different counterpart—typically, an electric utility) at a pre-defined price; and

❖ the new plant was project-financed based on having a secure fuel supply and a creditworthy buyer for the electricity.

Our team (led by Rich DiMichelle, Tani Nath, David Lewis, Eric Gadd, and lead negotiator Stewart Seeligson) turned that arrangement on its ears with this transaction, by thinking in multiple dimensions.

Sutton Bridge was structured such that:

a. We signed a tolling agreement with the Eastern Group (one of the few times that a trader has gone short a power plant). Eastern was a local distribution company in England that had about three million electric customers, and had been owned for about a year by the Hanson Group PLC, a company whose usual objective was to buy underperforming assets and turn them around.

b. We signed this agreement in late 1996, with the tolling to begin on May 1, 1999. This allowed us time to hedge the transaction by building a power plant at Sutton Bridge, Lincolnshire, a town about 140 kilometers north of London.

c. We built the 790 MW power plant over the next two years at a cost of about $550 million.

d. The tolling agreement was not tied to any specific plant (although Eastern probably assumed that the physical Sutton Bridge plant was our hedge), and did not require us to keep the plant. Once the plant came online, we were even more bearish about electricity prices, so almost immediately we put it up for sale and sold it to London Electricity (a subsidiary of EDF Energy) for $740 million, which included their assuming the debt on the plant. This gave us the option of using whatever vehicle we chose to meet our contractual requirements with Eastern.

e. For a monthly fee, the tolling agreement gave Eastern the option, but not the obligation, to give us natural gas on any day, and receive back electricity that was roughly equivalent to the same position they would have had if they were operating the Sutton Bridge power plant.

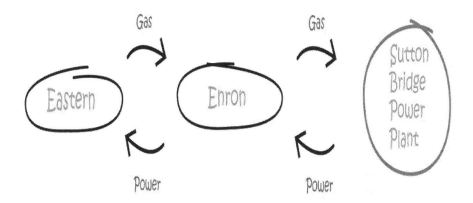

We made far more than the difference between the $740 million selling price and the $550 million construction cost because the value of our tolling agreement with Eastern had gotten much more valuable (to us) since we had signed it at the end of 1996. The trading value of the physical power plant had understandably dropped with the declining value of wholesale electricity.

The way large structured trades are booked at investment banks and trading houses is that the transaction is broken down into its component buckets of risk. When we did the transaction with Eastern originally, we were:

- ❖ long natural gas (which Eastern gave us),
- ❖ short electricity (which Eastern took back),
- ❖ short natural gas volatility,
- ❖ short electricity volatility,
- ❖ long the correlation of natural gas and electricity prices, and
- ❖ long the credit quality of the Eastern Group and its parent, the Hanson Group PLC (who was providing the parental guarantee).

Eastern had exactly the opposite positions, except they were initially long our credit quality and the credit of Enron Corp.

On day one, our positions were mostly offset (but not perfectly hedged) by having the physical power plant fully permitted and ready to construct.

We ran our models every day, and as prices changed, our positions changed. Keep in mind that we had to initially forecast our gas and electricity position for every 15-minute period for the next 17-1/2 years—over half a million buckets of time. For example, if natural gas got more expensive relative to electricity, we anticipated and modeled that our counterpart would toll less gas. Or if electricity got more valuable and natural gas prices stayed constant, we anticipated that the counterpart would toll more.

There were days that Eastern tolled gas when it made no economic sense based on the relative value of the natural gas and the value of electricity. And sometimes they didn't toll when the numbers indicated they should. This was simply a bonus for us, because our models assumed that they would exercise their daily option optimally, and every day that they didn't, we made more money than we anticipated—we got lucky.

WHICH PRINCIPLES APPLY TO SUTTON BRIDGE?

There's Always a Bear Market Somewhere. This was a period where we were bearish about the future UK electricity prices because so many new power plants were being built, compared to the changes in the demand for electricity. We consistently went short the power market during this time, and Sutton Bridge was the most profitable transaction we ever did in Europe.

Multiple Dimensions = Degrees of Freedom. The tolling agreement, construction of the physical plant, sale of the finished plant, and changing power costs all played a part in making this deal successful.

One reason the deal structure made sense was that Eastern's credit was not any better than Enron's. Traditionally, the excellent credit of a utility helps to keep financing costs down for an IPP. Since that was not the case, we were able to capture option value because Enron was originally the owner, operator, and controller of the plant.

Think on the Margin. The long-term nature of this deal demanded that we remain fluid, with our fingers on the pulse of the market. Forecasting had to be done on several levels: price changes, the rate of price changes, the market supply and demand, etc. We had no choice but to think, plan, and act on the margin, allowing us to extract even more value from the plant and agreements as time passed.

Do Not Ignore Pride of Ownership. From the time that Enron signed the first Eastern deal and the plant was operational, power prices dropped. Therefore, the "cash flow" value of the physical plant also dropped accordingly. Yet, we were able to sell the plant for more than both its cost to build *and* its trading value because of the "pride-of-ownership" premium we were able to charge for the physical plant. The day we sold the plant, we booked another substantial profit.

Strike While the Iron is Hot. After negotiating with General Electric to purchase the gas turbines for Sutton Bridge, but before the plant was operational, we developed encouraging data showing the original Eastern transaction would be more profitable than we first expected. The plant would be cheaper, more efficient, have higher capacity, and an all-round better deal than we had envisioned when we booked the deal. So what did we do? We signed a second transaction with Eastern on roughly the same terms as the first one. By that time, we were even more bearish on the UK power market, and knew that, at a minimum, we could build a second power plant to hedge our position. Eastern didn't benefit from this same fast feedback and information advantage because they were not building any physical power plants at the time. Enron never did build that second plant—it was always cheaper to simply buy the power and sell the gas in the traded market.

Find Free Options. The Sutton Bridge structure preserved free options (for Enron) that were normally wasted in a traditional IPP. In the customary arrangement, the Power Purchase Agreement (PPA) could not be amended without the approval of the banks, increasing the friction costs of any contract changes. In a traditional IPP, the power buyer (Eastern) has control over dispatching the plant. So, even if the plant should be running and Eastern chose not to operate it, value would have been destroyed because it would sit idle. That was not the case at Sutton Bridge, because Enron kept the rights to operate the plant based on its own criteria and needs. In a traditional IPP, the plant could not be sold without the approval of the power buyer (Eastern). In this case, Enron retained sole control of that decision and benefited greatly from that flexibility. Once we sold the power plant, we were free to find the most advantageous way to meet our gas and power positions.

Get Lucky. There was substantially more profit in the eventual power plant than the theoretical one that Enron had sold to Eastern. The tolling agreement was based on a very conservative set of figures, and Enron captured all of the upside with lower construction costs, higher capacity, and greater efficiency than was anticipated in the tolling agreement.

Enron also recognized that Eastern's occasional mishandling of their daily scheduling and exercise of their options was not always optimum (for them). We simply pocketed the extra money that this lucky twist brought us.

♦♦♦
♦♦♦

APPLICATION FOUR
ENRON DIRECT

In Europe, Enron had a very successful retail natural gas and electricity business. In the United States, it did not.

Here was the difference:

In Europe, we started Enron Direct by buying, for about $1 million, an existing small natural gas retailer that had a successful model of acquiring small- to medium-size business customers. We used outside agents to secure the customer base, which kept our customer-acquisition costs low. The transaction was championed by Dave Pope, whom I mentioned in the Free Option story.

A second major advantage was that the deregulated system was consistent across all of the UK, a nation with a population of over 60 million. The UK deregulation was practical and allowed real competition for customers. Niall Ferguson reminds us that deregulation is *not* bad, but bad regulation *is*.**

But that was only part of the formula. The most important thing is that we were extremely bearish on UK electricity prices, and this segment turned out to be a very efficient way of getting short electricity in this market. As a result, we could offer prices lower than those being charged by existing utilities, and still make a substantial profit—especially since we were more bearish than most of the other sellers in the market.

After Enron went into bankruptcy, this business was sold for over $150 million to Centrica (British Gas).

By the way, after getting Enron Direct up and running in the UK, Dave Pope moved back to Alberta and started the same retail natural gas business from scratch at Enron Canada; this business was ultimately sold for about $100 million Canadian.

Electricity and natural gas deregulation in the US was a totally different story.

First, each state had its own plan, or lack of a plan. So a business value proposition that worked in one state might be a loser in another.

Lucky And Good

California had the worst plan, with a cockeyed partial deregulation design for electricity.

Second, Enron was not bearish on wholesale electricity prices in the US (a much bigger market than the retail natural gas market). Remember that a big retail load is usually a "short position," and one that you don't want if you're bullish on wholesale prices.

Third, California electricity deregulation was subject to gaming, including players being able to send power from within California to outside the state and drive up prices in California even higher—a tactic which Enron, along with other wholesale players, exploited.

Fourth, California's incumbent utilities had been required to sell off most of their generation to third parties. And they were also required to drop the prices to their existing retail customers by 10%. So, in fact, very few retail customers had an incentive to switch to new suppliers. When wholesale prices started to exceed retail electricity prices, the utilities were stuck with having to supply their customers at a loss. The customers weren't given any price signals that would encourage them to use less, and the utilities weren't able to pass on the much higher costs to their customers. **It was a system that combined the worst of regulation and the worst of deregulation.** The result was rolling blackouts and the bankruptcy of Pacific Gas and Electric, a utility for which I had previously worked.

Electricity was successfully deregulated in Texas, the UK, and Norway, with none of these problems. These markets were successful because the deregulation was fully and intelligently phased in.

** The exact quote/reference being: "In my view, the lesson of the 1970s is not that deregulation is bad, but that bad regulation is bad, especially in the context of bad monetary and fiscal policy. And I believe the same can be said of our crisis, too. The financial crisis that began in 2007 had its origins precisely in over-complex regulation. A serious history of the crisis would need to have at least five chapters on its perverse consequences." *Niall Ferguson. "The Darwinian Economy." Recorded at The New-York Historical Society, New York City; first broadcast on BBC Radio 4 and the BBC World Service. 26 June 2012.*

WHICH PRINCIPLES APPLY TO ENRON DIRECT AND THE RETAIL ELECTRICITY BUSINESS?

Find Inflection Points. The best time to acquire retail customers is when prices have reached a peak and you expect them to decline.

There's Always a Bear Market Somewhere. The UK retail electricity business was a great way to short the market.

Multiple Dimensions = Degrees of Freedom. In the UK we bought a retail natural gas business, but quickly expanded it to the much more profitable retail electricity business.

Know the Long and Short of It. Retail customers are a short position—take them on only if you expect prices to drop.

Fight Friction Costs. Each regulatory market is different, and requires additional overhead to understand its rules and to manage the regulatory risk associated with its peculiarities. Also, in the UK, we had a low-cost way to acquire new customers.

♦♦♦
♦♦♦

APPLICATION FIVE
GOVERNMENT PENSION RETURNS

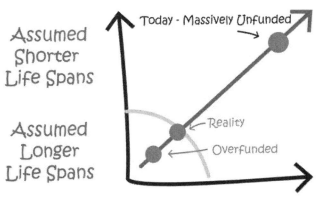

Let me contrast free and competitive markets (the UK power market, not the California power market) with the average US public pension's approach to estimating future rates of return. These estimated returns are set by politicians who do not (or who are not forced to) rely on independent, transparent, market-based mechanisms. The result is that public pensions have systematically underfunded their reserves.

These pensions continually overpromise and under save. Nationwide, unfunded liabilities are in the tens of trillions of dollars. Niall Ferguson, in *The Great Degeneration*, claims it is more than a hundred trillion, much greater than the traditional debt of our federal, state, and local governments.

Experience shows that, as markets and economies fluctuate, so too will the rate of return. One only need look at bank savings statements over the past several years to note that savings have been paying tiny interest rates—money might be relatively safe, but earnings are potentially nil. Obviously, if the pension managers brilliantly choose when to invest in the equities markets, real estate market, and debt markets, they can beat bank interest rates—but they have not historically done much better than the rest of us in picking their spots.

However, it's not politically correct to honestly assess and fight for a lower estimated investment return forecast, because that means that either taxpayers directly or the government (taxpayers, a bit more indirectly) have to come up with more money *today*. The reason is obvious. If the pension fund is going to make 25% per year, they don't have to collect much today to pay big pensions 20 years from now. On the other hand, if they're going to earn nothing, they have to collect every penny that they'll be paying out in the coming years. And if they're going to lose money (yes it happens), they have to collect even *more* than they are going to eventually pay out.

These flagrant political practices have caused those responsible for the public pension system to consistently overestimate pension fund earning expectations, providing the excuse to underfund the reserves. We don't have nearly enough to meet the promises, to pay the future pensions. If CEOs and CFOs of publicly-traded US companies took this same approach, they would be subject to criminal prosecution.

Lucky And Good

In March 2012, CalPERS (the California Public Employees' Retirement System, the biggest US public pension fund, accountable for investing retirement funds of many California state employees) made the "tough" decision to lower their expected investment return from 7.75% to 7.5 %.

Can you say "dreaming?"

Even with this minimal adjustment, California's state fund had to shell out another $167 million, and local governments and agencies also had to add more to the piggy bank. They were not happy campers. Another article declared that: "CalPERS could have socked the state for another $425 million. Instead, it chose a 'compromise' measure that's expected to cost $167 million."

I would label this a "compromise with reality."

What if CalPERS had reduced their investment return down to, say, 4%? (As I write this, the risk-free investment of 30-year Treasuries is returning an annual yield of about 3.5 %.) How would that have gone over?

At least for US Treasuries, there is a market; yields rise and fall, based on thousands of market factors that change every single day. Of course, the Federal Reserve frequently steps in and "tinkers" with the market, buying trillions of dollars of debt in order to manage interest rates, so even this is only a pseudo-market.

These factors obviously don't impact the estimates used by public pension managers, resulting in a distorted view of reality. For the fiscal year that ended on June 30, 2012, CalPERS announced an investment return of 1% for the prior 12 months versus the projected figure, 7.5%. Not even close!

The Teachers Retirement System of the State of Illinois (TRS) is considering lowering the estimated return on its $37 billion portfolio, according to the agency's chief. The current estimated rate of return is 8.5%, one of the highest in the country, and has remained at the same level for 25 years. (In this case, consistency is not a virtue.) The TRS investment managers are clearly superior to California's—NOT!

A *Wall Street Journal* article reported: "Lowering the assumed rate could increase liabilities at the fund." Idiot reporter! The liabilities are unaffected by a changed assumption; they would only be *acknowledged* as unfunded liabilities. (In the real world, this is referred to as: "getting real," "fessing up," or "facing facts." Based on the 8.5% assumed rate of return, the retirement system is still 46% underfunded. Imagine how underfunded the pension system would appear if they used a reasonable investment return (say, 4.5%). By any rational business measure, the fund is already insolvent, but nobody wants to take the pain today and come to grips with working through the problem. Collecting another $100 a month from each teacher is not going to solve the problem in Illinois.

Heck, Bernie Madoff only promised his investors 12% per year. These pensions are consistently underestimating life spans and overestimating the investment returns they will earn.

I won't address the bias in life span estimates—it will only increase your level of pessimism, if you are counting on a pension payment (unless you think that Obamacare will kill Americans at an earlier age). I do have a potential, although politically impossible, solution for estimating future investment returns.

Here goes: We should create a Pension Investment Return Prediction Market (PIRPM). Every year, CalPERS reports their actual investment return. In 2011 it was 1.1%. In the 12 months ending on June 30, 2012, it was 1%. If history repeats itself, we won't know the 12 month results ending June 30, 2013 until about April 2014 (slow feedback—maybe they are using an abacus to calculate their returns). So, there would be a traded market for the following years: 2014 might trade at 5%, 2015 might trade at 4%, and so forth. Based on market prices that are visible in the traded market, the pension fund managers would use an aggregate to determine how much money they needed in the piggy bank today.

Traders would be invited to speculate. Yes, they would gamble and bet—like punters (the English term for bettors) in the European markets wager on national elections, and the way we bet on the Super Bowl, or on movie prospects at the Hollywood Stock Exchange. Traders and speculators could bet on the investment returns that

CalPERS would earn, year by year, for the succeeding years. The latest price (for each year) would indicate what the market was expecting CalPERS to earn on its investments each year. Eventually, we could take the politics out of the investment-return estimating game. Government would be required to use the traded market value to estimate their future investment returns.

But this proposed market has no chance of being established because:

1) It would result in a very unpopular short-term outcome. Estimating a lower investment return would force an already insolvent State of California, and its cities, counties, and local agencies to cough up billions more to fund their pension promises. Even without this pension problem, California is on the verge of insolvency. Jerry Brown announced in early 2013 that he will balance California's budget: "For the next four years we are talking about a balanced budget." I'll believe it when I see it, Governor.

2) Other than the California taxpayer and the average California pensioner, who are *hoping* for a higher investment return, there are no "non-speculator" participants in this market who are naturally long or short, as there are in the pork-belly, gasoline, or electricity markets. In other words, the market would be almost entirely made up of traders and speculators—and the Commodities Futures Trading Commission hates that idea, because they worry that it looks too much like gambling.

3) If such a market were established, the estimated return would drop so quickly that speculators would be blamed for manipulating the market. Politicians and regulators would step in, adding rules and restrictions to impede the price movements. If you believe that government regulation and intervention in the US ethanol, corn, milk, cheese, and solar industries has distorted all the market signals, why would you expect politicians to keep their grubby hands off of this one? Nancy Pelosi and Harry

Reid would push for a Department of Justice investigation into the bastards who were shorting the market.

This idea won't happen. Although, if this market were established and allowed to function freely, it would shine a bright light on the problems in our public pensions and other unfunded/underfunded government liabilities. In the US, our unfunded liabilities, including pensions and health care promises, are at least five times bigger than our government debt. Now *that's* risky, and will eventually be unlucky for most pensioners and taxpayers. In the end, traders are probably lucky that this market will not be created, because who do you think would take the blame when pensioners stopped getting their pensions?

There is, however, an alternative approach in which this market might flourish. If a traded predictive market were developed based on wagering a pseudo currency, it also might be useful. Regulators are unlikely to go along with allowing the public to gamble with real money. But playing a "game" with quasi money, like Monopoly dollars, Farmville coins, or even the remaining credits on a pinball machine, has usually kept regulators out of the picture.

In *The Wisdom of Crowds*, James Surowiecki discusses how predictive markets can still be quite accurate in forecasting this type of variable, even without real money on the line. The challenge is that: 1) you need a diversity of participants; 2) you need to find a mechanism for insuring that no one is manipulating the market (don't have California regulators set up the rules); and 3) the participants have to have an incentive to make their best predictions.

WHICH PRINCIPLES APPLY TO GOVERNMENT PENSION RETURNS?

Unfortunately most of the principles below have been ignored:

Nothing is Risk Free. We used to think that a government pension was a sure thing. No longer.

Find Inflection Points. We have not yet reached the inflection points that will require fundamental change to public pensions. Regrettably, it will be extremely painful when the bubble bursts.

Fight for Fast Feedback. These public pensions have been operating for decades, and the voting public will only understand the size of the bubbles once pensioners start getting a haircut. A promise has been made, but the piper doesn't have to be paid yet—primarily the piper's sons and granddaughters will have to pony up.

Play the Odds. This requires honesty and objectivity—qualities uncommon in Washington and our state and local capitals. A predictive market would do a far better job of predicting the current odds than our politicians will ever do.

Beware of Idiotic Leverage. Unfortunately, this is all about idiotic leverage. If the pension funds were underfunded by a few percent, the problem would be manageable. But we have passed the point of any easy and painless resolution.

Think on the Margin. At the very least, politicians could keep the liabilities from getting any worse. They could restructure the promises on a go-forward basis, in which the existing promises are kept in place, but nobody would see any increase in their pension benefits. Over the last two decades, the private sector has been freezing its pensions, replacing them with 401(k)-type programs. In the private sector, the company simply starts paying a certain amount into the employee-managed retirement account. This is not happening in the public sector. Private companies have generally kept existing retirees' pensions as they were and have either cashed out those who have not yet retired, or given employees the option of transferring this asset into a self-directed 401(k) or IRA program.

♦♦♦
♦♦♦

APPLICATION SIX
ENRON CREDIT

One of the factors that always bothered me about Enron's trading and commodity businesses was the imprecision and sluggishness of our credit risk pricing, which I still believed to be better and faster than anyone else's in our industry. We also faced a lack of liquidity, poor transparency, and high transaction costs in hedging our credit risk.

Selling a small amount of natural gas or oil for six months to an A-rated, publicly-traded company was one thing. Selling a large amount of 15-year electricity to a subsidiary of a BBB-company was quite another.

My original premise was that our company's biggest cumulative risk by far was the trade credit Enron granted to our counterparts. That wasn't what eventually brought the company down, because the risk was split into thousands of uncorrelated buckets—but it might have, if we had not improved our processes based on the sheer size of these positions.

To address this issue, I assigned Bryan Seyfried to investigate whether there were better vehicles for evaluating and hedging our credit risk. If not, I asked him to consider whether we could use our international market presence to create a profitable market-making operation in credit.

At the time, we had two major alternatives for managing our trade credit: 1) ratings by the credit-rating agencies for evaluating the credit quality; and 2) the credit default swap market for hedging some of our risk. Both of these would come to major disrepute during the 2008 banking crisis.

As we increased internet transactions via Enron Online, a few things were happening:

- ❖ Our average margin per transaction was shrinking (the result of our market-maker model). We were making more in total, but probably less per transaction.

Real-World Applications

- Our volumes were swelling exponentially.
- Our total credit exposure was increasing every day.
- Credit risk was a part of every single transaction we did in every market in every country.
- The number of counterparts we had was growing.
- The amount of our bad credit reserves was a rough approximation, and not based sufficiently on prices in a real credit market.
- Our credit department evaluation of credit risk was not "real time."
- We didn't have any efficient means for hedging our credit risk.

The common thread among our trading businesses (energy, shipping, metals, pulp and paper), and our retail electricity business, was credit. I wanted a mechanism to price the credit risk in real time, and I wanted a vehicle to hedge the credit risk for a reasonable price, when we chose to do so. We were adjusting all of our other prices in real time, so the old system of sending a transaction to the credit department for review and getting an answer back in a few days just wasn't fast enough or precise enough.

CREDIT DEFAULT SWAP MARKET

The credit default swap market had already been in place for several years, but from my angle, it never did the job for several reasons:

First, at the time, credit default swaps only worked for hedging the credit risk of large counterparties that had publicly traded debt. The basic transaction involved paying a premium for the right to exchange a bond (if the bond went into default) for its full value. But most of our counterparts were not publicly traded companies.

For example, when we did our largest transactions with the Eastern Group, it was a privately-held subsidiary originally owned by the Hanson Group PLC. (Eastern Group was subsequently sold to TXU Europe, a subsidiary of TXU, a US-based energy company.) Our credit risk was generally with the Eastern Group, but we could only evaluate and hedge the Hanson Group PLC credit risk via a credit default swap.

Unless we got a full parental guarantee, we were at risk of the subsidiary going bankrupt without any obligation by the parent company to make up the difference. Even if we got a partial or full parental guarantee, the parent sometimes faced deterioration in credit quality as well.

Second, if a credit default occurred, (bankruptcy or nonpayment of their public debt), collecting on our hedge had plenty of additional friction costs. We had been trying to hedge the risk that we wouldn't get paid on a commodity transaction, but now we had to shift gears and buy a bond in order to trade it in for cash. Making money on trading in this bond (which would have dropped substantially in price with the default) for cash (we would receive 100% of the face value of the bond) would ostensibly make up for the money we didn't get paid by the customer. Since we were not a regular in the bond trading market, however, we were likely to get hosed by the investment banks in the process. (They saw us as Chumps ready for slaughter.)

Third, the investment banks' control over the credit default business was partially a result of their *not* providing transparency and liquidity to this market (a different business model than Enron's). This applied especially to JPMorgan, which had originally created the credit default market and dominated it at the time.

OUR VALUE PROPOSITION

We developed an alternative structure—the bankruptcy swap—via a new business entity called Enron Credit. The bankruptcy swap would trade the perceived probability that a legal entity would declare bankruptcy during a given time period. It might be traded at 0.3% by 0.35% (bid offer spread) for the next two-year period, and the percentages always went up as more time was added to the clock.

So, for an up-front premium of 0.35% (this figure is an example only) of the notional amount—say, $1 million—the transaction premium would equal $3,500 (.35% x $1 million). If Whizblast.com went bankrupt during the two-year period, we would pay our counterpart $1 million. Of course, our counterparts would also bear the burden of Enron's own credit risk. If both Whizblast.com and Enron went bankrupt, the hedge was useless (like buying fire insurance from an insurance company that goes bankrupt). I am happy to report that Whizblast.com never went bankrupt (it does not have a single liability as I write this—and, unfortunately, also no asset other than a cool name).

We hoped to spur an active market with multiple buyers and sellers of bankruptcy swaps. The credit market is one that doesn't work well with one dominant seller of protection, such as AIG in the credit default market, in early 2008.

If Enron bought a bankruptcy swap from another company for an up-front premium of 0.3% on a notional contract of $1 million, we would pay a premium of $3,000, and would receive $1 million if the traded company went bankrupt during the same two-year period.

The bankruptcy swap had many advantages from my perspective. Its transparency and liquidity reduced friction costs, and it could be quickly and easily transacted via Enron Online. Neither party would need to deliver or receive a bond in order to collect on it. So it could eventually cover many more companies, i.e. those with no publicly traded debt. Therefore, the bankruptcy swap might allow companies that were short the credit of other companies (a situation where one made money if another company went bankrupt) to earn some extra income from their short credit position.

For example, Intel is probably short the credit of their competitor Advanced Micro Devices. Verizon is short the credit of AT&T, because it is their biggest competitor. Finally, and of great importance to me, this market would give us a real-time price signal for credit risk for those companies that were being traded.

When we started this business, Enron's credit was BBB+. (It probably shouldn't have been that high.) Our senior finance people told me we had a reasonable chance of getting our credit rating raided to A-. (We didn't quite get there.) We were challenged by the fact that we generally had a poorer credit rating than the investment banks.

In his book *Enron: The Rise and Fall*, Loren Fox mistakenly stated that, "John Sherriff, the President of Enron Europe and the leader of the effort, figured that credit derivatives weren't much of a stretch from energy derivatives given that Enron relied on credit in its trading business." This was not quite right. I never thought competing in this business was going to be easy—I just thought credit evaluation, pricing, and mitigation were critical to our business, and a massive opportunity.

Fox, however, went on to correctly quote me: "Every part of our business involved granting and receiving credit. Really, we were in the credit business more than we were in gas or electricity or oil." Fox opined: "It also loaded more and new risks on Enron." Well, yes and no. We were already in the credit markets big time; whether we liked it or not; we already had plenty of credit risk on the books. I believed that we needed a market in which we could efficiently unload some of our credit risk. And so we tried to change the market with our usual method of entering a market by adding transparency and liquidity, and becoming a market maker.

Credit agencies like Moody's Investors Service, Standard & Poor's, and Fitch Ratings were, and continue to be, bureaucratic train wrecks in evaluating credit worthiness. They are slow, political, and oblivious to what the traded credit markets are telling them. In *The Signal and the Noise*, Nate Silver discusses how the AAA rating implied only a 0.12% chance of default during a five-year period. But Standard & Poor's own figures indicate that 28% of the mortgage-backed securities on which they placed this prized AAA rating defaulted. They were only off by a factor of 233.

As to the politics, the Italian Prosecutor summoned seven officials from both Fitch and Standard & Poor's to answer for a 2011 decision to downgrade Italy's sovereign credit rating. This political and legal pressure does not bode well for an independent appraisal.

Standard & Poor's affirmed Enron's credit rating on October 25, 2001, as BBB+, and only downgraded it to BBB on November 1, 2001. Enron was bankrupt 31 days later.

I have always placed more faith in the prices reflected in free and open markets than in those determined by a governmental bureaucrat or Standard & Poor's (a non-governmental bureaucrat). I wanted a real-time market that responded to what the market was seeing, as the credit-worthiness of our trading partners changed.

From my standpoint, the credit rating agencies had the same limitation as the credit default swap market—they only rated the credit quality of publicly traded companies. (There were a few exceptions in which someone was paying them for an initial rating, which was the case with many of the collateralized debt obligations that they started to rate before the 2008 banking crisis.) But there are far more companies that are *not* publicly traded and have no credit rating than there are those that are rated.

I hoped that we might eventually be able to adjust our other commodity prices, customer by customer (in real time), based on the prices from Enron Credit. We might raise the price of natural gas to one customer if we already had plenty of that credit risk. We also might give that same customer a slightly better bid (or buy) price because this might actually reduce our credit exposure by offsetting an existing position. But we never got that far.

*****

Keep in mind, a thriving bankruptcy swap market would not solve the entire credit risk challenge. If I have granted you credit, I have two separate but related risks: 1) the probability that you will declare bankruptcy; and 2) the uncertainty of my recovery if you do.

I might recover anywhere from zero to 100 cents on the dollar after the bankruptcy. In the case of Enron's bankruptcy, the creditors eventually received 53% of what they were owed (although they probably netted less after paying their legal bills fighting for their claims). This market was big enough that some hedge funds actually stepped in and bought bankruptcy claims early in the process for much less than 53 cents on the dollar, based on the expectation that the eventual payout would yield a nice profit.

If you estimated that a company would pay 50 cents on the dollar in bankruptcy, and they owed you $2 million, then you might only buy a bankruptcy swap for the other half ($1 million). Still, as in most situations, your hedge would be far from perfect.

WHICH PRINCIPLES APPLY TO THE BANKRUPTCY SWAP MARKET?

Start with the Big Picture and the Macro Trends. Enron had growing trade credit exposure; we were managing our price risk in real time but not our credit risk.

Multiple Dimensions = Degrees of Freedom. We needed to move out of the constrained world of hedging credit only on companies with publicly traded debt. The bankruptcy swap did just that by creating a mechanism that worked for small private companies as well as huge publicly traded companies.

Think in Opposites. We wanted to take a problem and not only resolve it, but make money from it.

Think on the Margin. Prices of credit risk reflected in the bankruptcy swap market changed in real time. And, of course, our potential exposure to each individual credit was constantly in flux. By recognizing and making the cost of trade credit transparent across our organization, we could give ourselves a much better chance to consistently make the best marginal decision. A deal originator or trader could eventually put a price on the credit risk, as he could on the other pricing dimensions of a transaction. We never got to the point where this was integrated real-time into our online pricing, but the evolution of this new credit market was getting us closer.

Know the Long and Short of It. We were long the credit of most of our counterparts (in other words we wanted it to get stronger, not worse). At best, we were flat if we had no business with a company. But let's say we had a provision that a transaction with negative mark-to-market value had the additional proviso that we could walk away from a deal if the other company went bankrupt. In this rare case, we might actually be short that company's credit.

Fight Friction Costs. Absent a liquid and transparent bankruptcy swap market, there is no way for many companies to efficiently hedge much of their trade credit risk. The expense prohibits it. Nothing has come close to replacing Enron Credit in providing liquidity and transparency in this massive market for hedging credit risk for companies without publicly-traded debt.

Don't Pick Up Dimes in Front of Steamrollers. If Enron only sold, but never purchased, bankruptcy swaps, we might have been guilty of this nasty habit. But we both bought and sold. Insurance giant AIG, started writing credit default swaps in the mortgage market and picked up plenty of dimes—but generally did not buy much protection. In September 2008, they had to be bailed out by the US federal government, making them the number-one example of the importance of following this principle.

Put Your Socks on Right. We initially listed the ECC (the Enron cost of credit) for over 10,000 companies, and provided real-time two-way bankruptcy swaps for over 400 companies. If our pricing was wrong, we would end up with plenty of losing trades. The details mattered.

Life Happens. Not considering that your customer might declare bankruptcy is denial. Counterparts go bankrupt, and depending on the amount of your business that customer represents and how much they owe you, their bankruptcy could be fatal. The real test of the bankruptcy swap market would have been in the chaos of the 2008 banking crisis. If we had remained in business, and had naively accepted too much exposure to AIG, Bear Stearns and Lehman Brothers, it would have been painful.

♦♦♦
♦♦♦

APPLICATION SEVEN
COVERING YOUR LEGAL BASES

ADVICE FOR CIVILIANS IN THE LITIGATION WORLD

Over the years, as a non-attorney, I have seen an awful lot of litigation. My current work requires regular contact with a variety of lawyers. I have great respect for some, and despise a few. I've heard the joke that 90% of attorneys give the other 10% a bad name. My experience is not as bad as the joke suggests, but I've learned to be very careful about which attorneys to trust.

Some might question how a trader can be so critical, but my bias is based on my own set of real-world experiences. I have several good attorney friends (Joe, Geoff, Jeremy, Frank, Sam, Ken, Alex, Elisha, Hugo, Jeff, Dave, Michael, Jon, Ron, Dianne, Donna, to name a few—I'm sure they don't want to be fully identified). There: I've come out of the closet and admitted it. The attorneys who are my friends are honest, hard-working, and smart (just like the traders whom I respect). **But my overriding philosophy is that "friends tell friends about lawyers."**

In my business, I offer business advice to non-attorneys who are about to begin dealing with lawyers (big business). I have a blog at HireAnAttorney.blogspot.com about how to hire, manage, and fire attorneys, specifically because I think the profession is pathetic and self-serving about giving non-attorneys advice about how to "manage" them.

People who call their state bar associations to request information about hiring an attorney usually get very little useful information. If you ask them to recommend a lawyer or two, you are likely to get the next name on their state's licensed attorney roster, without regard to that professional's skills or cost. Callers are typically given names of attorneys who are not currently under censure, but little thought is given to specific skill sets, costs, or experience in the area in which the caller needs help. They might go so far as to notice that the legal office is close to where you live—but it is a bad trade-off to have a poor attorney whose only redeeming value is that his office is nearby.

The industry is self-regulated. Disciplinary committees are usually inadequate and slow. They seem to have one primary goal: protecting the image of lawyers, and doing the bare minimum to make sure they are never ever regulated by non-attorneys. Although, in all fairness, I have seen a couple of jerks disbarred based on complaints that I have made. That has been a rare, but satisfying experience.

The more business you do, and especially for smaller companies, the higher the probability that you will end up in litigation. A network of good and trusted counsel is a real asset, especially friends (yes, traders and lawyers *sometimes* have friends) who will give you a quick take on things without charging by the hour.

I have been involved in a number of lawsuits, both in my history working for big companies as well as in my entrepreneurial endeavors. I am not an attorney, but I understand risk, and I appreciate how deals get done and how they fall apart. After all, virtually every business day, I talk to prospective clients who have gotten the short end of the stick on a business deal. Here are some suggestions about contracts, deals, and litigation based on what I've learned over the years. They may help you reduce the risk of misunderstandings and legal conflict in your business life:

When you strike a deal, write out the specifics yourself. How can your lawyer know the particulars, if you don't? Draft the contract with plenty of detail, so that both you and your counterpart understand exactly what the agreement says, in plain English. Once you have agreed on a draft, you must decide if you want an attorney to review it. If substantial sums of money are involved, or you are new to negotiating contracts, you are likely saving dimes relative to the major consequences of a poorly-drafted agreement. Encourage the lawyer to use simple English whenever possible, and to avoid legalese (for example, I can't stand the use of "whereas" and "shall"). Attorneys hate the notion of being "managed" by their clients, but tough luck. (I almost used another four letter word.) After all, they are the "service provider" and you are the customer, so by all means, don't be passive about the business relationship you form with your attorney.

What do you do when your attorney proudly presents you a paragraph like this?

> **Either Party may terminate this Agreement provided such terminating Party shall be in compliance with its obligations by giving written notice in the event (a) the Conditions Precedent set forth in Section 5.5 are not satisfied or waived on or before December 31, 2014 provided, Seller shall be entitled to terminate at any time it, in its sole discretion, concludes that an Incentive will not be made available for the System; or (b) pursuant to and in accordance with Sections 10.5 or 10.7 hereof.**

This is language designed to increase the demand for attorneys who are "long" legal disputes. Tell yours that if she can't write the agreement in simpler and shorter sentences, you will find a new "service provider." My proposition is that agreements written like this lead to misunderstandings because fewer people bother to read and understand what they are signing. And if you end up at trial before a jury of your peers, with an average IQ of 100, what are the chances that they will understand it? Finally, it is a bad idea to assume that your attorney actually knows what this means, either.

Always get your agreements in writing, especially when working with a new counterpart. A verbal agreement is as good as the paper it isn't written on.

Only deal with people that you fundamentally trust. In about 2005, my friend brought me an opportunity to make a loan to a Texas man who had a sterling reputation. It looked like a great opportunity and, at an 18% interest rate, quite lucrative. But before we got very far, the client requested that the deal be structured so that his wife wouldn't know about it. This was a red flag to me, and I nixed the deal. Fast forward to 2013. S. Mark Powell committed suicide, and the Feds have launched an investigation into his financial dealings as the list of those he never paid back grows. At this point, it is also not clear if the collateral that was used to guarantee his loans actually exists.

Research what, if any, litigation they have been involved in (especially in which they were the defendant). You should learn something about them during the due-diligence and negotiation process. Warren Buffet speaks frequently about doing business with honest people. This is fundamental in his evaluation of any opportunity. Even with this as a major criterion, he misses the boat occasionally (although you will not hear much about it in his annual letters). When you smell something wrong early in the process, your odds of being disappointed later increase dramatically.

A fourteenth century Italian merchant, Francesco di Marco Dadini, complained about his insurance underwriters: "For who they insure, it is sweet to them to take the monies; but when disaster comes, it is otherwise, and each man draws in rump back and strives not to pay." More recently Homer Simpson told his wife, "Marge, don't discourage the boy! Weaseling out of things is important to learn. It's what separates us from the animals! Except the weasel!"

As you carefully think about an agreement you are about to make, consider the situation that the other guy is in. I have usually found that folks under financial pressure are more likely to lie and cheat than those who have plenty of time and options. The very nature of my lawsuit-funding business means that most of my potential clients are in a financial pinch, so I need to exercise more caution than I might in other business settings.

When I need an attorney to review an agreement, I prefer to use a litigator rather than a transaction-only attorney. I have found that lawyers who only draft agreements but never experience the back-end results are less effective in explaining the pros and cons of specific clauses, and understanding what really matters if the agreement leads to litigation. My ideal attorneys are good at reviewing agreements *and* have litigation experience, as well.

Organize your material ahead of time so that you optimize your attorney's time. Since you're probably paying by the hour, be certain to prepare the draft agreement and background documents on your own clock, not your attorney's.

Use arbitration clauses in most agreements. While these clauses have both pros and cons (an attorney will be glad to charge you several thousand dollars to explain this in more detail), it is usually much faster and more efficient to get a decision via arbitration than in a public court. This disparity will become even more dramatic as cities, counties, and states face more budget cuts. Arbitration costs are substantially more expensive than court costs—a court filing fee for a complaint might be $500, while I recently invested in a complex litigation case where the costs for three days of arbitration totaled $30,000. Include a provision in your contracts that the loser pays these fees. (I assume that you are honest, ethical, and pay attention to details, so I will bet that you will prevail in most disputes.) The price differential between public courts and arbitration will probably shrink over time, as more charges are levied on the participants in civil cases. For example, in many California courtrooms, the parties involved in civil litigation now have to split the cost of the court reporter.

One disadvantage of arbitration is that it frequently awards more modest amounts for punitive damages than those awarded by juries. (Again, since you are reading my book, I assume you will prevail more often than you will pay a judgment.)

Pick your partners and counterparts carefully. You will find litigation to be expensive and time consuming, and it will probably take years to complete. Litigation is no fun (akin to a needed root canal where a dentist is not available for surgery for several years).

Realize that these things take time. If you do have to litigate, understand that most attorneys are horrible at returning phone calls, unless you have a prior relationship (sorry for the generalization). The process can be expedited if you have another attorney refer you. But I have found that the most valuable references are from former clients, rather than from other attorneys. Most new litigants think they can sign up new counsel in a day or two, and have the lawsuit filed within a month. Wrong!

Decide whether an hourly or contingency fee will best serve your needs. (I guarantee that your state bar will do nothing to help you make this decision.) If you're going to initiate a lawsuit, it will be much easier to get representation if you are willing to pay by the hour; it is also less likely that prospective attorneys will tell you your case is a waste of money. But, obviously, you have to have the cash to pay for the work as it's done. Remember, if you run out of cash, you are out of business. Unless your case is very simple, or unless the proceeds of the case are at least $50,000 (for a commercial case, it's usually much higher), you will have a hard time getting a law firm to take your case on contingency.

On average, attorneys who are being paid $500 an hour are willing to spend considerable time shooting the breeze with their clients. Those on contingency want to focus more on results, and devote less time and energy to the touchy-feely task of consulting with you—after all, that doesn't pay the bills.

The stronger and bigger your case, the more power you have to negotiate with prospective attorneys. When trying to enlist a contingency attorney, it is absolutely essential that you put together a great package. A contingency attorney can charge anywhere from 20% to 50% of the proceeds of the case; the typical percentage is 33%. Most contingency lawyers advance expenses as well, and are reimbursed when the judgment or settlement is collected. Some want the client to advance the expenses on the case, such as expert witness and court reporter fees for depositions. Remember that the contingency fee and the funding of expenses are all subject to negotiation.

Sell your case. When you meet a potential contingency lawyer, you're selling your case. Remember that the best contingency attorneys only take a few of the cases they are offered. In deciding whether to accept, they will perform a risk/reward analysis that is very similar to the evaluation that I make when I invest in a lawsuit. They care about how well the client can tell the story, the facts, and the law in the case. They want to get a feel for whether you will be a difficult client. Also, if they're going to invest a million dollars of time and expenses in a large contingency case, they're not looking to earn only 50% additional on their investment; they're looking to earn a large multiple.

Talk to a few potential attorneys in parallel, not sequentially. The process moves far too slowly to interview prospective attorneys one at a time; it will simply take too long to get the best offer on the table. If your case is a good bet, and you have interviewed and discussed it with a few lawyers, you may find yourself in the enviable position of being able to choose between more than one law firm to represent you. Having multiple firms vying to represent you also gives you a better chance of getting a better deal on the contingency fee. This is advice the state bar might consider blasphemy. (Free market principles applying to such a hallowed profession? Surely not!)

Understand the statute of limitations on your potential lawsuit. In some states, the statute of limitations for breach of contract may only be two years from the day that you uncover a breach. So, don't sit back and dawdle in selecting representation and filing your lawsuit. I have seen too many clients and more than a few attorneys ignore the statute of limitations, destroying the value of the case before it's even been filed.

Try to stay the course. Keep in mind that, if your attorney is on contingency and you fire him or he drops the case, it's twice as hard to get a second attorney. The second lawyer may have to hand over some of his contingency fees to the first one, and the second lawyer may be concerned that the first attorney has screwed up the case or that the client (you) is difficult to work with.

WHICH PRINCIPLES APPLY TO COVERING YOUR LEGAL BASES?

Nothing is Risk Free. This holds true for any business agreement that you consummate, and goes double for the litigation process.

Multiple Dimensions = Degrees of Freedom. Every business contract has multiple dimensions, and working beyond simple pricing provides an opportunity to increase the size of the pie.

Fight for Fast Feedback. A 10-year agreement is frequently more dangerous than a six-month agreement. The world changes, and having terms and conditions locked in with little ability to adjust based on the changing world can increase the chances that one of the parties ends up hating the agreement.

Play the Odds. Do your best to understand the numbers for your side of the deal as well as for your counterpart's. If you execute a deal that really disadvantages the other side, you are much more likely to have the hassle of litigation or breach of contract later on, when trying to enforce the agreement.

Some Things are Less Predicable than Others. Lawsuit results are impossible to predict. How well will your attorney play the game? Will you be lucky with the judge you are assigned? If it is a jury trial, will they be sympathetic to your position? Is there a quirk in the law that makes your claim a moot point?

Think on the Margin. I have often seen the "sunk cost fallacy" driving the decisions of defendants. They are thinking, "I've come this far; let's play this out." Both sides should be comparing the marginal cost versus the marginal benefit of settling, every step of the way.

Do Not Ignore Pride of Ownership. If you can keep your emotions in check, you have a better chance of settling the case and walking away with more money in your pocket. While the occasional insult or shouting match might feel good at the time, it is usually not the way to play the game from a financial perspective.

Fight Friction Costs. An attorney who charges $600 an hour might not be twice as effective as one at half the price. But, then again, she might be 10 times as good. I would quiz a potential attorney about how you can work together to get the most bang for the legal buck.

Never Run Out of Cash. When you are paying by the hour, whether as a defendant or a plaintiff, you need to assess early and often how long you can last. Getting close to the end zone without enough muscle to push the ball over the goal line, usually results in a loss.

Put Your Socks on Right. This is Job One when you are working on the original deal. Keep complete notes while the agreement lives and breathes. If you do end up in litigation, having all the details with written proof puts you in the driver's seat.

Think and Act with the Long Run in Mind. At all times, you should act rationally and in sync with the estimated costs and potential pitfalls of your litigation. If you find the case requires more time and money than you are willing to commit, be reasonable about settling or dropping the case. This is Objectivity 101.

Be Optimally Persistent. When considering whether to continue with a lawsuit or settle, fight only as long as it makes sense to fight (such blinding insight). You would be a fool to ever consider another transaction or agreement with the other side, anyway, so get what you can, bury your ego, and forget about trying to make a point. As James Surgwiecki explains in *The Wisdom of Crowds*, "People would rather have nothing than let their 'partners' walk away with too much of the loot. They will give up free money to punish what they perceive as greedy or selfish behavior." Holding your adversaries accountable would be great, but your priority should be deciding what is most beneficial to *you* (Think on the Margin). Why try to set an example that will cost you boatloads of money with someone you aren't going to do with business again, anyway? Success and financial freedom are generally the best revenge.

♦♦♦
♦♦♦

Real-World Applications

APPLICATION EIGHT
UNLOCKING THE FUTURE

Here is an opportunity that most of my friends think is trivial. They may be right. But then again, many innovations are viewed that way until they see the light of day.

In early 2013, my friend and partner Robb Sexton and I filed a provisional patent relating to anything that uses an unlock code. Robb has hundreds of inventions and patents under his belt. Initially we were focused on the smartphone market, but the concept applies to anything that uses a password to unlock (think personal computer, tablet, digital camera, and the as-yet-unidentified hottest digital device in the year 2020). You can read all about this idea at Qunlocker.com. The idea started with my frustration over the fact that the lock code on our cell phones is used for just one purpose—to unlock the phone.

Simply put, our concept is that you should be able to both unlock the phone and simultaneously initiate another action with one of many user-defined codes. For example, I might set up my phone so that the code "9478" simply unlocks the phone. And "21" unlocks my front door and then immediately relocks the phone. The code "31" might unlock and start my car, turn on the air conditioning, and then relock my phone, while "41" might open the garage door. Punching in "911" might initiate an emergency call and feed my location and name to the emergency operator and several nearby friends, while leaving the phone line open until the situation is resolved. This functionality is also capable of locking the device while leaving specific applications or functions enabled.

ENOUGH ABOUT THE IDEA (FOR NOW): WHAT IS THE OPPORTUNITY?

First, our full provisional patent is held confidentially, and establishes our priority date with the US and global Patent and Trademark Offices. By the end of the first year, we must file our full US non-provisional patent (or international patent), or our patent protection priority date becomes null and void. The details of provisional patents are not initially available to the public, although I have given you the short version here.

Before we filed the provisional patent, we conducted a patent search and found no "prior art"—patent-speak for the same idea at an earlier date. In other words, we *may* be the first out of the gate. However, if someone else filed a patent (full or provisional) a day before us, we wouldn't know that until their patent was made public (the earlier of when their full patent was approved or 18 months after they filed their full patent). Once a patent is made public, then it can be found via a patent search. So, if someone else beat us to the punch, we are literally a day late and a dollar short. And since we wouldn't be the Champs, you know that, by default, we'd be the Chumps. This time frame, however, protects us from unscrupulous readers (in the unlikely event that I have any) who would steal our idea, as you cannot now apply successfully for this same patent.

It is interesting to note that patent offices all over the world are in business not to grant patents, but rather to protect existing patents. Thus, getting a patent is a very tedious and detailed process—not for the faint of heart nor, unfortunately, for those who are short of financial resources.

We will only have a minimum investment (relative to the opportunity) in the idea before we learn if we actually are "first." About a year after we file our full US patent, we will file an international patent application that will protect us globally for another year. Finally, we must file country-specific patents. By the time we have to make that decision, we will have spent no more than $20,000 in total (plus an investment in marketing). Filing these patents country by country is substantially more expensive; we might spend another $100,000 or more to get that done.

It might be three or more years before we have the final patents approved in the major developed markets, and by that time, our investment may be more than $250,000 (plus marketing expenses).

Meanwhile, we will be pitching the concept to the smartphone operating-system developers (Google, Apple, Samsung, Microsoft, Motorola (a subsidiary of Google), and a host of the smaller ones). This will not be an easy sell. First, despite the innovation for which these companies are known, they generally hate outside "nuisance" patents (as ours may be viewed) that interfere with them doing what they want, when they want. Yet they all fight ferociously to protect their own intellectual property rights, many of which are smaller in scale than this one.

Don't expect a quick resolution to this story. If nothing comes of it, we will banish the tale and talk about baseball and poker. But what kind of changes will we see in mobile and smart phone applications in just the next few years? We will probably experience the smartphone being used to control everything from hearing aids to the tire pressure on your car. And the perception of who are the Chumps and who are the Champs in the business is likely to change. In early 2012, Apple looked like they had an insurmountable lead in smartphones. But as I write this, many are now arguing that Google and Samsung are the new Champs. Who will be the Champs in the 2018 smartphone market is anyone's guess.

WHICH PRINCIPLES APPLY TO THE LOCK DISPLAY PATENT?

Start with the Big Picture and Macro Trends. Several trends support this idea. We expect electronic chips to get smaller, cheaper, faster, and more powerful. (Boy, this is a unique insight, isn't it?) We assume, along with everyone else, that cell phones and other "smart" devices will continue to massively increase their power and versatility. And many "dumb" devices will get smart. Improvements in biometric security systems and voice recognition may pose a competitive headwind to our concept. Security, along with the need to protect individual devices and information, is rapidly gaining importance. And anything to make these devices simpler is powerful.

Multiple Dimensions = Degrees of Freedom. This idea started with my frustration about the many steps required to start an application on my phone. And then I asked—why are we using the unlock code to accomplish just one thing?

Combine an Information Advantage with Volatility. We are betting on volatility in technology. The faster it changes, the more chance we have to cash in on this idea. This business is an inexpensive out-of-the-money option that *might* pay off. If nothing changes, it is a sure loser.

Welcome Forks in the Road. The more new entrants and changes in the overall landscape, the more likely we are to find our first customer.

Fight for Fast Feedback. Once we "locked up" the idea with our patent application, we immediately started asking for feedback, far and wide. The majority of friends that I canvassed didn't think much of the opportunity. All the feedback was valuable, however, because it provided an early alert regarding concerns to be addressed as we begin to market the idea.

Play the Odds. Initially, this patent is an inexpensive option and a long shot. If we do sell the idea, we are not expecting a mere 2X return, we hope for north of 100X back on our investment.

The Numbers May Be Hazardous to Your Health. There are about six billion cell phones in use in the world today. Most of these are not smartphones, and in many areas such as India, fewer smartphone applications are used than in Europe and the US. But this may dramatically change within just a few years, simply because of the declining cost of technology. My brother has about 40 internet-enabled devices at his new home in Texas. This is an exponential, not a linear, trend.

Some Things Are Less Predictable Than Others. We know upfront that we really don't know what the cell phone market is going to look like in five years—and neither does anyone else. This uncertainty makes our inexpensive option potentially more volatile, and hence, more valuable.

Beware of Idiotic Leverage. Robb and I are not using debt to fund this project. We are keeping the leverage below the "idiotic" threshold.

Think on the Margin. Whenever we have to spend more money, we will be evaluating the prospects at that stage of the game.

Know the Long and Short of It. We are long in several areas: technology volatility, the number and general use of smartphone applications, number of smartphone users in the world, and the number of new devices that morph from dumb to smart. We are marginally short voice recognition systems like Apple's Siri. Our patent applies to voice commands, but if voice recognition becomes so good that it can use the voice itself as a reliable security device, and can handle more complex commands, our concept becomes less advantageous. Because voice recognition is currently less useful in noisy environments, we are probably long background noise. A combination of inexpensive and effective biometric security sensors, such as fingerprint, retinal, and facial recognition—blended with more powerful voice recognition—*might* make our concept moot.

We also recognize that the most sophisticated technology does not always win. When the first text message was sent on December 3, 1992, no one foresaw that this market would grow as it has. After all, emails can be far more detailed and lengthy, and a voice call has a much more personal feel. And yet? As recently as 2001, text messages in the US were a blip on the screen compared to voice traffic. But since 2002, SMS traffic has grown exponentially to about 75 billion text messages in 2008 in the US. By the end of 2012, about 8.6 trillion were being sent per year, globally (that is trillion with a "T").

Do Not Ignore Pride of Ownership. Robb and I are proud of this idea. But we are objective enough to separate the pride of ownership from the business reality. If the concept never gets traction, we both know we have plenty of other ideas to pursue.

Strike While the Iron is Hot. We did that by quickly filing our provisional patent. Now we can move more deliberately as we make the pitch to the operating system developers.

Never Run Out of Cash. We won't.

Find Free Options. This patent filing option is not exactly free; but when you can't get a free option, an inexpensive one with a big potential payoff is the next best thing.

Put Your Socks on Right. At this point, the rule applies specifically to how well we manage the details on our patent applications, each step of the way.

Think and Act with the Long Run in Mind. This business plan is the embodiment of working towards the long run. It is unlikely that we will ring the cash register any time soon.

Be Optimally Persistent. We're realistic about the possibility of having to fold our hand, but believe that our persistence has a chance for a nice payday.

*****

I offer one last comment for anyone thinking about patenting a new idea or innovation. The value or deterrence effect of patent protection is only as strong as the patent holder's willingness and ability to protect his intellectual property (IP) in the world's courts. Many times, a patent holder is unable or unwilling to spend the time, resources, or distraction to fight another company (especially big or foreign companies) to uphold its patent.

If you are the owner of Intellectual Property and do not defend your position when you learn of an infringement, the patent is essentially nullified. Simply said, if you are not willing or able to defend your patent, you are better off trying to use a first-to-market strategy rather than spend your time and money on the patent process.

CONCLUSION IN A NUTSHELL
(Or is that a Nut's Hell?)

"The road you don't travel is always smoother."
—Rep. Duncan Hunter, Sr. (R-CA)

In early November 2001, I came home from work to a new place that Lorraine and I had just rented in Leigh, a small village in Kent, south of London. We had decided to move out of Hampstead to the country. There I found Lorraine, our dog at her side, busy unpacking. I knew on that day that Enron was toast. I had had numerous trading managers from the industry call me directly that week demanding prepays on our commodity purchases—the writing was on the wall. When I walked in the door, I announced to my wife and dog: "You can stop unpacking." We sat down and discussed the odds of Enron surviving.

From that day forward, I still dutifully went to work, put on my game face, and wrestled with one crisis after another. It was like being down in a football game 57-0, with five minutes to play—you know the outcome, and those five minutes feel like years. But you still have to run onto the field and play the game. (It didn't make sense to continue unpacking, though.) Those were the worst days in my work life, and I know that they were for my colleagues, as well.

Let's look at the legal requirements for Administration—the UK's equivalent of bankruptcy. Once management knows that it can't pay the bills, the corporate directors *must* put the business into Administration—TODAY! Failure to do so creates personal criminal liability for the management. I like this law, and wish we had the equivalent in the US.

Lucky And Good

So, on the evening of Wednesday, November 28, 2001—the day that Standard & Poor's rating agency downgraded Enron's debt to junk status, and Enron Corp failed to wire-transfer $50 million to us (Houston was controlling most of the company's cash around the world)—I called up Enron's president and chief operating officer, Greg Whalley. Ken Lay had brought Greg into the role after Jeff Skilling's August resignation. I told Whalley that, the next morning, my directors and I would meet and vote to put Enron Europe into Administration. He was not surprised, and by then he knew that soon, (four days later, in fact), Enron Corp would itself file for bankruptcy.

On November 29, after my fellow Enron Europe directors and I voted to put the organization into Administration, we turned over the keys to the bus to the Administration team at PricewaterhouseCoopers. Their leader reminded us that they were now in charge, and not to do anything, say anything, sign anything, or—most importantly—spend anything.

We called mid-day floor meetings in which all of the employees were told by the Administrator, "We are in charge now. Don't pay any attention to those knuckleheads who were running things before." Actually, he was more diplomatic in delivering the news. But that was the gist of it. He told the employees that they were employed today and tomorrow, and would be paid for both days (wow, what a deal). Then he told them, "We'll let you know if we need you after that."

The next day, Friday, turned out to be the last day on the job for most of my colleagues. The reality was, if you were in Accounts Payable, you probably weren't needed. After all, the Administrators weren't going to be paying bills for some time. Although the Accounts Payable group had plenty of talent, and most would do very well in their next jobs, they were unlucky that day.

But if you happened to know more about a liquid and valuable asset, especially one that would quickly deteriorate in value, you had a chance to score. The prime example was our UK Enron Direct retail gas and electric business. A team of about 20 was assembled to sell the business, in exchange for a promise from the Administrator that they would share 10% of the sales price. Within a couple of weeks, this talented and lucky team sold the business for about $150 million US, and split a performance bonus of about $15 million. As I keep

Conclusion in a Nutshell

saying, I'd rather be lucky *and* good, and I was excited to hear how lucky this talented team had been.

I was personally devastated by the collapse of Enron. I loved the excitement of sitting on a trading floor—for me it was like being a boy in the candy store. It was great fun just to be around such smart and like-minded compatriots.

In the aftermath of the Enron collapse, the federal government did not stalk me like they did so many other Enron executives. But a couple of years later, I returned to my Lake Tahoe home from a vacation (some might ask, why do I have to go on vacation, if I live at Lake Tahoe) and checked the voice mail. The message said: "Hi, this is ____, I'm with the FBI in Houston, and we'd appreciate it if you would give us a call." What would you rather get—this phone call, or a sharp stick in the eye?

I hesitantly called the agent the next day, and we spoke. She told me that the FBI wanted to interview me about a meeting that had been held in Houston a few months before Enron's collapse. I said, "Fine, but first I need to find a Houston attorney to represent me, and then I will fly down to Houston and we can talk."

She said, "We are willing to travel to Lake Tahoe to interview you."

I responded, "No thanks. I need a Houston attorney who understands the case, and it will be less expensive if I fly there than if I have her fly to Tahoe."

A friend connected me with the lawyer he was using; the Houston attorney called up the agent and suggested a few dates for the meeting. The FBI agent said, "We'll get back to you." But guess what—we never heard from the bureau again. Bravo!

I have long suspected that the agents in question were more interested in a taxpayer-paid trip to Lake Tahoe than they were in speaking with me. Further, I believe that, if I had agreed to meet in Tahoe, we would probably still be meeting several times a month during each and every gorgeous summer, with my attorney fees stacking up like Obama's national debt. I dodged a bullet on that one—not because I had anything to hide, but the government would have cost me most of *my* money for *the government* to figure that out.

When the Feds started poking and prodding, my former colleagues who were on the receiving end of the government's pressure, spent a minimum half million dollars on legal expenses. One colleague had every one of his eligible tax returns audited, costing him hundreds of thousands of dollars. The IRS agent made it clear that this was driven by his association with Enron. The IRS didn't find a single error on his returns, but he didn't get any refund. And these semi-political IRS agents weren't even from their Cincinnati office.

The stakes went up tenfold for those who were indicted. It is clear to me that the government was guilty of prosecutorial misconduct (see Cara Ellison's excellent discussion of this at caraellison.wordpress.com). A riveting story about US prosecutors lying with impunity can be read in *A Price to Pay: The Inside Story of the Natwest Three* by David Bermingham. And you can see more folks speaking up at ungagged.net.

Many former colleagues were forced to choose between two stark possibilities: one, a trial costing millions in legal fees, *combined* with the chance of 20+ years of jail time, *or* a plea deal leading to a two- to three-year sentence. Regardless of my advice about playing the odds, I have actually never had to make that kind of decision for those stakes. So I cut *most* of these folks a great deal of slack in their choices, knowing that a few bad apples had spoiled the entire barrel for the rest of us. I viewed most of the proceedings with skepticism.

I always had a great relationship with both Jeff Skilling and Ken Lay, and found them amazingly supportive. But the government really had them in their sights as Enron went down in flames. When the final story is eventually told, now that everyone can speak without the threat of government prosecution, I think we will hear about even more prosecutorial misconduct. As I go to press, the government and court have just agreed to a reduction in Jeff's prison sentence based in part on the prosecution's wrongdoing. Jeff and Ken both made some great bets, and a few too many losing ones for which they both paid a huge price.

My lawsuit-funding business triggers almost daily discussions with businesspeople who have been swindled and cheated. I only accept clients whose stories ring true (cheated by partners, screwed by lawyers, lied to by politicians). And I have seen a greater magnitude of dishonesty in my lawsuit business than I ever saw on the trading floor.

Conclusion in a Nutshell

I entered the trading business late in life (at the ripe old age of 37—unheard of for a junior trader on Wall Street). For me, it didn't get any better. When, at the advanced age of 49, Enron came crashing down, I felt like I had been sucker-punched in the stomach (or lower). Granted, I took a financial hit, but the abdominal pains had little to do with money. I loved the trading business, and strongly suspected that I had seen my last days on a big trading floor. (I had always worked hard to avoid a private office.) Since I didn't want to live in New York, London, or Houston, and not many boards were looking for former Enron executives to lead their Lake Tahoe trading teams, I was going to have to find a new game to play.

Most of our traders, originators, and back office folks dispersed throughout the energy trading industry—oil companies, banks, and hedge funds; they did extraordinarily well. They continued the best aspects of the culture, and Enron's data-intensive, analytical approach to markets is now the norm in the energy-trading business.

After taking most of a year off, I recognized that, in the future, I would have to think and act more like an entrepreneur, particularly if I wanted to stay headquartered at Lake Tahoe. The benefit, this time around (compared to earlier days when I was young and poor), was that I had some money in the bank, and more experience under my belt. Plus, I still had the "advantage" of thinking like a trader.

Ok, enough sniveling, whimpering, and crying over spilt milk (this is very Chump-like). Stick with me while I remind my readers about the key points that I hope they will draw from this book.

*****

No matter what business you pursue:

1) **The Law of Supply and Demand** is still King in the world of capitalism. In making virtually any decision, when in doubt, go back to this fundamental. Study and understand how supply and demand will change and, most importantly, how your estimates differ from the consensus. Obviously, government actions and behavioral economics are important forces in shifting this balance.

2) **Don't be a Chump.** This requires that you both overcome your Lizard Brain or "feel good" but "money-losing" tendencies, *and* that you find a competitive advantage.

3) As the Dalai Lama said: **"Know the rules well, so you can break them effectively."** When making business decisions, if you don't occasionally break some rules, you're just not trying hard enough. There is no formula on when to do this other than to understand the details and logic behind the way things are currently being done, and recognize and act when the status quo just isn't good enough. Champs usually figure out how to break the right rule at the right time.

   If you get a little too contrarian and try to break too many conventions all at once, you'll have little time and energy remaining for the basics. So, when you break away, do so consciously and with care—then, quickly absorb each lesson as you learn it. If you always conform, other more adaptive players will eat your lunch.

4) As Warren Buffett explains: "Most managers have very little incentive to make **the intelligent-but-with-some-chance-of-looking-like-an-idiot decision**. Their personal gain/loss ratio is all too obvious: if an unconventional decision works out well, they get a pat on the back and, if it works out poorly, they get a pink slip. (Failing conventionally is the route to go; as a group, lemmings may have a rotten image, but no individual lemming has ever received bad press.)" Buffett probably hates the idea that a former Enron executive is quoting him—sorry Warren!

*****

Although my principles apply to all business, I favor one group more than others—entrepreneurs. Their success can help grow our economy. I hope (that dirty four-letter word!) that they will make smart bets, take intelligent chances, and, most importantly, act on accurate hunches about the future. Additionally, I hope many of them

Conclusion in a Nutshell

will be extraordinarily lucky. Their successes produce blessings for the rest of us in the form of more jobs, more tax revenues, and greater prosperity.

Entrepreneurs—past, present, and future—are my heroes.

May you have more profitable wins and less costly mistakes! Now go for it!

I would sure appreciate it if you took a few moments to rate and review this book, back at Amazon.com. THANK YOU.

Lucky And Good

♦♦♦
♦♦♦

EXHIBIT A
More (but not all) of the Current Macro Trends

- Starting in 1944, the US steadily increased its dependence on imported oil until about 2005. Since then, crude oil and petroleum product imports have been falling.
- After World War II, social democracy expanded in Western Europe as the predominant political system. (With the European financial crisis, the chances of a dictatorship or other totalitarian regime arising have increased from what we might have thought of as zero only a few years ago.)
- Since 1958, when New York Mayor Robert Wagner, Jr., issued an executive order giving public employees the right to collectively bargain for the first time, public-employee union memberships have grown dramatically in the US. Today, American public employees are nearly five times as likely to be unionized as those in the private sector.
- Conversely, in the US, private-sector union membership has steadily declined since 1955.
- From 1982 on, interest rates have fallen in the US (30-year mortgages recently hit 2.89%). It appears that this trend may have reversed as of August 2012.
- Islamic extremism has expanded since the late 1980s. (It is too early to tell if the Arab Spring will dampen this, but I doubt it.)
- Since 1989, China has grown as a manufacturing giant. During this process, Chinese workers have consistently gained higher wages which, in the long run, may dampen this trend.

- In the developed world, the threat of global warming is a growing concern. (This is considered of little consequence in the developing world, especially in China.)
- In the two decades starting in 1990, the volume of US patent litigation increased by more than 230%.
- The euro was established as a common currency in 17 countries in 1999, and was viewed as a roaring success for its first eight years.
- The US spends more on its military than the next 17 countries combined.
- For decades, expenditures on college education in America and total college debt have continued to increase faster than the rate of inflation, family incomes, and starting salaries for recent grads.
- Traditional government debt (by any measure) in the developed world has grown on steroids during the last few decades.
- In the US, the total amount of unfunded liabilities (promises made for which insufficient money has been set aside to later pay the bills) for things like public pensions, Social Security, and health care promises is at least four to five times as large as traditional government debt in the developed world. These unfunded liabilities continue to grow.
- Technology-based goods and services, like personal computers, tablets, cell phones, the Internet, search engines, and GPS tracking, continue to expand, change, and drop in price.
- It is getting cheaper and faster to create a new invention, but harder and more expensive to protect Intellectual Property in the global market place.
- China, India, and other Asian countries continue to modernize, urbanize, and westernize. This is resulting in greater private-property rights, greater manufacturing capacity, and global competitiveness in this part of the world. Money and power is shifting from West to East.

Exhibit A

❖ Many developed countries are quietly (notwithstanding Japan's recent loud announcements) in a race to devalue their currencies in order to boost jobs for their citizens. Which country will win the race to the bottom?

♦♦♦
♦♦♦

Lucky And Good

♦♦♦
♦♦♦

EXHIBIT B
Inflection Points

A few historical non-price inflection points:

- the development of the spice trade from Roman times through the Age of Discovery,
- the European bubonic plague of 1347,
- the end of slavery in the United States after the Civil War,
- World War I,
- World War II,
- the fall of the Berlin Wall in 1989,
- the end of the Cold War in 1991, and
- the September 11, 2001 terrorist attacks on the US.

A few significant price-based inflection points in the last few decades:

- US interest rates (the Federal funds rate) hit a peak in 1980 at 20%. As I write this in mid-2013, it's 0.25%.
- The US Consumer Price Index inflation rate, compared to the prior year, hit a peak of 14.6% in March 1980.
- During the 1973 oil crisis, OPEC countries joined forces and colluded to increase the price of their one and only product—oil. It worked. But, meanwhile, it disrupted global oil and gasoline flows and production, and dramatically increased the price of gasoline at the world's pumps. This was a big blow to the US, which had peaked in its own oil production in 1970, and was steadily increasing oil imports.

These potential inflection points in the global markets might send out big ripples:

- As a result of the debt crisis in the Eurozone, some or all of the remaining Euro countries may integrate more, financially, beyond sharing their currency.
- The richest region in Spain (Catalonia) is seriously talking about seceding from the country. About 1.5 million Catalonians (around 20% of the regional population) turned out in September 2012 in support of independence. This does not bode well for the concept of wealthy parts of Europe paying for the spendthrift habits of other regions.
- In France, President Francois Hollande recently proposed that the marginal tax rate for those earning more than one million euros per year be increased to 75%. At the end of 2012, the French Constitutional Court rejected the new tax rate because it was deemed unfair in how it would be applied to different households. But they didn't reject the percentage, so don't be surprised to see a "new and improved" tax soon.
- The UK might leave the EU.
- Dr. Gary Shilling and author Gordon Chang are predicting a hard landing in China.
- The development of nuclear weapons by Iran may result in more severe armed conflict in the Middle East.
- In the 10 years starting in mid-2002, the central banks of Japan, the US, Europe, and China more than quadrupled their assets from about $3 trillion to about $13 trillion. The electronic printing presses have been on a full rampage to a degree never seen in the developed world. What will be the consequences?
- There is potential deflation ahead in the US and Northern Europe. Oil prices might fall, interest rates are near their all-time lows, high unemployment is pushing down wages, and the real estate bubble may still be popping around the world. The Federal Reserve, Japanese Central Bank, and European Central Bank will battle hard to prevent this collapse. Few of

the "experts" are worried, but the central banks may run out of tools for the fight. This is Dr. Gary Shilling's prediction.

❖ With the economic challenges facing the world today, we may see a dramatic increase in trade protectionism. The countries with higher unemployment will face political pressure to reduce imports and bring jobs *home*. Hopefully we don't have anything as horrendous as the Smoot-Hawley Tariff Act of 1930, which contributed to the severity and the length of the Great Depression.

❖ The developed world may have taken on so much government debt that the result might be sweeping movements to the extreme right or extreme left. These shifts may cause losses in personal freedoms that, up until now, have improved steadily during the last century.

These potential inflection points in the US markets might change the game:

❖ Public employee unions in the US may be at a precipice. They lost in the 2012 recall election of Wisconsin Governor Scott Walker, and also lost in San Jose and San Diego, where the voters rolled back some of the pension promises being made to their city employees. In each of these cases, unions backed the losing side.

The Douglas County School District, a suburban community south of Denver, parted ways with their union when their contract expired on June 30, 2012. Their board declared that the expired collective bargaining agreement would henceforth have "no legal effect whatsoever." In Camden, New Jersey, the city disbanded its entire unionized police force, and has contracted with the county to provide the same services at a lower cost.

Public employee unions remain strong in many other state and local governments in the US, but we *may* have hit an inflection point on this issue. Based on the 2012 presidential election, however, they are likely to have few setbacks at the

national level under the Democratic leadership for the next four years.
- ❖ The US now has the highest corporate tax rate of any country in the developed world for those paying the full sticker price.
- ❖ The looming US trillion dollar-plus college loan bubble.

♦♦♦
♦♦♦

EXHIBIT C
Calculations for the Short Putt

The estimated probability that a golfer will win in sudden death is 70% if he ends up in sudden death. The 18+ putt offers a 60% chance of sinking the putt for a birdie four, a 40% chance to two-putt for a par five, and no chance that he will need more than two putts. (I am not talking my own golf game here.)

For the 30+ putt, he has an 80% chance of sinking the putt for birdie four, a 10% chance to two-putt for a par five, and a 10% chance to three-putt for a bogey six.

The average number of strokes (to complete the hole) for the 18+ putt is (60% * 4 strokes) + (40% * 5 strokes) = 4.4.

The average number of strokes for the 30+ putt is (80% * 4 strokes) + (10% * 5 strokes) + (10% * 6 strokes) = 4.3 stroke average.

But the chances to win the tournament are different.

Using these estimates, the probability of winning the tournament with the 18+ putt is 60% + (40% * 70%) = 88%.

The probability of winning the tournament with the 30+ putt is 80% + (10% * 70%) = 87%.

♦♦♦
♦♦♦

Lucky And Good

♦♦♦
♦♦♦

EXHIBIT D
More Examples of the Long and Short of It

This is a continuation of the discussion of the principle Know the Long and Short of It.

- ❖ The US Postal Service is long the demand for mail service (good luck with that one; everyone knows that demand is dropping rapidly), and long the willingness of the federal government to make up their losses. They are short gasoline and labor costs—specifically, pension costs.
- ❖ An entrepreneur has developed a new lightweight stanchion for crowd control. He's short inflation (because he must fix his prices with his big customers for the next year), transportation costs between China (where his product is manufactured) and the US, cardboard (for packaging and shipping his product), and cash. He's long hustle, and trade credit (all his suppliers want to get paid up front).
- ❖ CNN is long big stories that are 24/7 and garner worldwide attention. They are long advertising rates and short the cost of reporting.
- ❖ Weightwatchers is long the number of overweight people, and short food prices as they sell their Weightwatcher meals to their customers.
- ❖ Al Capone was long the 18th Amendment (Prohibition), short the 21st Amendment (which repealed the 18th Amendment), and short effective and honest policing.
- ❖ Anti-American terrorists are short US Homeland Security, suicide bombers, and long covert funding and anti-American sentiments.

- The Oprah Winfrey Network (OWN) is long Oprah (they want her to remain personally popular), long advertising rates, long regular viewers (they want more), and short content. (During the first week of its launch in 2011, OWN was watched by an average of 505,000 viewers. In February 2011, viewership fell to an average of 135,000 viewers, although OWN ratings started to increase in 2012.)
- LinkedIn.com is long visits per month per viewer, advertising rates, number of users, and the number of recruiters using it for hiring. It is short the cost of cloud computing.
- McDonalds is short other fast food outlets, food costs, labor costs, and advertising costs, and long their own perceived convenience, speed, and consistency. They are also short diets.
- Toby Keith is long good songs (he can never have enough) and long the overall popularity of country music.
- Major League Baseball is long subsidized stadiums, television advertising, and League game attendance. It is short baseball labor costs and short all other amateur and professional sports other than youth baseball programs.
- A recycling company that does curb pickup is long wholesale plastic, paper and metals, and short diesel, labor, the mob (in certain cities), and the cost of new trucks.
- Dunkin Donuts is short sugar costs, labor costs, coffee bean prices, Starbucks, and the Michael Bloomberg nanny state restrictions on diet. They are long the economy, high employment rates, and consumer spending.
- A liquefied natural gas (LNG) facility that imports liquid natural gas into the US is long American natural gas prices, short LNG shipping costs, and short natural gas prices in the rest of the world, where underutilized export LNG capacity exists.
- An LNG facility to export liquid natural gas from the US to China and Japan is short US natural gas prices, LNG transportation costs, the cost to liquefy the natural gas, and the cost to convert the liquid into gas. They are long energy prices in Asia and Europe.

Exhibit D

- Ethanol producers are long gasoline prices, total gasoline consumption, and ethanol government subsidies—and short corn prices.
- Dairies are short electricity, the price of dairy cows, cattle feed costs for alfalfa, corn, proteins and grains—and long the price of wholesale milk.
- Life insurance companies are long longevity when they sell term life insurance policies. But they are short longevity when they sell annuities.
- Ammonia producers (which use huge amounts of natural gas as a feedstock for producing their product) are short natural gas prices, short nitrogen and hydrogen prices, and long ammonia prices.
- On D-Day, the Allies were long good weather, and the Axis powers were short good weather.
- The San Francisco Giants are long runs produced and short runs given up. They are short the Dodgers, and long the San Francisco Bay Area economy and TV advertising rates on televised Giants games.

♦♦♦
♦♦♦

Lucky And Good

♦♦♦
♦♦♦

EXHIBIT E

Sherriff's Core Business Principles (Summary)

Nothing Is Risk Free

Start with the Big Picture and Macro Trends

Find Inflection Points

There's Always a Bear Market Somewhere

Multiple Dimensions = Degrees of Freedom

Think in Opposites

Combine an Information Advantage with Volatility

Welcome Forks in the Road

Fight for Fast Feedback

Play the Odds

The Numbers May Be Hazardous to Your Health

Correlation is Not Causation

Some Things Are Less Predictable Than Others

Beware of Idiotic Leverage

Think on the Margin

Know the Long and Short of It

Do Not Ignore Pride of Ownership

Don't Jump the Gun

Fight Friction Costs

Decide to Decide

Strike While the Iron Is Hot

Don't Pick Up Dimes in Front of Steamrollers

Never Run Out of Cash

Avoid Gambler's Ruin

Find Free Options

Put Your Socks on Right

Think and Act with the Long Run in Mind

Life Happens

Get Lucky

Be Optimally Persistent

♦♦♦
♦♦♦

ACKNOWLEDGMENTS

"I can't protect you from everything, but I can read you stories that make you believe I can protect you from everything."

—Cartoon in *The New Yorker*, July 29, 2013

James Altucher's blog (Jamesaltucher.com) offers advice for writers, along with plenty of other interesting topics about living well. The suggestion that caught my attention, and which I have tried to follow, is to read good writing each day before sitting down to write myself. By following this advice, I am sure that my work is at least slightly better than it otherwise would have been. Many of the authors below have influenced my thinking, but more importantly, I hope that they have helped me shape my story into a better tale.

The one writer that I read virtually every day is Mike "Mish" Shedlock. Always time well spent. I find his blog on the web at: http://globaleconomicanalysis.blogspot.com.

About halfway through writing this book, I started to read the works of Nassim Nicholas Taleb, including *Fooled by Randomness, The Black Swan,* and, most recently, *Antifragile: Things That Gain from Disorder*. Nassim has a far more eloquent and philosophical writing style than mine. His work is brilliant and a must-read. Of course, I'm thrilled that he frequently agrees with me and I with him. I found that I had already addressed a few of his themes, although with far less rigor. I hope that I have added a helpful twist to a couple of his hypotheses.

When my first draft was nearly finished, I came across Nate Silver's *The Signal and the Noise: Why So many Predictions Fail–But Some Don't*. It's a fabulous read from a guy in the prediction business who also happens to like talking baseball and playing poker.

Daniel Kahneman's latest work, *Thinking Fast and Slow,* wonderfully summarizes decades of his collaborative research about how folks make decisions, and how they view risk.

I've been a fan of Bill James for decades. He's the father of the Sabermetrics application of statistics to baseball. Although he writes about a sport, James' thinking style and problem formation are great illustrations for any trader, investor, or entrepreneur to study. Likewise, Michael Lewis, in both *Moneyball* and *Blindside,* applies economic market theory to baseball and football, all the while providing critical business lessons.

I think that John Stossel, Libertarian commentator for Fox Business Network, is the most important journalist in the world today. I haven't actually used any quotes or examples from his shows here, but no other member of the media is as significant. He consistently asks the right questions on his weekly show.

John Mauldin is a big influence in economic and political discourse these days. His newsletter is read by millions, and his writing is an absolute joy to read. His two latest books, *The Little Book of Bull's Eye Investing,* and *Endgame: The End of the Debt Supercycle and How it Changes Everything* (co-written with Jonathan Tepper), brilliantly discuss long-term trends and their impact on investment opportunities.

Warren Buffett has always been a great source of interesting and commonsense quotes on investing. I share some of them in this book.

I admire the work of Jessica Hagy, a *Forbes* contributor who uses Venn and XY diagrams to get her points across. This throws a few people for a loop because, typically, X-Y graphs convey real observed and recorded data, rather than an overall trend or opinion. I have borrowed her technique and appreciate the concept.

Dr. Robert Shiller is the author of several books, including *Irrational Exuberance.* His discussion of bubbles and efficient markets is a must-read for any trader or investor.

And, of course, Dr. Gary Shilling, author of *The Age of Deleveraging,* is one of my favorites—an economist, yet he can conceive (and actually step out and predict) that some assets will drop in price. He is no Pollyanna.

All of these authors had no idea, and could probably care less, that I was inspired by their writing. But the following friends and

Acknowledgments

family took the time to read through my various drafts and give me detailed suggestions and comments: grandson Alec Sherriff, Dale Surbey, Rex Shelby, Andrew Casey, Mike Nunamaker, Dave Pope, Doug Eger, Mike Mumford, Dave Redmond (the originator of the term "better bettor"), Lyn Salomone, Bill Echols, Tom Kearney, Harry Arora, Mitzi Crawford, Dave Altscher, Jerry White, Linda Hein, George Gaskin, Tim Belden, Don Chigazola, Rahil Jafry, Dr. Vince Kaminski, Tomas Valnek, Joel Staib, Stu Staley, Perry Lamy, George Shiau, Valerio Fabbri, and Robb Sexton. Thanks to all of you for your time and encouragement.

Thanks to my editors, Tom Hauck, Nancy Osa, Kathryn Galán, and Heather Parry. It takes a village to write a new book (at least mine did).

Jonathan Spence from Belfast, Northern Ireland converted my back-of-the-envelope and hard-to-read drawings into the colorful graphics shown here. He is a graduate architect, and shows his whimsical side in his graphic designs.

My wife, Lorraine, invested the most time in this book, other than me, and she was always a great sounding board—and is, of course, a far better writer than I am.

I want to acknowledge Bob Shiring, who brought me into the natural gas trading business in 1991, and gave me a start as a trader.

My brother Jim is always an inspiration to me. He is smart, hardworking, honest, and amazingly creative. Rain or shine, I can always count on this great friend. He also happens to be the one person in the world who gives me the most joy when I *occasionally* beat him at the poker table.

Naturally, I want to thank my biggest "fan," who opined at my valueofcollege.blogspot.com website: "You are an idiot. Your poor grammar and spelling show just how incompetent you really are. To try to convince others to eschew an education in favor of so-called 'better' post-high school alternatives, is both misguided and a misrepresentation of reality. Your guidance, while perhaps pertinent to you (I assume your intellect would not thrive in the University environment) should not be used to discourage others from making what is almost always a worthwhile investment. I award you no points, and may God have mercy on your soul."

This fan identified himself as Claude Kemble, B.A. Latin, Greek, Archaeology, University of Michigan; M.Phil, Medieval German, Oxford University; Ph.D. Medieval German, Harvard University. I suspect that Claude might be a fraud, since I have trouble digging up any of his accomplishments on Google, but I absolutely reveled in his harangue, whether real or prank. I hope to get such detailed and supportive feedback on this book, once it is released.

Finally, and more seriously, I want to thank my colleagues at Enron (with few exceptions), who inspired me every day that I worked there. I hope this book makes them proud.

◆◆◆
◆◆◆

ABOUT THE AUTHOR

> "Wow. What an ignorant bastard you are. Enjoy your 8-hours-a-day of television you ignorant capitalist prick."
> —Another big fan,
> commenting on the author's blog
> at *ValueofCollege.blogspot.com*

John Sherriff is the former CEO of Enron Europe, based in London, which was one of the largest commodity-trading organizations in the world. Enron traded in European, Australian, and Japanese electricity, European natural gas markets, and worldwide oil, credit, and metals markets.

Prior to joining Enron in 1994, he was a vice president at American Hunter Energy, and before that, he acted as director of corporate sales at Pacific Gas & Electric Company in San Francisco.

For the last 10 years, his business has been investing in commercial lawsuits with Lake Tahoe Financial http://www.fundinglawsuits.com, in which he buys a share of the plaintiff's potential proceeds in their litigation. This is a high-risk, high-reward business.

John holds a B.S. in Mathematics and an M.S. in Computer Science from Cal Poly, San Luis Obispo (earned in a prior millennium). He never ever thought about going to law school.

He has blogs at:

- http://valueofcollege.blogspot.com/ about the value of college,
- hireanattorney.blogspot.com about how to hire, manage, and fire an attorney, and
- getbackjack.blogspot.com on all the world's other problems.

His website, valueofcollege.com, tries to discourage college students from going deep into debt to get any college education (especially one in the bottom quartile).

You can contact John at **BeLuckyNGood@gmail.com**.

Or please join the discussions related to this book on Facebook at **facebook.com/luckyngood**.

He would love to connect with you at LinkedIn.com. His LinkedIn address is **http://www.linkedin.com/in/johnsherriff**.

Or invite him via **infoltf@gmail.com**.

♦♦♦
♦♦♦

COPYRIGHT NOTICE

Copyright © 2013 by John Sherriff. All rights reserved

"... my problem isn't piracy, it's obscurity."
—Cory Doctorow

ISBN-13: 978-1492275282

ISBN-10: 149227528X

    Unless the quote is totally flattering, only sections of 100 words or less from this book may be reproduced in any form or by any electronic, chemical, extrasensory, physical, metaphysical, or mechanical means, including information storage and retrieval systems, without written permission from the author. The only exception made is for reviewers and literary savants, who may quote excerpts of up to 250 words. You are allowed to remember things.

    Past results of business decisions are not indicative of future outcomes. You risk losing every last penny if you ignore my advice and *perhaps* slightly less if you pay attention. But I make no guarantees. You may suffer from adverse tax consequences (especially if you live in France, Illinois, or California), or you may simply be unlucky. Life is volatile, many people lose their investments, and if you do anything other than put your money in an FDIC-insured account or in US Treasuries, you have a chance of losing it all. In fact, the way this government is spending like a drunken sailor, you might lose it all even if you leave it in cash in your gun safe at home.

    Life involves risk, and I try to remind you of this every chance I get. My hope is to make you comfortable with taking this uncertain world head-on. But, even if you listen carefully to what I have to say, you might be dumber than a fence post (I doubt it, if you made it this far) when it comes to using this information. Only significant self-analysis (and psychotherapy) will tell you if you should even attempt to put these ideas into practice.

You may have figured out by now that I don't put much stock in this kind of legal disclaimer beyond what it might do to save my butt, and you will be pleased to know that I wrote it myself, without the benefit of a $700-an-hour attorney. In general, the legal profession thinks in opposites and pays attention to the details (both great concepts that I discuss in this book). Unfortunately, when asked to write legal disclaimers, attorneys draw them out interminably (it seems that some are paid by the word), and suggest wildly catastrophic consequences that might result from using whatever they are disclaiming. Through their long-winded, creative writing, they convince most of us to never even read their warnings. Yet, they are paid to inform you in thousands of words that you would be a fool to ever consider buying the product or service offered. You have definitely not been a fool to buy or read this book.

Back to a few more caveats of my own. The information presented herein represents the views of the author on the date of publication and, as a trader, he may change his mind tomorrow. If this book helps you to make money, the author deserves much of the credit. **If you lose money, then you're on your own; this is your risk, your decision, and your bet.** I make no promises about preventing male pattern baldness, either—and that goes double for women. Don't say I didn't warn you.

My name is John Sherriff, and I approve this message.

♦♦♦
♦♦♦

Lucky and Good

♦♦♦
♦♦♦

Made in the USA
Charleston, SC
18 September 2013